THE INDIAN EQUATOR

Also by Ian Strathcarron

Joy Unconfined! Lord Byron's Grand Tour Re-Toured
Innocence and War: Mark Twain's Holy Land Revisited

THE INDIAN EQUATOR

MARK TWAIN'S INDIA REVISITED

IAN STRATHCARRON

Signal

SIGNAL BOOKS
OXFORD

First published in 2013 by
Signal Books Limited
36 Minster Road
Oxford
OX4 1LY
www.signalbooks.co.uk

A catalogue record for this book is available from the British Library

ISBN 978-1-908493-75-0 Paper

Design & Production: Tora Kelly
Cover Design: Baseline Arts
Cover Images: Ian Strathcarron; Wikipedia Commons
Illustrations: © Ian Strathcarron pp.17, 31, 38, 54, 82, 84, 104, 112, 132, 146, 156, 160, 178; Dover Publications pp.1, 22, 42, 98, 141, 187, 221; Wikipedia Commons pp.I, 26, 89, 168, 180, 190, 195, 211, 216
Printed in India

CONTENTS

PROLOGUE

"Dear me! It is a strange world. Particularly the Indian division of it."
Mark Twain, *Following the Equator*

As noted below in a series of clippings from *The New York Times,* Mark Twain's publishing company was declared bankrupt in 1894. Although he was under no legal obligation to pay off any of the company's debts of $250,000—about $4,000,000 in today's money—he felt a moral obligation to pay them in full.

By then fifty-eight years old, his plan was to raise funds by two means: a worldwide lecture tour and a subsequent book about the tour. The one hundred-date lecture tour, which took him across North America, to Australia, New Zealand, India, Sri Lanka, Mauritius, South Africa and England, lasted from July 1895 to July 1896. On tour he took extensive notes, which in late 1896 and early 1897 in London he turned into the book. It was published as *Following the Equator* in New York and *More Tramps Abroad* in London in November 1897. The mission was successful and a year later all his debts were repaid.

Two years later he wrote, "How I did loathe that journey around the world!—except the sea-part and India." Although he was only in India for just over two months his exploits and observations there take up forty percent of the book—and by common consent are by far the best and liveliest part of it.

He loved India and its exotic splash of humanity then; I'm sure he would love it still; I certainly did as I followed him around that extraordinary country, truly a country without padding.

The New York Times

May 10, 1894
CHARLES L. WEBSTER & CO.'S AFFAIRS
The Liabilities Placed at About $80,000—"Mark Twain" Sails for Europe
Samuel L. Clemens, (Mark Twain) senior partner of the publishing house of Charles L. Webster & Co., sailed for Europe yesterday on the steamship New York. Before his departure Mr. Clemens held an extended conference with Bainbridge Colby, the assignee of the company. Later, Mr. Colby made the following statement:

"The liabilities of the firm will not exceed $80,000. The largest claim against the company is one for $25,000. There is no truth whatever in the report that

Mrs. U. S. Grant has a large sum of money due here on the Grant "Memoirs." Her claim will not exceed a few hundred dollars. I am convinced there is only one way to realize on the assets of the Webster Company, and that is to sell them in the usual course of business. I still have hopes that some plan may be perfected which will make it possible to sell the stock which is on hand without resorting to such a costly alternative as an assignee's sale.

"Mr. Clemens feels keenly the condition in which his affairs are involved, and whatever the result of the plan which he has adopted for the working up of the assets and the continuation of contracts, I do not think that he will consider himself relieved of the moral obligation to repay his creditors."

Mr. Colby said Mr. Clemens sailed for Europe to be absent indefinitely. He has a number of important engagements abroad, but will return at once should there by any need here for his presence.

The New York Times
September 19, 1894
BUSINESS TROUBLES
The schedules of Charles L. Webster & Co., book publishers at 67 Fifth Avenue, in which firm Samuel L. Clemens ("Mark Twain") and Frederick J. Hall are the partners, were filed yesterday. They show liabilities of $94,191, nominal assets of $122,657, actual assets of $69,164, less $15,000 hypothecated to the United States National Bank, and net actual assets of $54,164.

There are more than 200 creditors scattered all over the United States. Among the creditors are: Mount Morris Bank, $29,500; United States National Bank, $15,000; George Barrow, Skaneateles, N. Y., $15,420; S. D. Warren & Co., Boston, $6,332; Jenkins & McCowan, $5,363; Thomas Russell & Son, $4,623. There is due for royalties: Estate of U. S. Grant, $2,216; Col. F. D. Grant, $727; estate of Gen. P. H. Sheridan, St. Paul, Minn., $374; Mrs. E. B. Custer, London, $1,825.

The New York Times
July 12, 1895
EXAMINING MARK TWAIN'S ASSETS
Supplementary Proceedings on a Judgment Resulting from Failure of C. L. Webster & Co.—Mr. Clemens in Poor Health
Samuel L. Clemens, (Mark Twain,) the humorist, was yesterday examined in

supplementary proceedings at the office of his lawyers, 40 Wall Street. Mr. Clemens was a partner in the publishing house of Charles L. Webster. The firm was organized in 1885, failed in 1890, was reorganized, and failed again in April 1894, with assets of $25,000, and liabilities of $80,000. The firm published Grant's Memoirs, and made a success of it, but in the late business depression the firm became embarrassed.

The examination of Mark Twain yesterday was upon a judgment against him and Frederick J. Hall, another member of the firm, that Thomas Russell & Sons, printers of 34 New Chambers Street, obtained in the sum of $5,046.83. Upon the return of the execution unsatisfied, Justice Patterson issued an order for the examination of Messrs. Clemens and Hall.

Mr. Clemens returned from Europe about six weeks ago and went to Elmira. He was there served with the order for the examination, and came here yesterday morning.

Bainbridge Colby, assignee of the firm of Charles L. Webster & Co., said that Mr. Clemens had lost all of his money trying to keep the firm solvent, and that in its failure he had lost everything.

When the firm needed money and Mr. Clemens had no more to give it, Mrs. Clemens made loans, until, at the time of the failure, it owed her $70,000. For this she has never made a claim against the firm's assets.

With the exception of Russell & Sons, the creditors of the firm have taken no action against Mr. Clemens, knowing that Mr. Clemens will do what he can to pay them in full.

At the time of the failure, Mr. Clemens became ill through worrying over his business affairs, and has not yet fully regained his health. If he regains his health sufficiently he will start West. He expects to leave Vancouver Aug. 16, on a lecture tour around the world, that he contemplates making.

The New York Times

August 17, 1895
MARK TWAIN'S PLAN OF SETTLEMENT
Samuel L. Clemens Proposed to Pay the Indebtedness of His Firm with Proceeds of Lectures and Book

VANCOUVER, B. C., Samuel L. Clemens, (Mark Twain,) who is leaving for Australia, made a signed statement today concerning the purposes of his worldwide lecture tour and his business troubles, in part, as follows:

"I intend the lectures, as well as the property, for the creditors. The law recognizes no mortgage on a man's brain, and a merchant who has given up all he has may take advantage of the rules of insolvency and start free again for himself; but I am not a business man; and honor is a harder master than the law. It cannot compromise for less than a hundred cents on the dollar, and its debts never outlaw.

"I had a two-thirds interest in the publishing firm, whose capital I furnished. If the firm had prospered, I should have expected to collect two-thirds of the profit. As it is, I expect to pay all the debts. My partner has no resources, and I do not look for assistance from him. By far the largest single creditor of this firm is my wife, whose contributions in cash, from her private means, have nearly equaled the claims of all the others combined. In satisfaction of this great and just claim, she has taken nothing, except to avail herself of the opportunity of retaining control of the copyrights of my books, which, for many easily understood reasons, of which financial ones are the least, we do not desire to see in the hands of strangers. On the contrary, she has helped and intends to help me to satisfy the obligations due to the rest.

"The present situation is that the wreckage of the firm, together with what money I can scrape together with my wife's aid, will enable me to pay the other creditors about 50 per cent of their claims. It is my intention to ask them to accept that as a legal discharge, and trust to my honor to pay the other 50 per cent. as fast as I can earn it. From my reception thus far on my lecturing tour, I am confident that, if I live I can pay off the last debt within four years, after which, at the age of sixty-four, I can make a fresh and unencumbered start in life.

"I do not enjoy the hard travel and broken rest inseparable from lecturing, and, if it had not been for the imperious moral necessity or paying these debts, which I never contracted but which were accumulated on the faith of my name by those who had a presumptive right to use it, I should never have taken to the road at my time of life. I could have supported myself comfortably by writing, but writing is too slow for the demands that I have to meet. Therefore I have begun to lecture my way around the world. I am going to Australia, India and South Africa, and next year hope to make a tour of the great cities of the United States. In my preliminary run through the smaller cities on the northern route, I have round a reception the cordiality of which has touched my heart and made me feel how small a thing money is in comparison with friendship.

"I meant, when I began, to give my creditors all the benefit of this, but I begin to feel that I am gaining something from it, too, and that my dividends, if not available for banking purposes, may be even more satisfactory than theirs."

Names

I am using "Mark Twain" throughout the book rather than dipping in and out of Sam Clemens because it was as Mark Twain that Sam Clemens made the Grand Tour of India.

Accompanying him throughout were his wife of twenty-six years Livy and their twenty-two-year-old daughter Clara, only ever known as Mrs. and Miss Clemens, along with his tour manager, Carlyle G. Smythe[1] and bearer Satan. To simplify matters, when they are all together, I've called them "the Twain party".

I have mostly used the place names as found in Mark Twain's time, although I also use Mumbai and Kolkata to refer to the modern-day cities. Bombay is still known as Bombay to many of its inhabitants anyway, some of whom point out that the main enthusiasts for the Mumbai version of Bombay are local politicians; by Bombaying the citizens do protest. Delhi is still Delhi, although in Twain's time New Delhi had yet to be built; he was in what is now Old Delhi. Calcutta is now Kolkata but the Bengalis pronounce it somewhere in between so either version is easily accepted on the ground. Benares had yet to become Varanasi but the local people still call the Ganges front area, which was in Twain's time most of the city, Benares. I found that while the sign on the front of the train said "Varanasi" most passengers reckoned they were going to Benares. Cawnpore has become Kanpur and hasn't improved with the name change. Baroda is now called Vadodara but again is still widely known as Baroda, not least by those that live there. Lastly, Poona has become Pune but is still pronounced Poona.

The great Indian revolt against British rule that occurred in the summer of 1857 is known to the British as "The Indian Mutiny" and to the Indians as "The First War of Independence". Neither is really satisfactory: the former is euphemistic and the latter overblown. I've called it the Sepoy Uprising because that is what is was, an uprising by Indian soldiers, known as sepoys,[2] against their British colonial rulers. Although the uprising happened 39 years before

---

[1] Carlyle Greenwood Smythe was 41 at the time of the India tour. Trained as a journalist, after a brief spell in Europe editing the *Belgian Times* in Brussels he returned to Australia to inherit his father's lecture management business. Also in their stable were Sir Arthur Conan Doyle, Annie Besant and Captain Amundsen, amongst others.
[2] From the Urdu *sepahi* (soldier).

Mark Twain's Grand Tour, the heroic legends arising from it and its aftermath had a big effect on him and on the British Raj side of India that he saw.

Lastly, the word Raj[3] and the concept of India. Strictly speaking, the Raj refers to the direct rule of India by the British Crown from the Sepoy Uprising to Independence, so for the ninety years from 1857 to 1947. For one hundred years before 1857 India was ruled—amazingly enough—by a private stock company, the Honourable East India Company. Nowadays most Indians use the word Raj to describe the whole period of British rule and I've followed suit.

India as we know her today did not really exist as one unified country until the takeover of Goa from the Portuguese in 1961. At the time of Mark Twain's Grand Tour "India" included what we now call India, Pakistan, Bangladesh, parts of Nepal and Burma or Myanmar, and was actually a collection of 560 princely states under British "protection" with the land in between them under direct British control. For the sake of simplicity I've called the whole area he visited "India".

Money

There were rupees (Rs.) in India then and there are rupees here now. Like the place names the text has kept with the original values.

It is always troublesome to compare values over the centuries even without the complication of calculating the changes across currencies. However from *Following the Equator*, Livy's letters and historical value websites we can piece together some clues:

Mark Twain paid his general factotum Rs. 30 a month, which he noted was 27 cents a day or $8 a month. That was "a princely sum for the native switchman on a railway and the native servant in a private family get only Rs. 7 per month, and the farm-hand only 4; $1.75 and $1 per month respectively."[4]

This makes Rs. 1 worth US$0.25 at 1896 values, or about US$28 today. Nowadays Rs. 50 is worth a dollar.

---

[3] From the Hundi *raj* (reign).
[4] Like now Westerners were always charged well over the odds, firstly because they could afford it, secondly because it was expected—and as the cost of living is so low most find it fun spreading the wealth around.

THE INDIAN EQUATOR

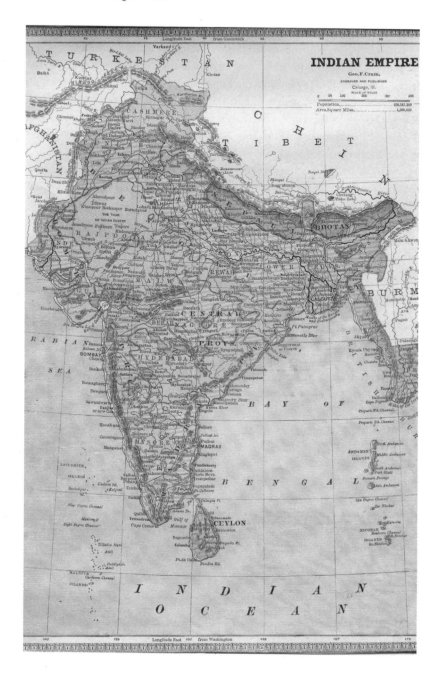

VIII

PART ONE
BEWITCHING COLOR, ENCHANTING COLOR

A MAD SEASON.

1. BOMBAY

I KNEW WE were going to find someone better than Satan. Mark Twain's Satan had come to him highly recommended, as indeed had the equally highly recommended bearer before him, the poor old butterfingered and confused Manuel.

A bearer—or two—was considered essential for all pre-World War 2 travelers in India and every visitor's first task was the hiring of one. Thus on the Twain party's second day in Bombay, 19 January 1896, the hapless Manuel was waiting to be interviewed in the lobby of Watson's Hotel in downtown Bombay. Mark Twain was feeling ill and had confined himself to bed to starve out the bronchial infection he had picked up on the rust bucket steamship *Rosetta*[5] as she sailed north across the equator from Ceylon. He had six days in which to recover before the first of his three Talks in Bombay, Talks which needed him to be on stage, alone and unamplified, for up to an hour and a half. Twain's wife Livy, his daughter Clara and tour manager Carlyle G. Smythe had left him well wrapped and in peace in their suite of rooms at Watson's Hotel. On their way out they saw the hapless Manuel waiting in the lobby and sent him up to be interviewed.

As Twain wrote,

> ...the bearer—a native man-servant—is a person who should be selected with some care, because as long as he is in your employ he will be about as near to you as your clothes. He is messenger, valet, chambermaid, table-waiter, lady's maid, courier—he is everything.

> In India your day may be said to begin with the bearer's knock on the bedroom door, accompanied by a formula of, words—a formula which is intended to mean that the bath is ready. It doesn't really seem to mean anything at all. But that is because you are not used to bearer English. You will presently understand.

A tall, stooped, rather pathetic old Indian man stood at the end of Mark Twain's bed and touched his forehead in salute.

"Manuel," said the patient, "you are evidently Indian, but you seem to have

---

[5] "...a poor old ship, and ought to be insured and sunk"

a Spanish name when you put it all together. How is that?"

Manuel looked perplexed. "Name, Manuel. Yes, master," he replied placidly.

"I know; but how did you get the name?"

"Oh, yes, I suppose. Think happen so. Father same name, not mother."

"Well—then—how—did—your—*father*—get—his name?" asked Twain with early signs of the exasperation that was to follow.

"Oh, he Christian—Portygee; live in Goa; I born Goa; mother not Portygee, mother native-high-caste Brahmin—Coolin Brahmin; highest caste; no other so high caste. I high-caste Brahmin, too. Christian, too, same like father; high-caste Christian Brahmin, master—Salvation Army."

An awkward silence fell between them and then suddenly Manuel was in full flow. Twain held up his hand.

"There—don't do that. I can't understand Hindustani."

"Not Hindustani, master, English. Always I speaking English sometimes when I talking every day all the time at you."

Within an hour Manuel had his own bearer and Twain had his first taste of the twists and turns of the Indian caste system. Rather than clean the bathroom himself Manuel "put a coolie at the work, and explained that he would lose caste if he did it himself; it would be pollution, by the law of his caste, and it would cost him a deal of fuss and trouble to purify himself and accomplish his rehabilitation. He said that that kind of work was strictly forbidden to persons of caste, and as strictly restricted to the very bottom layer of Hindoo society, the despised Untouchable."

Three days later, with the Twain party in despair, Smythe fired Manuel and set about finding a replacement. This time the recovering Mark Twain interviewed… well, he never did get to the bottom of his name but they all soon settled on Satan.

Satan was a whirlwind and all Mark Twain's "heart, all my affection, all my admiration, went out spontaneously to this frisky little forked black thing, this compact and compressed incarnation of energy and force and promptness and celerity and confidence, this smart, smiley, engaging, shiny-eyed little devil, feruled on his upper end by a gleaming fire-coal of a fez with a red-hot tassel dangling from it."

"You'll suit. What is your name?" Twain said.

"Muzzererivathayana," Muzzererivathayana replied.

"Let me see if I can make a selection out of it—for business uses, I mean; we will keep the rest for Sundays. Give it to me in installments."

"Muzz-erer-ivath-ayana," Muzzererivathayana replied slowly.

"There does not seem to be any shorter, except Mousawhich—suggesting mouse. It is not in your character, too soft, too quiet, too conservative, not of your splendid style. Mousa is short enough, but I don't quite like it. How do you think Satan would do?"

"Yes, master," replied the newly christened Satan, "Satan do wair good."

Well, every chap needs a Satan—especially in India. Much as I would have loved a bearer, or a whole bevy of bearers, for the Mark Twain footsteps task in hand a research assistant is far more useful.

Mine swings into our lives haphazardly. Through a friend at the British Foreign and Commonwealth Office in London I am introduced to the Cultural Attaché from the Indian High Commission, Shaurya Mark. Before a slow lunch at Romanov's in Aldwych he writes me a sort of "To Whom It May Concern" get-out-of-an-Indian-jail letter of safe passage to tuck into my back pocket. I explain about the research done with the Mark Twain Project at UC Berkeley and he asks what more needs doing.

"Well, the next stage is to hire an intern in India to do some more research over there and come on the trip with us, interpreting, generally helping us out."

"Us?"

"Yes, there's my wife and photographer Gillian too."

"Ah, good, so you can have a female researcher."

I must have looked quizzical. "Yes," he said, "in India this is important. Chaperoning is still in vogue. In this case you are in luck."

"My four favorite words, but how so?"

"My niece Charusheela John has just finished her studies at Lancaster University and is now back home in Bombay. She needs some work experience for her CV, you need an Indian intern, hey presto!"

"What did she study?" I ask.

"English Literature. 1.1, if I'm not mistaken."

"Ouch," I reply, "out-qualified again. And her second name John, would she be Anglo-Indian?"

"No, no, her family—and mine—are Christian. We take the father's first name as our last. Her father is John. His brother, my father was Mark. Her brother is Paul, and so on."

"What if you have more than twelve boys?" I ask.

"Then you start over."

*

The Twain party's Watson's Hotel is no longer habitable and we are staying at the Royal Bombay Yacht Club; hardly a hardship posting. An interview with Charusheela had been arranged and she breezes into the august old club, swirling past the wood paneled, trophy-covered walls, a vision of modern India in jet black designer ringlets, pendulum designer earrings, fake designer jeans and slightly-too-tight-but-who-am-I-to-judge fake designer tee-shirt. The interview starts, the dynamic changes and after several cups of Darjeeling's finest brew I'm pleased to say we seem to have passed and will start with her in a few days.

I mention how Mark Twain had grappled with Muzzererivathayana and settled on calling him Satan. "Look, I hope you don't mind me saying so but Charusheela doesn't exactly roll off the tongue either. The idea behind the story is then-and-now. I can't call you Satan. Maybe I can call you Angel?"

Gillian leans forward imperceptibly and an eyebrow raises towards the conversation. "Maybe not Angel," I stumble, "What is the name of your favorite Hindu goddess, for example?"

"Sita," she replies, "She's not *really* a goddess but I like her name."

"And do you like her?"

"Yes, of course, she is Rama's consort."

"Then Sita you are. Sita and Satan. I think you are going to make quite a pair." And they did.

*

Watson's Hotel ain't what it used to be. It was built as the finest hotel in Asia in the mid-1860s and by common consent for a generation it was just that—if you were white, for that was its policy. If you were non-white you would have been among the six hundred staff working to service the 150 rooms all of which could be adjoined to make suites; but then you had to be white again, and female, to work in the restaurant; and white again and male to work in the lobby. A popular untruth is that when the Indian tycoon Jamsetji Tata was refused a room in 1903 he built the Taj Mahal Hotel next to the Gateway of India in retaliation. Not so, he had already determined that Watson's was in incurable decline and Bombay was booming enough to warrant a replacement. And, like a good Tata, he was absolutely right: today the ludicrously overpriced Taj still stands tall and full and

THE INDIAN EQUATOR

Watson's is condemned and crumbling—but, this being India, still full.

The construction was unusual and serves to show how much the Empire benefited Britain. Private money was raised to employ the civil engineer who cut his teeth on St. Pancras, a Gothic-revival main line train station in London; he used the same system of Lego-linking cast-iron steel girders that had been used at London's Crystal Palace, built ten years earlier for the Great Exhibition. The four thousand beams were made over three years in three factories in the Black Country in the English Midlands, then shipped by canal to Manchester, by barge to Liverpool and by a series of freighters to Bombay. Like many buildings designed by engineers it wears its heart on its sleeve, or in this case its girders on its façade. It is, even now in its death throes, rather magnificent—albeit more so as a monument to the financial and imperial confidence of the early Raj period than to its aesthetic merit.

The Twain party arrived there on the morning of 18 January 1896 and were immediately bedazzled by their early impressions of India. "The lobbies and halls were full of turbaned, and fez'd and embroidered, cap'd, and barefooted, and cotton-clad dark natives, some of them rushing about, others at rest squatting, or sitting on the ground." Their suite of rooms was on the fourth floor and a long procession of Indians carried their numerous possessions up to the suite. Each man carried one item as is still the case in smart hotels today. "Each native carried a bag, in some cases, in other cases less. One strong native carried my overcoat, another a parasol, another a box of cigars, another a novel, and the last man in the procession had no load but a fan."

Gillian and I travel somewhat more modestly: two large suitcases and two carry-ons. All glide along on wheels—the suitcases are four wheel drive—and are easily self-driven but it's impossible to avoid a scurry of porter activity as soon as you are spotted. The subsequent tipping regime remains unchanged—"each man waited patiently, tranquilly, in no sort of hurry, till one of us found time to give him a copper, then he bent his head reverently, touched his forehead with his fingers, and went his way"—although the copper has been replaced by a ten-rupee note per bag. Also unchanged is the first impression: "They seemed a soft and gentle race, and there was something both winning and touching about their demeanor."

Fortunately though *this* has most certainly changed:

> The door opening onto the balcony needed cleaning and a native got down on his knees and went to work at it. He seemed to be doing it well

6

enough, but perhaps he wasn't, for a burly German in charge put on a look that betrayed dissatisfaction, then without explaining what was wrong, gave the native a brisk cuff on the jaw and then told him where the defect was. The native took it with meekness, saying nothing, and not showing in his face or manner any resentment. I had not seen the like of this for fifty years. It carried me back to my boyhood, and flashed upon me the forgotten fact that this was the usual way of explaining one's desires to a slave.

Sita's research had revealed that the World Monuments Fund, a US-based NGO, had managed to enlist Watson's as one of the "100 World Endangered Monuments" but being a mere NGO did not have the power to make the landlord repair it; the landlord anyway cited the city's rent freeze as making restoration infeasible. Meanwhile in a monsoon a large chunk of masonry had fallen from the old hotel's western façade, killing a beggar below, frightening the life out of passing worthies and damaging various vehicles. Town Hall declared the building unsafe to survive another monsoon and ordered its evacuation and a demolition report. The engineers reported the building was not only evidently unsafe but also economically indestructible and Town Hall were faced with a Watson-22: given its prime downtown location and massive girder construction the old hotel would be so expensive and disruptive to demolish that it had to remain in situ, but to have it remain in situ would mean evacuating it and under an old Raj-era by-law compensating the landlord as if it were in prime condition—compensation he would not be due had they been able to afford to demolish it. Welcome to the labyrinthine world of British-derived Indian bureaucracy.

We arrive to find Mark Twain's old hotel not only booming but bursting with ramshackle offices and stalls. The illegal temptation to have a free downtown office next to the High Court is too much to resist for dozens of advocates as well as for the shoal of printing, copying and faxing pilot fish attending the legal—well, illegal—sharks. The electric wiring alone is a masterpiece of daring, crackling improvisation; most of the glass from the famous old atrium is smashed and shards lie dagger drawn ready to fall from on high, while others lie in wait in the corridors; litter is piled to shoulder height and the lawyers with offices at the rear of the building have had to cut a path through it to reach their shack-offices.

We are keen to reach the fourth floor where we reckon the Twain party stayed; to rephrase—I am keen to make the climb but Gillian takes one look at the holes in the treads of the stairways and stays firmly grounded. I tread the treads but by the third floor it is clear that each one of the old hotel rooms has been divided and subdivided into so many lawyer's cubicles to make them unrecognizable as the finest rooms in Asia that they were. More fun is to be had reading the overlapping lawyers' signs, part directions, part advertisements, part pleas for any sort of legal work in the illegal surroundings and all bottomed off by a plethora of buckets to catch the leaks.

*

That afternoon there is a matinee performance of Bollywood's *Tanu Weds Manu* at the Excelsior Cinema just around the corner from Watson's. Sita has a crush on the lead supporting actor Jasjit Singh Gill, who trades under the name Jimmy Shergill, but the official reason for standing outside the Excelsior is that this is where Mark Twain opened his lecture tour of India when the Excelsior Cinema was known as the Novelty Theatre. Waiting outside we pass around the advertisement Sita had found in an old *Times of India*:

FIRST APPEARANCE IN INDIA

of the

GREATEST HUMOURIST OF THE AGE

The Author of 'The Innocents Abroad'

MARK TWAIN

who

In the presence of

HIS EXCELLENCY THE GOVERNOR

And party will

TO-MORROW (FRIDAY) AFTERNOON

at 5-30 in the

NOVELTY THEATRE

give his

FIRST MARK TWAIN 'AT HOME'

Humorously And Numerously Illustrated With

LIFE AND CHARACTER SKETCHES

THE SECOND 'AT HOME' with Entirely Different subjects will be on

MONDAY at the same time.[6]

PRICES OF ADMISSION: Rs 4;3;2;1
Tickets maybe purchased and seats secured at Messrs. SOUNDY & CO.

Inside, the auditorium is unchanged in space but has lost its ornate decorations and gained a shabby nylon carpet. There are and were five six-seat boxes on each side of the hall and forty-one rows of seats at thirty-two to a row. I can feel Smythe beside me now, pencil scratching on the back of an envelope: 1,372 x av Rs 2.50 = Rs 3,430 – 500 exps. = 2,930. 293 for CS, 2637 for MT.

By the time Mark Twain stood up in front of the audience at the Novelty Theatre on 24 January he had already delivered 726 lectures—or as he would insist on calling them, Talks. The "At Home" world tour lasted for exactly a year, from 15 July 1895-6 during which time he gave the At Home Talk 160 times; that first night in Bombay was the 99th date. Why At Home? To include the words "At Home" on a formal invitation to an informal party was a British Empire convention and it was this informal atmosphere in a formal setting that he wished to create. He told the *Bombay Gazette* the day before the opening how he saw the difference: "A lecture could appear in print by virtue of its calculated form and graceful phrasing. A fine speech might be badly delivered yet it would read perfectly well in print. A Talk is a very different thing. It is the delivery that makes a Talk effective not the phrasing… The audience plays a vital role in completing the Talk… The best and most effective parts of the Talk are acted not spoken."

To develop this further, in his introduction to *How to Tell a Story* he notes that:

There are several kinds of stories, but only one difficult kind—the humorous. The humorous story depends for its effect upon the manner of the telling; the comic story and the witty story upon the matter.

The humorous story may be spun out to great length, and may wander around as much as it pleases, and arrive nowhere in particular; but the comic and witty stories must be brief and end with a point. The humorous story bubbles gently along, the others burst.

---

[6] We hope Mark Twain didn't see the advertisement as there wasn't enouugh material for two Entirely Different shows.

The humorous story is strictly a work of art—high and delicate art—and only an artist can tell it; but no art is necessary in telling the comic and the witty story; anybody can do it.

The humorous story is told gravely; the teller does his best to conceal the fact that he even dimly suspects that there is anything funny about it. Very often the rambling and disjointed humorous story finishes with a nub, point, snapper, or whatever you like to call it. Then the listener must be alert, for in many cases the teller will divert attention from that nub by dropping it in a carefully casual and indifferent way, with the pretence that he does not know it is a nub.

On stage he was really an actor, playing the part of a bumbling country innocent who had no idea why people were laughing at what he said. Off stage he was the opposite, urbane, well connected, fond of luxury and protective of his reputation. I often think the stress of performance must have been worsened by having to change character so profoundly.

The Talk would typically last for an hour and a quarter and although delivered entirely without notes followed a fail-safe formula. He had up his sleeve eight well rehearsed, amusing anecdotes of about fifteen minutes each and on any evening he would use any five of these to suit his mood and how he judged the audience. He also had a choice of two set readings from *Tom Sawyer* or *Huckleberry Finn* if he needed a break from adlibbing. He believed in the old adage that an amateur rehearses until he has it right, whereas a professional rehearses until he cannot get it wrong. From the same *Bombay Gazette* article we find:

I prepare carefully for the lectures. I am not for one moment going to pretend I do not. I don't believe that any public man has ever attained success as a lecturer to paying audiences who has not carefully prepared, and has not gone over every sentence again and again until the whole thing is fixed upon his memory.

It is all very well to talk about being not prepared and trust into the spirit of the hour. But a man cannot go from one end of the world to the other, no matter how great his reputation may be, and stand before paid audiences in various large cities without finding that his tongue is far less glib than it used to be. He might hold audiences spell bound with unpremeditated oratory in past days when nothing was charged to hear him, but he cannot rely on being able to do so when they have paid for their seats and require something for the money unless he thinks all out before hand.

The theme of "At Home" was moral regeneration, told with the irony that the more wicked you are now the less likely you are to sin in the future. He used the then-current advances in medicine as a physical parallel: just as doctors inoculate patients against deadly diseases by giving them a harmless dose of the same disease, he proposed that we apply the same logic to sinning. To sin then becomes a virtue; there are 462 (or any number he made up on the night) sins and the best we can do is through then whole gamut until we are sin-proof.

His stagecraft was as much a part of the allure as the anecdotes. Dressed all in white,[7] either a morning suit with collared shirt or in morning dress with wing-collar shirt, either of these with a white bow-tie and waistcoat and gold chain, he would wander onto the stage unannounced in a cloud of cigar smoke and stand there looking perplexed when the applause started. Then he would wait for the audience to settle down and pause, still without speaking, until the first nervous sniggers came up to the stage, and then, feet apart, a puff on the cigar, in a very slow syllable-stretching, exaggerated drawl he was off: "I intend to put before the world a scheme for the moral regeneration of the whole human race. I hope I can make it effective but I can't tell yet—but I know it is planned out upon strictly scientific lines and is up to date in that particular. I propose to do for the moral fabric just what advanced medical art is doing the physical body. I propose to inoculate for sin."

The review in the same *Bombay Gazette* two days later could have referred to any of the seventeen At Home Talks in India

The prominent points about Mark Twain's personal appearance are his long untidy hair, the ferocious moustache and the deep furrows falling outwards from the thin nose to the sides of his mouth which are the external and visible signs of the nasal drawl that characterizes the very thoughts of the man before he had given utterances to them. With his feet planted some little distance apart, the hands sometimes in his trousers, sometimes near his chin, his eyes are oftener than not as they

---

[7] ...or black; white mostly in India.

would be in the presence of a group of familiar friends.

Mark Twain used many devices to create an atmosphere of intimacy in the audience. One of them was the easy conversational style that brought about familiarity between the speaker and gathering. His reminiscences of the Mississippi and Nevada days, the narration of anecdotes, often personal and the utterly natural and spontaneous utterances broke the barrier of distance between him and the audience. At times he used anticlimactic sentences, puns and jingling words to surprise and catch the listener's attention. But the greatest of his devices was the sudden purposeful pause that created a strange expectancy in the audience. The people receive a rude jolt when they discovered something unexpected. It was entertaining to watch the audience—the smile, the anticipatory chuckle, the unrestrained laugh of hearty enjoyment.

The reviews throughout the tour were universally positive, partly because the Indian press were—and still are—suckers for celebrity and partly because Smythe made sure the press was squared before each performance. The routine was always the same: the Twain party would arrive in a city and the local newspaper would pop around to the hotel for an interview; they had their celebrity columns inches and Mark Twain and Smythe had their publicity for that town's At Home. Indian newspapers were—and again still are—nothing if not verbose and it is easy to see how Twain must have spent as much time in pre-performance interviews as he did on stage. Reading them now, the interviews[8] are as formulated as the Talks: the journalists obliged with the same questions, the humorist obliged with the same answers.

The Bombay Talks started at 5.30 p.m.—which in India means 6 p.m. (or as he would have it "The Trouble Starts at 6.00 pm") and it would have been all over by 7.30 p.m. The Twain party liked to visit the Royal Bombay Yacht Club, which by happy coincidence is where the Strathcarron party is staying. It still is one of the great clubs in the world, delightfully old-fashioned yet with modems in each of the rooms (typically, still known as "chambers"), the rooms themselves being the size of a small apartment built in the days—the mid-nineteenth century—when space and labor were plentiful and affordable. The day starts with a knock on the door and a bearer brings in "bed-tea" and the *Times of India*. He throws

---

[8] All found in *The Complete Interviews* edited by Gary Scharnhorst.

open the blinds and the view throws onto the Arabian Sea, with the Gateway of India to its left and the Taj Mahal Hotel to its right. It remains a kind of paradise, a last pocket of resistance, more so given the chaos of Bombay that lies, unseen and unheard, behind it.

Like a good Mark Twain footsteps hound I had offered to do a Talk there myself, this one on my book *Joy Unconfined! Lord Byron's Grand Tour Re-Toured.*[9] I am nervous about the presentation as no matter how sophisticated and poly-this and poly-that the audience—and this one was as poly as they come—one is still unsure as how far an adventure so quintessential British as Byron's Grand Tour will be understood. As it happens there were a sprinkling of Brits in the audience and their sniggers and guffaws seemed to encourage our hosts and by halfway through everyone was laughing together.

The writer is an Honorary Member of the Royal Bombay Yacht Club and they offered Mark Twain the same privilege but made the mistake of asking him to pay for it. In his notes he wrote: "Rs 16 for a month's honorary membership. A Club should not pay a compliment it cannot afford. It may be that some body asked for this honor for me—as to that, I don't know. In that case they ought too change the title to of it and call Temporary Membership. I have (taken membership)."

*

It wasn't until two days after the first At Home that Mark Twain felt strong enough to take Livy and Clara for lunch with Governor and Lady Sandhurst. He had previously met Lord Sandhurst at the Garrick Club in London and of course the governor and his family had been to the first Talk and had actually invited the Twain party to lunch as soon as they arrived a week before; an invitation the bronchial cough had forced his guest to decline.

It is a six-mile foray around Marine Drive, the crescent of the old "Bom Bahia", the "good bay" that the Portuguese found so enchanting on first arriving

---

[9] The Talk is billed as: "Two hundred years ago, between 1809-11, Lord Byron completed his Grand Tour of the Mediterranean. He was 21 when he left London. After catching a packet from Falmouth to Lisbon, his entourage rode down to Sevilla and Cadiz. He then sailed from Gibraltar to Sardinia, Sicily, Malta, Greece, Albania, back to Greece then Turkey, Malta again and then with a heavy heart home to England. His voyage was exotic and poetic, erotic and eccentric. On June 14th 2008 Solent sailors Ian and Gillian Strathcarron boarded their Freedom 40 'Vasco da Gama' at Bucklers Hard and sailed off to recreate Lord Byron's Grand Tour. Their own voyage was propitious and perilous, mysterious and mischievous—but seldom abstemious."

in 1508. In 1534 they murdered the heathen (actually Muslim) ruler and took the main island, Mumbai, outer islands and shoreline for themselves. The Portuguese then gave Bom Bahia to the British in 1661 as part of Catherine of Braganza's dowry to King Charles II. Seven years later Charles leased it to the Honourable East India Company for £10 a year and Mumbai started to become Bombay. Riding along Marine Drive in their two-horse barouche[10] allowed Twain his first proper look at India. He later recalled:

> Bombay! A bewitching place, a bewildering place, an enchanting place—the *Arabian Nights* come again? It is a vast city; contains about a million inhabitants. Natives, they are, with a slight sprinkling of white people—not enough to have the slightest modifying effect upon the massed dark complexion of the public. It is winter here, yet the weather is the divine weather of June, and the foliage is the fresh and heavenly foliage of June.

> It is all color, bewitching color, enchanting color—everywhere all around—all the way around the curving great opaline bay clear to Government House, where the turbaned big native chuprassies[11] stand grouped in state at the door in their robes of fiery red, and do most properly and stunningly finish up the splendid show and make it theatrically complete. I wish I were a chuprassy.

Then as now Governor's House—since renamed Raj Bhavan—occupies the promontory at the end of Malabar Point, the tip of the bay's crescent, with fabulous views back across the bay and to the city waterfront, and is thus the prime piece of land in Bombay. It was also Twain's first proper look at the splendors of the Raj:

> Government House, on Malabar Point, with the wide sea-view from the windows and broad balconies; abode of His Excellency the Governor of the Bombay Presidency—a residence which is European in everything but the native guards and servants, and is a home and a palace of state harmoniously combined.

> That was England, the English power, the English civilization, the

---

[10] A one-driver, four-passenger, two-horse carriage.
[11] Official, uniformed messengers.

modern civilization—with the quiet elegancies and quiet colors and quiet tastes and quiet dignity that are the outcome of the modern cultivation.

One has to agree: Raj Bhavan is still as magnificent as when it was called Governor's House and is still quietly elegant, quietly colored, quietly tasteful and quietly dignified—also the outcome of modern cultivation. Our own lunch is with the current governor, the eighty-year-old Shri Kateekal Sankaranarayanan, one of India's most distinguished politicians who apart from his myriad achievements in a lifetime devoted to the public good has also just won the prize for having the most "a's" in his name. In attendance is Shrikant Deshpande, Secretary to the Governor, and Anuradha Aru, Secretary to the Secretary to the Governor, so a bit of a full house, governor-wise.

If the charm of the governors and their palace remains the same, the governor's role has changed completely. Whereas Shri Sankaranarayanan's role in largely ceremonial, to be the local representative of the president (not unlike a governor-general in some Commonwealth countries), Lord Sandhurst was a powerful man indeed. He was only one executive level below the viceroy, and head of the Bombay Presidency, a vast area of twenty-five million people comprising what are now the states of Gujarat, the western two-thirds of Maharashtra, northwestern Karnataka as well as what are Pakistan's Sindh province and Aden in Yemen. As elsewhere in India only about two-thirds of the country was under direct Raj rule, the remainder being a hotchpotch of "princely states"; in the case of the Bombay Presidency no fewer than three hundred and fifty three of them.

The princely states have been unkindly described as the rump of the Moghul Empire, which ran India for nearly three hundred years before the East India Company and then the Raj. Certainly many of the rulers were Muslim but of the kinder, pre-Wahhabi persuasion.[12] The Pax Britannica arrangement was, by and large, a win-win: the princes kept their thrones and their states and were largely autonomous but they signed away to the British responsibility for external relations and defense—for which delegation they had to pay a sizable tax. In each princely state was a British Resident, a political agent who ensured that "the British voice was heard" "for the greater good of all", an appointment of some influence. The first rule of the British Resident was not to interfere and except in

---

[12] The most famous exception was in Kashmir, where the last maharaja was Hindu and decided at Independence to join his largely Muslim subjects to India rather than the more logical Pakistan - the consequences of which decision still rumbles on.

cases of gross misgovernance the rule was followed. The ceaseless civil wars were brought to an end and prosperity, at least for the rulers, reigned with the rulers.

And prosperous they were. In terms of wealth the modern equivalent may be the Gulf Arab royal families but the Indian princes had a far longer-standing sense of moral and social responsibility; the Arabs were, after all, desert nomads until—relatively—just the other day. Being Indian they also had their own inter-prince caste system to add to the British-ordained "Warrant of Preference" being determined by the number of gun salutes their arrival or departure attracted. In this way the highest ranking princes[13] like His Exalted Highness the Nizam of Hyderabad and His Highness the Maharaja of Mysore claimed the full 21 salutes,[14] His Highness the Nawab[15] of Bhopol had to keep his head down for just the 19, while His Highness the Maha Rao Raja of Bundi had to get by with 17. In descending order His Highness the Maha Rawal of Banswara heard just 15, His Highness the Deewan of Palanpur had to live with only 13, whereas His Highness the Thakar of Gondal could claim 11, and poor old His Highness the Saraswati Desai of Sawantwadi and His Highness the Thakore Sahib of Rajkot just had the 9 apiece.[16]

The British and the princes shared a love of protocol and hierarchy. The British published a so-called Blue Book which laid down an Order of Preference; no hostess or aide-de-camp could be without one for it determined who sat next to whom at dinner, who stood where in a greeting line, if the wife of a member of the India Civil Service with twelve years standing outranked a District Judge from Burma, if a Chief Engineer of the Royal Indian Marines was superior to a Sanitary Engineer of eight years standing, if a Director of Land Records in a princely state outshone an Officer, 3rd Class Indian Civil Service, how an Agricultural Chemist fared against the Assistant Inspector-General of Forests and so on. Unintentionally the British had created a hierarchy as complex as a Moghul court—and one that attached just as much importance to following the

[13] None ranked higher than prince to leave protocol space between them and the Empress Victoria.

[14] Gun salutes were an old Royal Navy tradition originating in the need to empty guns peacefully. The larger ships - with the more important captains - carried the greater guns and so greater salutes. By an old sea superstition even numbers foreshadowed death, thus odd numbers only were used.

[15] As a rule a Maharaja was a Hindu ruler and a Nawab a Muslim ruler.

[16] General Wavell invented the mnemonic, Hot Kippers Make Good Breakfast, to remind himself of the precedence: Hyderabad, Kashmir, Mysore, Gwalior, Baroda. These five alone were entitled to 21 guns.

correct protocol and etiquette.

Happily for the British they shared just as much in common with the Hindu ruled as with the Muslim rulers. Hindu society is divided up into four castes with numerous sub-castes. British society in India happened to mirror these divisions. At the Hindu head are the Brahmins of upper and lower rank, who

corresponded to the viceregal Indian Civil Service and the regional equivalents. Next come the Kshatriyas, the warrior caste and their sub-castes resembling the British Army and the Indian Army. The British businessmen, the successors to the East India Company pioneers, were wealthy but of low caste, known as "box-wallahs" to those above them, and they had their Indian equals in the Vaisyas, the merchant caste. Like the Vaisyas the mercantile class divided into two: those in commerce—bankers, insurance brokers, shippers and the like—and those in trade: shop owners, buyers and sellers who actually handled goods. At the Hindu bottom were the Untouchables who had their British equivalent, those who had "gone native", or were of mixed blood.

No doubt over lunch the conversation turned to the princes and their princely states and the fabulous wealth and extravagant palaces and exotic imaginings going on within. Mark Twain was fascinated by the titles: "the princely titles, the sumptuous titles, the sounding titles—how good they taste in the mouth! The Nizam of Hyderabad; the Maharajah of Travancore; the Nabob of Jupillipore; the Begum of Bhopal; the Nawab of Myscenah; the Rance of Gulnare; the Ahkoond of Swat; the Rao of Rohilkund; the Gaikwar of Baroda." In his notes he had further fun inventing some more:

> ...the Jimjam of Jubbelpore, The Nizam of the Maharaja the Rajah, the Rao, The Nawab, the Guicowar, The Thakore of Manta (now in dispute), the Slambang of Gutcheree, the Ahkoond of Swat, the Hoopla of Hellasplit, the Breechclout of Buggheroo, His Highness the Juggernaut of Jacksonville, the Jamram of Ramjam.

Governor Sandhurst GCSI, GCIE, GCVO, PC couldn't quite match these, being merely the first Viscount Sandhurst, but he had taken his seat in the House of Lords on his 21st birthday having inherited the lesser title of Baron Sandhurst from his deceased father. He was a rather uninspiring Liberal career politician who had been made governor of the Bombay Presidency the year before. A mere safe pair of hands was he. His wife, Lady Victoria, was the daughter of Frederick Spencer, the 4th Earl Spencer. Through her brother Charles she was—although she didn't know it—the great, great, great aunt of another Spencer, Diana, Princess of Wales.

*

A private lunch with the governor and his staff in the Governor's Dining Room is as splendid now as it was then. The table setting is formal and follows exactly the rules of its own etiquette, just as it has done a thousand lunches before. Moghul-style uniformed waiters hover discreetly behind one's left shoulder, and serve in the British "silver service" style. There is no scraping and no scrunching. Conversation is small talk and chitter chatter. Napkins blot the mouth as needed then fall to the lap. A glass of Indian red wine[17] is expected to last a course, the lead taken from the governor. This is no leisurely lunch, moving as it does at a steady clip, not rushed but not dallied over. After lunch the menu is presented to the guests as a memento. I'm looking at it now:

Dhan Dar

or

Cold Yoghurt Soup with Mint
******

Lamb in a Cashew Nut Sauce
or
Masala Dosas
Black Pepper Rice
Carrots Stir-Fried with Green Chillies
Baigan Achari
******

Pista Kulfi
Falooda

After lunch an aide-de-camp shows us around the current governor's great passion, the fifty acres of private parkland with its own botanical gardens. In Mark Twain's time Governor's House was only fifteen years old and the grounds were still being planted and landscaped; now, one hundred and fifteen years of care and maturity later they have blossomed and bloomed and are as immaculate—and as unnatural—as only a corps of gardeners can make them. The centerpiece is the croquet lawn, where the governor also holds his quarterly garden parties (sadly, we'll be long gone in Baroda when the next one is held). I fear for the head gardener's composure as he sees two hundred guests trampling all over his billiard-table smooth croquet lawn. Unfortunately the aide-de-camp doesn't play croquet—which seems a bit odd, I thought that was what aides-de-camp did—and steers us over to the cliff top walk. He stays well inland, maybe worried I am going to push him over for not playing croquet.

In the grounds now are also discreet, secluded bungalows where India's leaders come to relax; we take tea in the one preferred by Jawaharlal Nehru; next door is an English country cottage preferred by his daughter Indira Gandhi. It was also a venue where Nehru carried on his infamous affair with the vicereine,

---

[17] Indian wine consumption in India is growing as fast as its middle class. Cabernet Sauvignon is the most reliable variety and Grover's La Reserve and York brands aren't bad at all. Reveilo Reserve Syrah and Chateau Indage's Ivy Shiraz are delicious but far too expensive and hard to find. If a restaurant does serve wine it will probably be Riviera, a bland blend but just about quaffable. Whites tend to be sweet and warm. The biggest problem is the price: expect to pay $15-$25 for anything drinkable and quite often the wine part of the meal will cost twice as much as the food. Vineyard tourism north of Bangalore, in the Himalayan foothills and near Poona—our next stop—is just catching on. Not a bad way to see the country as it happens.

Edwina, Countess Mountbatten of Burma and I regret to say that when the aide-de-camp is showing Gillian something or other in the cottage kitchen I have a vicarious stretch on the lovers' bed.

*

After thanking and leaving the Sandhursts, Mark Twain, Livy and Clara made a short trot in their barouche to "a scene of a different sort: from this glow of color and this sunny life to those grim receptacles of the Parsee dead, the Towers of Silence".

The Parsees, as the Indian Zoroastrians are known, can lay claim to belong to the oldest religion in the world, a straightforward battle between the forces of Good and Evil with revelations aplenty. In Twain's time they were a small but highly influential group, much favored by the British administration. "The Parsees are a remarkable community. There are only about 60,000 in Bombay, and only about half as many as that in the rest of India; but they make up in importance what they lack in numbers. They are highly educated, energetic, enterprising, progressive and rich."

Today unfortunately they are in decline, partly because after Independence the favoritism was removed, partly because the Hindu and Christian communities in particular have caught up with them educationally and partly because as each of their new generations has been exposed to reason and the world the religious side of Zoroastrianism has declined. In the last census ten years ago there were still 40,000 adherents in Mumbai, but when one considers that the population of the rest of the city has increased twentyfold since Twain's visit the relative decline has been dramatic.[18] Their strength is now secular and tribal.[19] What has remained is the way they look after each other and the less fortunate: as Twain noted, "the Jew himself is not more lavish or catholic in his charities and benevolences"; not surprising then that the Tatas and Godrejs, two of India's richest and most philanthropic families, are Parsees.

Twain was fascinated by the Parsee funeral ritual. They hold that "the principle which underlies and orders everything connected with a Parsee funeral is Purity. By the tenets of the Zoroastrian religion, the elements, Earth, Fire, and

---

[18] The current estimate is about 35,000 Parsees resident in Muumbai.
[19] Once the population of a group falls below 25,000 the Indian government reclassifies it from a "community" to a "tribe". Sometime in the 2020s, therefore, the parsees expect to be officially and not just figuratively tribal.

Water, are sacred, and must not be contaminated by contact with a dead body. Hence corpses must not be burned, neither must they be buried." Instead they used vultures to pick the body clean, after which the bones were left exposed to the tropical sun and rain—and the sacred elements—for a month, when the powdery remains were placed in a well with a drain and eventually found themselves in the Arabian Sea.

Today, alas, the famously efficient Bombay vultures have vanished, poisoned by the twentieth century with its industrial pollution and agricultural chemicals. In their stead the Parsees have installed solar mirrors above and to the side of the funeral Towers and these are maneuvered to reflect intensified solar rays on to the bodies. The vultures are much missed: decomposition by vultures took as little as thirty minutes, whereas the same process by solar can take a week or so. The Parsees are now rearing fifteen vultures and plan to train them back in the ways of their ancestors, human and avian.

What do remain are the spectacular location and the rather dismal ceremony. "On lofty ground, in the midst of a paradise of tropical foliage and flowers, remote from the world and its turmoil and noise, they stood—the Towers of Silence." All three Towers[20] are located in extensive and beautifully maintained forested grounds in Mumbai's exclusive Malabar Point, just north of Raj Bhavan. The parkland must be worth billions of any currency that comes to mind. Only the burial preparation area of the grounds is open to the public and has the air of a well tended upcountry field hospital. Photography is strictly prohibited anywhere on the site but a fair impression of the park and the Towers of Silence can be seen on Google Earth at 18°57'33.14»N; 72°48'23.24»E.

The dismal ceremony? "None may touch the dead or enter the Towers where they repose except certain men who are officially appointed for that purpose. They receive high pay, but theirs is a dismal life, for they must live apart from their species, because their commerce with the dead defiles them, and any who should associate with them would share their defilement."

The Towers have a circular flat floor with surrounding walls—not unlike a squashed bull-ring, or as Twain put it, "a gasometer". The solar panels are above and beyond the walls. The floor is divided into three concentric rings: the bodies of the Parsee men are arranged around the outer ring, women in the middle ring and children in the innermost ring. In the centre is a circular pit where the bones

---

[20] There are three Towers, two main ones for general use and one for Parsee women who have been misguided enough to marry outside the faith.

are left to be bleached by the sun and washed by the rain, and thus powdered and cleaned are eventually washed into the sea nearby as before. Not so much dust-to-dust, ashes-to-ashes as powder-to-powder, water-to-water.

The illustration below, with the vultures awaiting their next meal, explains the Towers of Silence better than the thousand words I am hereby spared writing.

One animal disposal accessory that has survived since Twain's time is the dog which accompanies the body on its final voyage to the Towers; not the same dog of course, but a random ceremonial dog chosen for life, as it were, from the Parsee community. Even then the reason for the canine involvement in the ritual was lost in time: "The origin of at least one of the details of a Parsee funeral is not now known—the presence of the dog. Before a corpse is borne from the house of mourning it must be uncovered and exposed to the gaze of a dog; a dog must also be led in the rear of the funeral."

ONE OF THE TOWERS OF SILENCE.

Twain was an early American advocate of cremation and he compared it with the Parsee vulture system: "as a sanitary measure, their system seems to be about the equivalent of cremation, and as sure. When cremation becomes the rule we shall cease to shudder at it; we should shudder at burial if we allowed ourselves to think what goes on in the grave."

Two days and two Talks later Mark Twain was ready to make his first foray on the road, a Talk and overnight stay at Poona, five hours away to the southeast by train. Smythe went with him; Livy and Clara stayed behind at Watson's Hotel. By then Mark Twain had seen enough of India, albeit still only of Bombay, to remember:

> This is indeed India! The land of dreams and romance, of fabulous wealth and fabulous poverty, of splendor and rags, of palaces and hovels, of famine and pestilence, of genii and giants and Aladdin lamps, of tigers and elephants, the cobra and the jungle, the country of a hundred nations and a hundred tongues, of a thousand religions and two million gods, cradle of the human race, birthplace of human speech, mother of history, grandmother of legend, great-grandmother of tradition, whose yesterdays bear date with the mouldering antiquities of the rest of the nations—the one sole country under the sun that is endowed with an imperishable interest for alien prince and alien peasant, for lettered and ignorant, wise and fool, rich and poor, bond and free, the one land that all men desire to see, and having seen once, by even a glimpse, would not give that glimpse for the shows of all the rest of the globe combined.

It seems that like so many of us, he was smitten—but more of that later.

2. POONA

THE JOURNEY TO Poona was also Twain's first experience of Indian railways—what was to become, after Independence, Indian Railways. The train left from Bombay's famous Victoria Terminus, known to one and all as VT, a massive Victorian Italianate Gothic Revival pile, like Watson's Hotel modeled—or so it would seem—along the lines of St. Pancras train station in London. It had been opened just nine years before Twain's visit and named after the Queen Empress Victoria herself. Today renamed Chhatrapati Shivaji Terminus, or CST, it is still widely known to Mumbai taxi drivers and its three and a half million daily commuters—and lovers of the Gothic—as VT.

Twain's first impressions will be instantly recognizable to any VT visitor today:

> What a spectacle the railway station was! It was very large, yet when we arrived it seemed as if the whole world was present—half of it inside, the other half outside, and both halves, bearing mountainous head-loads of bedding and other freight, trying simultaneously to pass each other, in opposing floods of patient, gentle, long-suffering natives, with whites scattered among them at rare intervals. Wherever a white man's native servant appeared, that native seemed to have put aside his natural gentleness for the time and invested himself with the white man's privilege of making a way for himself by promptly shoving all intervening black things out of it. In these exhibitions of authority Satan was scandalous.

> Inside the great station, tides upon tides of rainbow-costumed natives swept along, this way and that, in massed and bewildering confusion, eager, anxious, belated, distressed. And here and there, in the midst of this hurly-burly, and seemingly undisturbed by it, sat great groups of natives on the bare stone floor, young, slender brown women, old, gray wrinkled women, little soft brown babies, old men, young men, boys; all poor people, but all the females among them, both big and little, bejeweled with cheap and showy nose-rings, toe-rings, leglets, and armlets, these things constituting all their wealth, no doubt.

If he thought it was teeming then he should see it now! Working the late afternoon arrival time at Poona of their five-hour journey backwards, Smythe and Mark Twain were on the Hyderabad Express, which still leaves at midday, a period of slightly lesser mayhem.

Mayhem in all its madness, pandemonium in all its confusion, bedlam in all its uproar, merely scratch the surface of VT at rush hour. They arrive on the carriage roofs; they arrive hanging from the window bars; they arrive clinging to the door frames; they arrive balancing on the bogeys; four and a half thousand die from these antics every year[21]—and the trains are not some super smooth Japanese contraptions, nor the tracks the latest in German seamless welding technology, but rickety old Raj-era jigger-buckets which give every impression of trying to shake their passengers off like a dog in from the rain.

Yet the real amusement for the first timer comes when any of the three and a half million daily commuters tries to disembark. It's out of the question to wait for the train to stop; much more fun to jump from it as soon as it is alongside any part of the platform. The first fliers inevitably stumble as they land and their trick is to be up and away before, mere seconds later, fliers from the following carriage land in the same spot. Pile-ups inevitably occur every few steps along the way but never a cross-word is heard. The driver joins in the fun too: instead of pulling alongside the platforms at walking speed he barrels in at a good trot looking backwards at the flying fun behind, then brakes hard as he approaches the stoppers and then has time for a last look behind as any stragglers are thrown off by the sudden stop.

By now those inside the carriages are starting to leap out, pushed from behind by the hundreds on board anxious to join in the fun on the platform. Each carriage is so full that it seems to take a minor eternity to empty itself. Eight hours later the process is reversed when after the gates open the Platform Olympic Games sees thousands of commuters sprint, hurdle, high jump and long jump first into and then over each other onto the carriages; just when you think the train is full, just when the train is full, just when it you think it is overflowing, just when it is overflowing, a fresh layer of desperadoes climbs on top of those already on top to make their way up onto the roof... and off it shudders through the slums.

It's a funny thing about the Indians that although so many of them spend

---

[21] 4,327 to be exact in 2008 on all three Mumbai suburban lines.

so much time—and danger and discomfort—commuting, they haven't learnt Lesson One: let 'em off before you let 'em on. This phenomenon is best observed on the commuter trains or, better still, the metro. First you notice something strange: between stations commuters shuffle and shove for position within the carriages, some moving towards the doors and some backing off. The reason becomes clear as the overpacked carriage arrives at a station. The moment the doors open an inch the pushing and heaving starts in equal measure: those trying to get in, try to get in and those trying to get *out*, try to get out. It's a crush, it's a scrum, it's a heaving scramble. The trick to getting out is to line up in the second row behind one of the larger commuters and then when the doors open use him as your battering ram, as you yourself will be used from behind. The trick to getting *in* is to line up in the third row and when the pushing stops you will be just outside the doors at which point you haul the man in front back and take his place just as the doors close. It's more fun than it sounds.

Train travel between cities is a lot less fraught and can be quite comfortable; it is always slow and always absorbing. When Twain caught the Hyderabad Express on 29 January there were three classes. "The natives traveled third class, and at marvelously cheap rates. There was an immense string of those third-class cars, for the natives travel by hordes; and a weary hard night of it the occupants would have, no doubt."

Now there are no fewer than eight classes. The old First Class, by which the Twain Grand Tour traveled when not in a special VIP "Palace-on-Wheels" carriage laid on by one of their hosts, is now only fourth in the hierarchy of comfort. Indian train journeys are built around overnight travel, partly because the distances are so long and the speed so slow, and partly because it is so much more comfortable to travel in the cool of the night. Top spot now goes to Air-conditioned First Class (AC1), which has only two berths in a lockable compartment; AC1 is now a rare class as the deregulated airlines[22] have taken the money of those who can afford AC1's relatively high prices. AC2 (as in two-tier bunks per compartment) is half the price of AC1 and has four-berth curtained off compartments, with fresh sheets and pillows and blankets supplied each night. AC2 is how the Indian middle class and most tourists travel; it is how the Strathcarron Re-Tour travels (although Sita looks a bit glum: her family normally travel AC1).

After AC3, which means three tiers of bunk, so six per compartment, comes (non-air-conditioned) First Class in fourth spot and not much changed from that day in 1896.

It was a car that promised comfort; indeed, luxury. The floor was bare, but would not long remain so when the dust should begin to fly.

Across one end of the compartment ran a netting for the accommodation of hand-baggage; at the other end was a door which would shut, upon compulsion, but wouldn't stay shut; it opened into a narrow little closet which had a wash-bowl in one end of it, and a place to put a towel.

On each side of the car, and running fore and aft, was a broad leather-covered sofa to sit on in the day and sleep on at night. Over each sofa hung, by straps, a wide, flat, leather-covered shelf—to sleep on. In the daytime you can hitch it up against the wall, out of the way—and then you have a big unencumbered and most comfortable room to spread

---

[22] Jet Airways and Kingfisher are excellent and affordable airlines. Indian Airways, now lumped in with Air India, is still equally awful and strike- and cancellation-prone. As Sita was to discover in Jaipur later there have been numerous scandals about Indian pilots buying their ATPL licenses from the state authority—justified in one Times of India report by the latter saying, in effect, "what's the problem? These things fly themselves anyway." Unless one is in a hurry—in India?—it's train time.

out in.

No car in any country is quite its equal for comfort (and privacy) I think. For usually there are but two persons in it; and even when there are four there is but little sense of impaired privacy. Our own cars at home can surpass the railway world in all details but that one: they have no cosiness; there are too many people together.

At the foot of each sofa was a side-door, for entrance and exit. Along the whole length of the sofa on each side of the car ran a row of large single-plate windows, of a blue tint-blue to soften the bitter glare of the sun and protect one's eyes from torture. These could be let down out of the way when one wanted the breeze.

Air-conditioning has really done for First Class. To keep out the heat the dark blue tinted windows that Twain described are actually almost black, which means one cannot see the great Indian countryside, and they need to be left a bit ajar for ventilation, which fills the compartment with heat and dust. After these come various versions of non-a/c discomfort known as Second Class, which Twain would have known as Second and Third class. He noted also that: "The Indian trains are manned by natives exclusively. The Indian stations except very large and important ones—are manned entirely by natives, and so are the posts and telegraphs. The rank and file of the police are natives. All these people are pleasant and accommodating." Actually a large part of the trains and stations were manned by Anglo-Indians and we'll see how they fared later.

*

Twain's and Smythe's visit to Poona was a bit of a damp squib. Poona itself was at its colonial finest. The British had discovered a pretty little mountain town a hundred miles southeast of Bombay—but more importantly 1,500 feet above the rank humidity of the monsoon-prone coast. From June to September the governor and his government decamped to the hill station and moved their whole operation into Poona's Governor's House. Scattered around the surrounding hills were the old Peshwa palaces, with pride of place going to the Parvati hill temple—all remnants of past Hindu glories and all giving the area an added oriental heritage and zest. By 1896 Poona was a full-scale, but still small-scale, Raj summer resort and year-round military headquarters centered in the cantonment area.

This was Twain' first cantonment experience; over the next two months he would experience many more cantonments as he was to a large extent under the care of the military side of the Raj and it was in cantonments that they were based. In small towns like Poona the cantonment quickly became the centre of activity and to visit a cantonment now is to experience an India that was: freshly painted buildings, swept and uncrowded streets and a strange sense of order and functionality. The Indian Army, Raj-like in so many ways, keep the cantonments all over India not just intact but spick and span, and Poona, being the headquarters of Southern Command, is especially spick and not a little span.

Fifteen years before Twain's Talk here the British had built the Poona Gymkhana Club adjoining the cantonment. "Gymkhana" is an Urdu and Hindi word for any form of sporting contest; the Indian nuance tips towards racket games, especially squash and badminton, and the British nuance towards equestrian events, especially polo and show-jumping. By the time Twain visited Poona on 30 January 1896 the Club had a large enough cricket ground to play two games simultaneously, numerous tennis and squash courts, two polo pitches and the beginnings of what is now an 18-hole golf course scattered across Poona's cantonment area.

When not disporting themselves on the sports or the battle fields Gymkhana Club members could enjoy tiffin in the day or cocktails in the evening, all served by uniformed bearers on the long veranda that joined onto the cricket pavilion. The bearers and the other staff were the only non-royal Indians allowed into the club. Royal Indians, with their boundless wealth and anyway tending to be more British than the British, were more than welcome—and more than paid their way. The founding fathers of the Poona Gymkhana Club were indeed the great and the good of Anglo-Indian society, proclaimed on a varnished and gold-leafed plaque above the entry to the veranda:

His Exalted Highness The Aga Khan
Nawab Shah Rookh Yar Jung Bahadur
Sir Cowasji Jehangir
Aga Kasim Shah
Sir Nusserwanjee Wadia
Aga Jalal M. Shah

Sir Jehangir (Kothari)
Sir Dhanjbhoy Bomanji
His Highness The Nawab of Junagadh
Sir Victor Sassoon
His Highness The Maharaja of Jodhpur
His Highness The Maharaja of Rajpipla
Sir Sasoon David
Sir Dorab Tata
Sir Cusrow Wadia
His Highness The Gaikwar of Baroda

It is hard to stress too highly the importance of club life in the Raj days. Most, like the Poona Club here or my Royal Bombay Yacht Club, started off as sporting clubs as sport was the overwhelming leisure activity of the Europeans in India. But the real value of club life for its members came off the polo pitch, tennis court or golf links, when the military and civilians could meet in the cool of the evening at bridge or cocktails or dinner. The club was where a major could compare notes with a sessions judge, a captain could confer with the district forest officer, a colonel could rub shoulders with a headquarters tax-collector and so on.

Membership was strictly controlled by rank, so a dashing young, independently wealthy lieutenant or solicitor would not have been admitted to the Poona Club whereas a newly arrived, gnarled and penniless captain or senior architect would. This was hardly a disaster as there were other, lesser clubs for the lesser orders and in big cities like Calcutta, to where we are heading, there were a dozen. They all shared formality in common with strict dress codes, tuxedos for dinner and ties at all times in the clubhouse. They also shared a system of credit: before credit cards there were chits, a sort of informal IOU, with the rule that all accounts had to be settled by the 7th of the following month.

Perhaps the biggest beneficiaries of the clubs were those not allowed to be members—women, or more precisely wives. The husbands went off every day to work, militarily or civilly, leaving their wives at home. Even the lowest paid officer or civil servant had a bearer, a maid, a cook and if with child, a nanny. There wasn't much, or anything really, for the wives to do. The clubs were where they passed the afternoon with their fellow wives, and spent most evenings with their husbands—and being British in the tropics, others' husbands too.

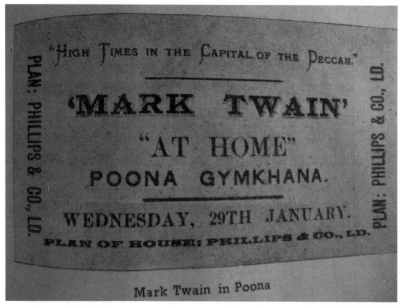

"HIGH TIMES IN THE CAPITAL OF THE DECCAN."

PLAN: PHILLIPS & CO., LD.

'MARK TWAIN'

"AT HOME"

POONA GYMKHANA.

WEDNESDAY, 29TH JANUARY.

PLAN OF HOUSE: PHILLIPS & CO., LD.

PLAN: PHILLIPS & CO., LD.

Mark Twain in Poona

So why was Twain's visit such a damp squib? At the end of January Poona was empty of the big cheeses who brought it to life in the season. There was really only the nearby cantonment, and one imagines quite a few inhabitants of the Officers' Mess were too arrogant to think they could be entertained by an American humorist. Certainly no one from the club met him and Smythe at the end of their five-hour train journey. Smythe recalled that the audience was really inadequate in numbers for the At Home Talk and *The Century* magazine reported that Twain's voice was creaking and croaking—either he hadn't totally shaken off the bronchial infection which had haunted him since Ceylon or the reporter wasn't used to the slow drawl of a Mark Twain Talk.

The *Bombay Gazette* reported that the Bishop of Bombay, who happened to be in Poona and in the audience, took exception to a rather tame morality joke about Adam and the serpent "and left the room therewith and not in the best of tempers. I am sorry that the Lord Bishop did not remain to hear Mark Twain on morals." Further on the appreciative reviewer noted that "one woman disturbed every body by her loud laughter", and was, when describing the audience, moved to rhyme:

A rather gushing one in cream

THE INDIAN EQUATOR

A perky one in black
A fair hared one in blue
Sitting next to one in 'lac
A lovely black fared
with the palest pink
With bow to match
The effect was really swell.

Unfortunately the old three-story wooden wedding-cake that was the clubhouse burned down in 1945, the only surprise being that it hadn't happened before. The open fires in the kitchens caught the blame but one can imagine a stray cigar butt being as likely a culprit. The fire took the library with it and so we have lost not only all the club records but also a wonderful reference to a slice of Raj history.

The Poona Gymkhana Club has now become the Poona Club Ltd. and styles itself, quite possibly correctly, as "South Asia's largest sporting club". I was shown around by my host, the club secretary Lt. Col. KSS Jamwal (Ret'd). The cricket facilities are wonderful and in January county players from the English leagues stay to keep their eyes in. Games are running all the time. The 18-hole golf course has been completed; the swimming pool keeps itself cool under a fine net shade; next door the squash courts resound to the thump-whack of dull rubber balls; beyond young girls take tennis lessons from older pros. There's a running track and a gymnasium; it's exhausting just thinking about the place.

Off the track and field things aren't so bright. The rebuilt clubhouse is attractive enough, its large open veranda off a ground floor with its high ceiling and token fans reminding one of a Serengeti safari lodge, but the service is dozy and grudging. One suspects the waiters have been on call since the great fire; there was no hurry then and there's even less hurry now. The female cleaners squat and sweep like grounded Cossacks, their old horsetail twizzles missing whole swathes of dust and stirring up the rest. The rooms are nothing special and the room service non-existent. Trying to communicate with them by phone or e-mail is a frustratingly one-sided affair. Worse, some bounder has put water in the bar gin.

Outside the club Poona is—to put it mildly—in full swing. It's growing so quickly that officials can only guess at the population, and their guess is four million. It feels like they are all on the same piece of road at the same time, all rushing and racing in a mass of ambition and endeavor. The city is expanding in all directions all at once without, it would seem, any direction at all. There is no room for pleasing lines or subtle shades in the cost-controlled concrete building rush. Being a pedestrian is a fearsome pastime: traffic lights and crossings and even pavements—if one can find one—are simply ignored. India is famously a structured society and pedestrians are near the bottom of the transport hierarchy, just above dogs and just below bicycles. The only consolation for not being able to amble about aimlessly is that one doesn't really want to amble about aimlessly; ugliness and pollution cure the foot-borne wanderlust and send us scurrying back to the sleepy veranda and the second innings at the Poona Club, where I'm writing now and still waiting for the Kingfisher beer I ordered at the start of the paragraph before last—or was it the one before that?

Poona the city and Poona the club are fine examples of the patronizing dilemma of the India lover; the India lover wants the India that was, while the India liver wants the India that is—and that the latter is far better off cannot be denied. And, as the songstress stressed, we are living in a material world.

3. BARODA

SITTING HERE IN the public library in Baroda it seems that researching Indian history is not as simple as one might hope. The problem for the researcher is that in the eyes of most Indians their country's history does not start until Independence in 1947. Before that "India" had not existed, not in the sense that Indians understand it now. In 1525 Babur and his Moghul army—directly descended from Genghis Khan and his Mongol hordes—swept into the Punjab from Afghanistan and colonized the hundreds of northern principalities that comprise the northern India, Pakistan and parts of Bangladesh of today. When the British Crown took direct control from the East India Company in 1857/8 "India" was a patchwork of those princely states that had sworn allegiance to the Crown (some more willingly than others), but nevertheless "India" was ruled by a system of suzerainty and paramountcy rather than as a unified bloc. Thus one can see the librarians' point that "Indian History" before 1947 is an oxymoron.

This hotchpotch of a history means that when one enters, for example, this or any other library and asks about local history in January/February 1896 there are only blank looks and shrugged shoulders. Attempting to dig deeper soon seems impolite as the modern Indian librarian seems rather sheepish about the lack of Indianity for most of the last five hundred years—and if he or she *were* to dig deeper forever, before that too.

The BBC recently re-ran a documentary that started with the proposition that the greatest gift the British had left India was Indian Railways. I disagree. Indian railways is surely a remarkable legacy, a superb vision[23] of investor and political confidence executed by a stunning feat of engineering and millions of hours of sweat and toil—and indeed hundreds of lives. However, all these factors also required to create success a common country across which to build the railways, and then a common language with which to direct the enterprise and a then a common rule of law and civil administration to ensure its operation.

One hates to question the received post-colonial guilt wisdom of the BBC, but the greatest gift the British left India was surely India itself, even if

---

[23] Still the largest private investment, in real terms, ever made.

it still speaks twenty official languages and experiences all the inter-regional tensions such a vast, artificially created country is bound to feel. English is the Esperanto, the common language, a useful enough legacy in itself. The rule of law and the civil service may not be what it was at Independence but it is still better than it was five hundred years ago, before the Moghuls, let alone the British, arrived. Indian Railways is even more remarkable now than when the British left it, but surely a mere convenience compared to the fundamentals of the ninety-year legacy of the British Raj—but just don't mention any of this to the librarian at Baroda if you want to look at the one pamphlet referring to an (irrelevant) event in January 1896.

*

Mark Twain and Smythe left Poona twenty-four hours after they arrived, presumably with slim regrets to go with the slim pickings, to rejoin Livy and Clara back in Bombay's VT for the change of trains up to Baroda, in this case the overnight Dehradun Express. Livy and Clara would have taken one compartment, Twain and Smythe another. Then and now it arrives at crack of dawn.

> We arrived at 7 this morning. The dawn was just beginning to show. It was forlorn to have to turn out in a strange place at such a time, and the blinking lights in the station made it seem night still. But the gentlemen who had come to receive us were there with their servants, and they make quick work; there was no lost time. We were soon outside and moving swiftly through the soft gray light, and presently were comfortably housed—with more servants to help than we were used to, and with rather embarrassingly important officials to direct them. But it was custom; they spoke Ballarat English, their bearing was charming and hospitable, and so all went well.

The entourage deposited the Twain party at the Soni Pati Bhavan, the Maharaja of Gwaekor's visitors' guesthouse, just opposite the main gate. Since then the solidly cubed eight-room guesthouse has fallen on hard times, being a crumbling squat for the lowest castes, feral dogs and listless—if still holy—cows. This being India, the humans are intrigued and hospitable, the dogs wary at first and then easier and the cows pre-occupied with eating the garbage, a holy enough occupation hereabouts.

35

Time then for a wholesome English breakfast[24] and then an eventful tour of Baroda.

Breakfast was a satisfaction, after which the day began—and a sufficiently busy one.

We came to the city, by and by, and drove all through it... And the houses—oh, indescribably quaint and curious they were, with their fronts an elaborate lace-work of intricate and beautiful wood-carving, and now and then further adorned with rude pictures of elephants and princes and gods done in shouting colors; and all the ground floors along these cramped and narrow lanes occupied as shops— shops unbelievably small and impossibly packed with merchantable rubbish, and with nine-tenths-naked natives squatting at their work of hammering, pounding, brazing, soldering, sewing, designing, cooking, measuring out grain, grinding it, repairing idols—and then the swarm of ragged and noisy humanity under the horses' feet and everywhere, and the pervading reek and fume and smell! It was all wonderful and delightful.

By and by to the elephant stables, and I took a ride; but it was by request—I did not ask for it, and didn't want it; but I took it, because otherwise they would have thought I was afraid, which I was. The elephant kneels down, by command—one end of him at a time—and you climb the ladder and get into the howdah, and then he gets up, one end at a time, just as a ship gets up over a wave; and after that, as he strides monstrously about, his motion is much like a ship's motion. Among these twenty-five elephants were two which were larger than any I had ever seen before, and if I had thought I could learn to not be afraid, I would have taken one of them while the police were not looking.

Later Clara remembered the incident thus:

Father seated on an elephant defies description. There was something

---

[24] In the same way the British champion Indian dinners, the Indians have perfected the English breakfast.

funny about the sight, and Father, suspecting what I was giggling about, said "What are you laughing at, you sassmill?"

"'If you could see yourself, Father, you would laugh too. The elephant looks so unreal with all his important trappings and you have had such a troubled air, as if you realized your hat did not match the blue-and-red harness."

Father never minded being laughed at, so he replied he did not believe the picture could be any stranger than his feelings. What could he do if the elephant decided to run? Nobody could answer this question, so he decided to forget it and enjoy the picturesque little streets and unfamiliar architecture.

*

I had worried that Mark Twain's Grand Tour of India seemed a bit light on the maharaja audiences. One of the richest of them, actually the second richest and by general consent the most enlightened, was that of Baroda, in the modern state of Gujarat, where Sayajirao III, the Maharaja of Gwaekor, ruled in fabulous splendor and general munificence. As Twain noted: "This is indeed one of the oldest of the princedoms of India, and has always been celebrated for its barbaric pomps and splendors, and for the wealth of its princes."

His full form and title was His Highness Farzand-i-Khas-i-Daulat-i-Inglishia, Shrimant Maharaja Sir Sayajirao III, Gaekwad, Sena Khas Khel Shamsher Bahadur, Maharaja of Baroda, GCSI, GCIE, KIH. He had been on the throne for twenty years when Twain met him and in that time had just finished building the amazingly ornate, massively overwrought Laxmi Vilas Palace in the then-fashionable Moghul-British Indo-Saracenic style. It was four times the size of Buckingham Place and was said to have cost £200,000, a staggering sum considering that the labor was practically free. Perhaps he considered £200,000 was a sensible amount for a palace-cum-safe in which to keep his £3,000,000 (worth £12 million and £180 million today respectively) collection of jewelry—a collection which included the famous Brazilian diamond, the Star of the South and no fewer than four carpets made of pearls with diamonds, rubies and emeralds sewn into the silk. Every time the maharaja or maharini left or entered the palace the household guard, with their white breeches, blue and gold jackets and black boots, would strike up the Baroda anthem.

By the time of Twain's lecture tour he had already visited Europe five times—no small undertaking in itself—and in his library were several of Twain's books

among many thousand others. Twain observed: "The prince is an educated gentleman. His culture is European. He has been in Europe five times. People say that this is costly amusement for him, since in crossing the sea he must sometimes be obliged to drink water from vessels that are more or less public, and thus damage his caste. To get it purified again he must make pilgrimage to some renowned Hindoo temples and contribute a fortune or two to them. His people are like the other Hindoos, profoundly religious; and they could not be content with a master who was impure." The maharaja sent his personal representative, his Vakeel, Rao Bahadur Baskirao Balinkanje Pitale, to Bombay to persuade Twain—for the princely sum of 1,000 rupees—to lecture in the Durbar Hall at Laxmi Vilas Palace.

Twain was then shown the maharaja's two palaces: the older Makapura Palace, now purloined by the Indian Air Force for knocking its officers into shape, and the newer Laxmi Vilas Palace where he was to lecture later that day.

He much preferred the former, which he found "oriental and charming", and damned the latter as being without merit "except for its costliness". He saw the silver and gold cannons built by successive maharajas in a gilded display of one-upmanship, which "seemed to be six-pounders. They were not designed for business, but for salutes upon rare and particularly important state occasions. This sort of artillery is in keeping with the traditions of Baroda, which was of old famous for style and show. It used to entertain visiting rajahs and viceroys with tiger-fights, elephant-fights, illuminations, and elephant-processions of the most glittering and gorgeous character."

Although the Laxmi Vilas Palace was "not a good place to lecture in, on account of the echoes, it is a good place to hold durbars in and regulate the affairs of a kingdom, and that is what it is for. If I had it I would have a durbar every day, instead of once or twice a year." Baroda made a deep impression on Twain, who thought it all "intensely Indian, crumbly and mouldering and immemorially old"; I can echo that impression having, like Twain, arrived here from downtown Bombay and cantonment Pune—this for the first time on his Tour and indeed on our Re-Tour was "India".

*

Two hundred and fifty specially invited guests, who had been summoned by gold-leafed invitations to hear the "Yankee humor", attended the At Home Talk. Twain considered the Talk a success although Smythe noted that the female part of the royal household watching from behind the mezzanine screens didn't laugh at his jokes as heartily as the men did and the acoustics in the cavernous Durbar Hall caused each joke to be told several times.

Like a good footsteps hound I was keen to meet the current scion of the Gaekwad dynasty and visit the Durbar Hall and Laxmi Vilas Palace. Through connections at the American Centre in Bombay I made an appointment for an audience for Gillian and me with the heir to the throne, Yuvraj (Prince) Samarjitsingh Gaekwad, Yuvaraj Sahib of Baroda. He further promised that his secretary, Mr. Mahendrasinh Chauchan, would show us around later, which he did.

Actually I had already paid the Laxmi Vilas Palace a visit the day before as an anonymous tourist to see how the general public would see it. It was not, one might say, overly impressive. The palace itself is still, just about, overly impressive but tourists are left to feel they are only allowed in through grated teeth. To buy a ticket one has to visit a subsidiary library a quarter of a mile off the beaten track. Once in the palace it is clear that only half a dozen or so rooms—and all in one wing of the ground floor—are open to inspection. No-one in a uniform knows anything about the history of the building; in fact no-one speaks English even though it is the lingua franca of tourism. For some bizarre reason photography is forbidden inside the palace, even though high-resolution images are freely available on the internet and digital throw-away photography is the essence of modern tourism. Welcome one is not made.

But the Durbar Hall is still as magnificent as it was in its pomp and prime and on the night that Mark Twain lectured there. The Venetian mosaic floor, the Flemish stained glass windows, the Moghul-style panels with their intricate inlaid and relief mosaics, the French chandeliers and the Genoan lacquered ceiling are all present and correct, glimmering and glittering in a dazzling display of opulence and extroversion. Compared to the interior, the Grand Entrance—by Fellici—is a bit shabby. It features an Italianate courtyard with water fountains and sculptures in bronze, marble and terracotta. As a design feature the concept "intricate" is an over-simplification.

Paintings show the wonderful grounds that were landscaped by William Goldring, largely responsible for Kew Gardens; they are now a golf course and like many a golf course it has soon and unintentionally turned itself into wildlife sanctuary.

The prince, 44, with a flurry of silver hair and complexion polished by a life of ease, is very handsome and gracious and received us in one of the ground-floor reception rooms. An accomplished sportsman and Uppingham old boy, it is clear his interests lie in the golf course rather than the palace, in the pleasure of sporting competition rather than the pain of accountancy and commerce. The family fortune has been decimated by taxes and internecine pay-offs and is in need of urgent rebuilding. With his Bollywood good looks and easy charm he would make the perfect film star—one well-paid way to restock the assets. There is vague talk of him turning the palace into a hotel and conference centre as other maharajas have done. What a venue it would make, but it seems unlikely to happen. One cannot imagine the prince feeling too comfortable with the great unwashed swarming all over the place.

All around the structure is slowly on the crumble and I fear that within two generations—and his only child is a daughter in a regime of primogeniture—it may be beyond affordable repair. In the meantime his family can wander along the labyrinthine corridors, explore the countless rooms (the prince didn't know how many there were) and gaze in awe at the paintings and mosaics that look down on the slow decline. For the grandmother in the wheelchair there are wonderful memoirs of shimmering parties; for the children scampering along the endless cracking tiles there is the innocence of the inheritance; and for the prince, perhaps a wistful sideways look at the tumble of life's dice, which have given him a six when he could have done with a seven.

PART TWO
THE HINDU HEARTLAND

THE WELL OF FATE.

4. ALLAHABAD

THE TWAIN PARTY left for Allahabad by a night train for "it is the custom of the country to avoid day travel when it can conveniently be done. It was a long journey—two nights, one day, and part of another day; but it was always interesting, and not fatiguing." Livy and Clara were in a ladies' four-berth compartment, and Mark Twain and Smythe in a male-only one down the corridor. Nowadays one can reserve the more desirable lower berths but in 1896 the etiquette was that whoever laid out their baggage on the lower berth first "bagged" it. The trick was to have "your Satan arrive before somebody else's servants, and spread the bedding on the two sofas and then stand guard till you come and all will be well; but if they step aside on an errand, they may find the beds promoted to the two shelves, and somebody else's demons standing guard over their master's beds, which in the meantime have been spread upon your sofas."

This is exactly what happened. Satan had laid out Livy and Clara's bedding on the lower berths in the female compartment and then gone to the male compartment to do the same for Twain and Smythe. "Clara's satchels were holding possession of her berth—a lower one. At the last moment, whilst Satan was attending to Smythe and me, a middle-aged American lady swarmed into the compartment, followed by native porters laden with her baggage. She was growling and snarling and scolding, and trying to make herself phenomenally disagreeable; and succeeding. Without a word, she hoisted the satchels into the hanging shelf, and took possession of that lower berth."

Slowly the old steam engine chugged them across the endless plains of northern India:

> Out in the country in India, the day begins early. One sees a plain, perfectly flat, dust-colored and brick-yardy, stretching limitlessly away on every side in the dim gray light, striped everywhere with hard-beaten narrow paths, the vast flatness broken at wide intervals by bunches of spectral trees that mark where villages are. All day long one has this monotony of dust-colored dead levels and scattering bunches of trees and mud villages. You soon realize that India is not beautiful; still there is an enchantment about it that is beguiling, and which does not pall.

You cannot tell just what it is that makes the spell, perhaps, but you feel it and confess it, nevertheless.

Perhaps the spell was helped when "Satan got left behind somewhere that morning, and did not overtake us until after nightfall. It seemed very peaceful without him. The world seemed asleep and dreaming."

*

When Mark Twain arrived on the morning of 3 February he promptly christened Allahabad by its direct translation, Godville. Actually, god-wise, he had rather missed Godville's glory days but he was in the right place and the right time—a once every twelve years right time—to see the most extraordinary outpouring of goddom, the Hindu festival of Kumbh Mela.

For Hindus it is the place where Brahma created the universe untold millions of years gone by; after the Moghuls arrived five hundred years ago they built mosques and forts all over northern India, and one of the best surviving ones is here, the wonderful Akbar fort on the banks of the Ganges; when the British took over two hundred years after that numerous churches and missionary schools were built, the most outstanding church being All Saints Cathedral,[25] modeled on Paris' Notre Dame and completed only ten years before Twain's arrival.

The city had played a part, albeit a minor a part, in the Sepoy Uprising of 1857, a series of mutinies and revolts whose memories were increasingly to preoccupy Twain as his Grand Tour proceeded.

*

I think now would be a good time to say something about the Sepoy Uprising. As Twain traveled east towards Calcutta from here then headed back west to Delhi he journeyed through the Uprising country and was hosted by the same British Army whose attitudes to India had been changed so much by the mutinous events thirty-nine years before.

The events and heroics of the revolt inspired him, even if he only came across the British view of them: "The military history of England is old and great, but I think it must be granted that the crushing of the Indian Mutiny[26] is the greatest chapter in it. The British were caught asleep and unprepared. They

---

[25] Designed by Sir William Emerson of Victoria Memorial fame—more in Calcutta.

were a few thousands, swallowed up in an ocean of hostile populations. It would take months to inform England and get help, but they did not falter or stop to count the odds, but with English resolution and English devotion they took up their task, and went stubbornly on with it, through good fortune and bad, and fought the most unpromising fight that one may read of in fiction or out of it, and won it thoroughly."

Like many great events in history the *casus belli* of the Sepoy Uprising was not one single catastrophic eruption but a series of minor tremors, each survivable on its own but which when thrown together became combustible. The most major of the minor incidents was the decision—motivated purely by greed—in the spring of 1857 by the ruling East India Company to annex the Kingdom of Oudh. As Twain noted: "It seems to be settled, now, that among the many causes from which the Great Mutiny sprang, the main one was the annexation of the kingdom of Oudh by the East India Company—characterized by Sir Henry Lawrence as "the most unrighteous act that was ever committed."

This being India, caste—and the protection of caste rights—also played its part. Luckily for the British the revolt was confined to only one of the three armies, the one from Bengal,[27] and this was the only one recruited from the higher-caste Rajputs and Brahmins. Ironically, this recruitment was done in the early days of Company expansion as it was thought the caste system, with its inbuilt respect of hierarchy, would provide greater loyalty. In fact of the 140,000 sepoys—indigenous infantry privates—in the Bengal Army only 8,000 remained loyal.

As the Company's empire spread west and the newly acquired lands came under British control the ruling castes lost some of their perks and privileges, causing disquiet; this disquiet, allied to the better education which their higher caste had given them, fermented into revolt—and well-led revolt at that. According to Twain: "The leaders moved from camp to camp undisturbed, and painted to the native soldier the wrongs his people were suffering at the hands of the English, and made his heart burn for revenge. They were able to point to two facts of formidable value as backers of their persuasions: In Clive's day, native armies were incoherent mobs, and without effective arms; therefore, they were weak against Clive's organized handful of well-armed men, but the thing was

---

[26] He would only have heard the uprising called the Indian Mutiny or Great Mutiny.
[27] The Bombay Presidency's Army saw only minor disturbances and the one from Madras (now Chennai) none at all.

the other way, now. The British forces were native; they had been trained by the British, organized by the British, armed by the British, all the power was in their hands—they were a club made by British hands to beat out British brains with. There was nothing to oppose their mass, nothing but a few weak battalions of British soldiers scattered about India, a force not worth speaking of."

There was a related issue to caste: religion. In the early days of British expansion the East India Company had concentrated on its main aim, commerce. As the unofficial empire expanded more force was needed and the army presence grew. With the army came chaplains and religiously minded officers, some in very high rank, whose own interpretation of their mission was as much to save the heathen Hindu from his sins as to establish trade routes for the Company. Inevitably this postulating from the Christians leaders, who made the mistake of seeing Hinduism as a religion—and an inferior one—led to resentment among the sepoys who made the mistake of seeing Christianity as another philosophy—and an inferior one—to which they were not about to descend. As the Christians were in power and Hindus subjugated, the latter felt the need to make a stand to protect their way of life—and for them was Hinduism is just that.

The most infamous cause of the uprising—and certainly the most ineptly handled by the British—was the issuing of ammunition greased in animal fat. The army had recently been re-equipped with the Pattern 1853 Enfield rifle. This new technology needed better shot which had to be tightly wrapped in greased paper. The drill was for the sepoys to bite off the end of the cartridge to release the powder. The shot now came pre-greased with tallow made from animal fat, either from a cow or a pig; the vegetarian Hindu sepoys could tolerate biting neither tallow and the Muslim sepoys could not tell from which beast it derived and so chose the abhor them both as *haram*.

Amazingly the British ignored all warnings about the unacceptability of the sepoys biting into tallow and insisted, to the point of court martial, that the new shot was used as designed. When unrest became restless the British tried denying there was animal fat in the tallow but as the high-caste sepoys could see the low-caste tallow-wallahs at work the denial only aroused suspicions. When the British then re-issued the shot with hand-torn cartridges the original suspicions were only confirmed.

Finally, there was a less tangible, more Indian factor at work, best explained by Twain as follows: "...the bravest and best Indian troops had a wholesome dread of the white soldier, whether he was weak or strong. But, against that, there was a prophecy—a prophecy a hundred years old. The Indian is open to prophecy at all times; argument may fail to convince him, but not prophecy. There was a prophecy that a hundred years from the year of that battle of Clive's which founded the British Indian Empire, the British power would be overthrown and swept away by the natives."

It is hard in retrospect to see how the British did not see the trouble brewing. The reason was in large part benign neglect; the older and more senior East India Company British officers had developed a strong attraction to India and felt they had a special relationship with the sepoys, and the sepoys with them, and as a result the sepoys would never revolt against them. They had after all learnt the native language—no sepoy was allowed to speak English to an officer and no officer allowed to speak English to a sepoy. Younger officers who sounded the alarm were ignored as inexperienced types who didn't understand the native mind and spirit. In Twain's words: "…a mutinous spirit was observable in many of the native garrisons, and it grew day-by-day and spread wider and wider. The younger military men saw something very serious in it, and would have liked to take hold of it vigorously and stamp it out promptly; but they were not in authority. Old-men were in the high places of the army—men who should have been retired long before, because of their great age—and they regarded the matter as a thing of no consequence. They loved their native soldiers, and would not believe that anything could move them to revolt."

We shall see how the Sepoy Uprising affected Twain's visits to the northern cities as he passed through these places For now suffice to say that the revolt failed and the British retribution was unjust and terrible, "disproportionate" as we would say now. A further tragedy was the breakdown in trust between the British and the Indians. Before 1857 the British in India called themselves "Indians" and the Indians "natives", with no hint of disparagement. After the slaughter of British women and children, in particular, the feelings of bonding turned to disgust—and fear, the feeling of "the degradation of fearing those we had taught to fear us" in the words of Sir John Kaye. H. G. Keene in his *Anglo-Indian Sketches* wrote that "a terrible abyss has opened between the rulers and the ruled; and every huckster, every pettifogger who wears a hat and breaches, looks down upon the noblest of the natives." Even Sir Bartle Frere, an ex-Governor of Bombay and in many ways the father of the modern city, said, "You have no idea how much India has altered. The sympathy which Englishman felt for the natives has changed to a general feeling of repugnance."

As Twain pointed out, the British won a heroic victory against seemingly impossible odds but they were helped enormously by the chaos on the Indian side. The Muslims in particular divided against themselves, Sunni and Shia, or against the Hindus by supporting the British when Hindu success seemed likely. Other Indian groups, like the Sikhs, the Pathans, the Ghurkhas and other Nepalis and the Aga Khan's Muslims, openly supported the British from the start. Meanwhile the sepoys, at heart an unpaid, officerless peasant army, had no central command or even a cohesive goal, and split more geographically than ideologically were easily picked off by the disciplined—and at the time, desperate—British.

When the British regained control, that control passed from the East India Company to the British Crown whose first priority was to make sure no future uprisings could give them such a run for their money. Entire native towns were cleared across the northern plains, of which Allahabad was one. In the Sepoy Uprising the British areas had been badly damaged and in their place the British built wide, tree-lined boulevards with large, tree-lined bungalows behind even larger tree-lined walls; a vision of European civilization in the tropics. From these bungalows they ran the districts and in many cities, including Allahabad, they called these areas Civil Lines.

*

Civil Lines in Allahabad Mark Twain described thus: "I saw the English part of the city. It is a town of wide avenues and noble distances, and is comely and alluring, and full of suggestions of comfort and leisure, and of the serenity which a good conscience buttressed by a sufficient bank account gives. The bungalows (dwellings) stand well back in the seclusion and privacy of large enclosed compounds (private grounds, as we should say) and in the shade and shelter of trees."

Twain's hotel was at the western edge of Civil Lines, next to All Saints Cathedral. It still stands and will soon be a functioning hotel again, albeit with the rather unfortunate name of Hotel Harsh. Built in 1875 on two floors with a castellated roof, it is long and low and white and had what Mark Twain described as "a long yellow veranda", a feature which still zigzags around the front of the hotel now.

In 1896 it was known as Barnet's Hotel; its proprietor was Sir G. H. Barnet about whom even Sita cannot find anything noteworthy.

I meet the current owner, Mr. Adinath Harsh.

"We are rebuilding it. It has not been a hotel for more than twenty years. But now Allahabad is busy again. Aspects are propitious."

He shows me around. There are no records surviving, no guest book of 3 February 1896 for us to pore over.

"This room is typical room of where they would have stayed. We have yet to divide it."

"Divide?"

"Yes, the rooms are too big for today. Typically they are four hundred square feet with twenty-five foot ceilings. Imagine the cost of cooling that. So we are lowering the ceilings and dividing the rooms. Indians like smaller confines and we get twice as many rooms."

"I hope you don't mind me saying, and you speak such good Engl…"

"The name," Adinath says. "Yes, I know. In Hindi *harsh* means comfortable—and fortunate. But really the problem is that it is part of our family name and my father is insistent."

"It's his hotel?"

"It's his money. And as you say, 'he who pays the piper plays the tune'."

That evening's Talk was at the Railway Club, a short *tonga*[28] trot away. Mark Twain noticed how everyone had their own carriage and took it for even the shortest distances: "all the white citizens have private carriages; and each carriage has a flock of white-turbaned black footmen and drivers all over it. The vicinity of a lecture-hall looks like a snowstorm—and makes the lecturer feel like an opera."

Railway Clubs were the most racially integrated meeting places in India. While, to quote Rudyard Kipling, East is East and West is West, and never the twain shall meet,[29] there was one group where they did meet, the largely unfortunate Anglo-Indians. In the early East India Company days many European men were entranced by the Moghul and Hindu civilizations and, being single, took Indian wives, frequently beautiful widows who otherwise would have been left to wither on the vine. Their offspring, inevitably wealthy and often beautiful, were brought up without stigma; rather the opposite. By the time of Twain's visit

---

[28] A light two-person, one-horse carriage, often self-driven, from the Hindi *taga*—not to be confused with the nippier Victoria which was for one person and one horse—what we would call a sulky.

[29] From "The Ballad of East and West", written one year before Mark Twain's visit.

the more interesting, freethinking Europeans had been replaced by stuffier, less imaginative men—and their wives—and affairs between well-born Europeans and Indians were taboo. An Anglo-Indian at the Railway Club that night was more likely to have been the result of a liaison between a British squaddy[30] and an Indian prostitute—and as a result not readily acceptable to either side. Nevertheless they were fiercely racist against the "wog"[31] natives themselves and equally obsequious to the whites. They would only speak English, made the Indian railways their cause and were invaluable as drivers, engineers and junior managers; every major terminus and junction had its "railway colony" of Anglo-Indians. What few privileges their tint gave the twilight Eurasians were lost at Independence and most have now emigrated throughout the Commonwealth—anecdotally at least, largely to Canada.

Allahabad had become an important junction, but after Independence Indian Railways stopped supporting the club and it declined like so many other Raj institutions. In 1984 it was rescued by a local businessman who saw the need for a school and a community center. The Railway Club's wing is now the thriving Coral Club Medium School (not I presume, a school for mystics) and the main building a large empty shell used mostly for Hindu weddings. As a Hindu wedding is not a short-lived affair the main hall is in more or less permanent use.

The stage is still set at one end of the main hall, and as it is made of brick I can only assume it is as it was when Twain delivered his "At Home" there. The *Allahabad Pioneer*,[32] the paper on which his new friend Rudyard Kipling used to work, reported that "Mark Twain's humor is often of the ladies' postscript sort—in a casual incidental way he introduces a circumstance that puts quite a new color on a detailed story…The charm of his delivery is so delightful that no one who hears him could wish to have been content with a report."

*

---

[30] A British foot soldier, so called from having to march in a squad around the parade ground.
[31] Nothing to do with the children's book character, Gollywog, but an acronym for Westernized Oriental Gentleman—and used disparagingly. It was originally coined by the British to describe the Eurasian Anglo-Indians, who in turn took it to refer to native Indians, forgetting the meaning behind the acronym.
[32] Now a daily paper, *The Pioneer*, published from Lucknow.

Mark Twain and Rudyard Kipling were arguably the two most celebrated writers in the English language in the late nineteenth century. They formed a mutual admiration society.

Twain told the *Calcutta Hindoo* Patriot in an interview the following week that he had met Rudyard Kipling several times and "I like him very much. I admire his work prodigiously. There is no question as to his genius and that must be confessed by everyone. He has genius and plenty of it. I have an amazing fondness for his *Plain Tales from the Hills* and I think that some of his ballad work is inimitable. I don't see how anyone could possibly surpass it."

They first met in the summer of 1890 in Elmira, NY and gave back-to-back accounts of their encounter; Kipling's on meeting Twain in the *New York Herald* of 17 August 1890 and Twain's on meeting Kipling in the *New York World* a week later. Mark Twain was 55; Rudyard Kipling was 25.

Kipling's piece starts with an imaginary address to an audience in India:

You are a contemptible lot out there! Some of you are Commissioners and some Lieutenant-Governors and a few of you are privileged to walk about the Mall arm in arm with the Viceroy; but I have seen Mark Twain this golden morning, have shaken his hand and smoked a cigar—no two cigars—with him and talked with him for more than two hours! Understand I do not despise you—indeed I don't. I am only very sorry for you all from the Viceroy downwards. To soothe your envy and to prove I still regard you as my equals I will tell you about it.

I was impressed that Mark Twain had time to entertain an escaped lunatic from India, be he ever so full of admiration. I was smoking his cigar, and I was hearing him talk—this man I had learned to love and admire 14,000 miles away.

The *New York World* piece started:

The young story-writer of old England paid his respects in earnest person as well as in luminous prose to the veteran humorist of New England. The latter opined: "It would be a good thing to read Mr. Kipling's writings for their style alone if there were no back story to it. But, as you say, there always is a story there and a powerfully interesting one generally. How people have gotten to read and talk about his stories! Why, when a young man not yet 24 years of age, succeeds in the way Kipling has succeeded, it simply shows, doesn't it, that the general public has a strong appreciation of a good thing when it gets hold of one?

"His great charm to me is the way he 'swings nervous' English! It is wonderful. That it seems to me is one great secret of the hold he takes on his readers. They can understand what he is at. He is simple and direct."

*

The next morning, wrote Twain:

In the early brightness we made a long drive out to the Fort. Part of the way was beautiful. It led under stately trees and through groups of native houses and by the usual village well, where the picturesque gangs are always flocking to and fro and laughing and chattering; and this time brawny men were deluging their bronze bodies with the limpid water, and making a refreshing and enticing show of it; enticing, for the sun was already transacting business, firing India up for the day. There was plenty of this early bathing going on, for it was getting toward breakfast time, and with an unpurified body the Hindoo must not eat.

Then we struck into the hot plain, and found the roads crowded with pilgrims of both sexes, for one of the great religious fairs of India, the Kumbh Mela, was being held, just beyond the Fort. It is wonderful, the power of a faith like that, that can make multitudes upon multitudes of the old and weak and the young and frail enter without hesitation or complaint upon such incredible journeys and endure the resultant miseries without repining. It is done in love, or it is done in fear; I do not know which it is. No matter what the impulse is, the act born of it is beyond imagination marvelous to our kind of people, the cold whites.

Early this morning, as Gillian and Sita head off for the museum and library, I team up with my guide, a personable young Brahmin, Rajesh Giri. The reason I need a Brahmin will become clear soon. I jump on the back of his scooter and we head off for the fort. The reason we need a scooter will also become clear soon.

As we duck and weave in and out of the blaring traffic it seems hard to imagine that "Part of the way was beautiful. It led under stately trees..." None of the way is beautiful now, in fact for rank ugliness, what Twain called "uncomeliness", dirt and depravity, it is as bad as anything seen in India so far—a bar not set too low.

For Allahabad has spread way beyond Civil Lines and is one of the many places in northern India to claim the title "fastest growing city". It is a town divided by the railway tracks and, as always, there is the right side of the tracks and the wrong side of the tracks. Civil Lines and its wide streets and low-rise houses are on the fancy side; Chowk, an Indian version of souk, isn't fancy-side at all. Even on a scooter it takes twenty minutes, pedestrian speed, to clear the main street, leaving plenty of time to look around at all the garbage piled high: the fruit and vegetable trash being chewed by cows, the bag trash being inspected by dogs, the paper trash being slept on by goats, the metal trash being sifted by scavenger children, the glass trash being bagged by their parents, the bright trash being carried off by crows, the traffic trash just sitting there reproducing—and the smell of trash just hanging aimlessly in the air. The aural backdrop is the blaring horns. Right behind us is a particularly noisy and noisome old Ambassador.[33] The driver just holds down his horn a few feet behind me. None of the cars, motorbikes, pedal- or auto-rickshaws, cows or ox carts can go anywhere where they are not already going; can't go any faster either. I turn around and give him—always a him—a shrug sign. He just blows another blast. I get off the pillion and walk back a few feet.

"I tell you what. I'll sit in your car and blow the horn and you sit on the back of the scooter and try and get out of the way."

"Why?" he asks.

"Why what?"

"Why problem?"

"Why problem because I'm sitting a few feet from your horn. Your horn isn't making any difference. None of us can go anywhere we are not already trying to go."

He ceases. In the meantime the traffic has moved forward four feet. That is enough to get up a barrage of klaxoned abuse from those behind him. I walk forward and jump back on the pillion. He resumes his position an inch from our tail. And then he resumes his position on the horn.

---

[33] The standard issue government car, the venerable Hindustan Motors Ambassador is based on the 1946 Morris Oxford III.

"What's the problem?" asks Rajesh, blowing his tinny horn at the cycle rickshaw in front of him and the cow in front of that and everything and everyone on the road in front of them.

"Nothing," I reply and chalk another one up to irreconcilable cultural differences, patience and courtesy on the road not being part of the Indian DNA—like asking an Italian to wear a seatbelt or an Englishman to jump a line (there being no Hindi word or Indian concept for line[34]).

Eventually, nerves tattered and eardrums shattered, we reach Akbar's splendid old fort. We need a break from the madness and find a *chai* stall. I ask Rajesh about his life as tourist guide.

"I'm only doing it as I was hopeless at mathematics so couldn't do computer sciences like all my friends at school."

"Is that what they are all doing now?" I ask, "Hardware, software, that sort of thing?"

"You've seen the billboards for computer training courses?" I have, they are everywhere. "The whole country is going IT mad. I worked in a call centre after

---

[34] Sometimes one sees the English word "queue", as in a sign saying Queue Here, lost in translation to mean "Push and shove, please use elbows".

college."

"How was that?"

"I didn't like it for lots of reasons. We Brahmins speak the best English but even we had to take the MTI course."

"What's that?"

"MTI? Mother Tongue Influence. They try to make us sound less sing-song. I had to learn Australian slang too."

"So you speak 'Strain?"

"Yeah, Ozzie too, I guess. No probs, mate. I was on railway inquiries."

"You had to keep Ozzie hours too?"

"That's right, up all night our time. And four-hour shifts. And some rude and racist people on the other end too. It was sweat shop."

"But a well paid sweat shop."

"It is well paid, two US bucks an hour, about twenty thousand roops a month. Much more if you are selling something. On commission. My God, you can treble that. But I like this guiding. Not so much money but outdoors. And meeting interesting people, not just talking on the phone."

We look up as the old fort. It must have been completely splendid when it was built four hundred years ago and it still is relatively splendid even now. Twain described it: "The Fort is a huge old structure, and has had a large experience in religions. In its great court stands a monolith which was placed there more than 2,000 years ago to preach (Buddhism) by its pious inscription; the Fort was built three centuries ago by a Mohammedan Emperor—a resanctification of the place in the interest of that religion. There is a Hindoo temple, too, with subterranean ramifications stocked with shrines and idols; and now the Fort belongs to the English, it contains a Christian Church. Insured in all the companies." Very droll.

No insurance is needed now as three-quarters of the old fort has been taken over by the Indian Army. It looks in fine shape: painted buildings, mown lawns, a polo pitch. Left-right, left-right on the parade ground. I'm not quite sure why the third biggest army in the world needs to be here, as far as they can be from any border, mucking up our sightseeing but I am sure it's all for the best. The quarter not taken over by the Indian Army is going to the mange-dogs, physically and proverbially. There are four impromptu Hindu temples, surrounded by overgrowing general shrubbery; the civilian part of the fort will soon be of interest to archaeologists only.

From the turrets, now out of bounds, Twain could see the view I cannot see now. To reach the object of the view I need Rajesh, the Brahmin on the scooter.

Two rivers join at that point—the pale blue Jumna, apparently clean and clear, and the muddy Ganges, dull yellow and not clean. On a long curved spit between the rivers, towns of tents were visible, with a multitude of fluttering pennons, and a mighty swarm of pilgrims. It is a fair as well as a religious festival. Crowds were bathing, praying, and drinking the purifying waters, and many sick pilgrims had come long journeys in palanquins to be healed of their maladies by a bath; or if that might not be, then to die on the blessed banks and so make sure of heaven.

There were fakirs in plenty, with their bodies dusted over with ashes and their long hair caked together with cow-dung; for the cow is holy and so is the rest of it; so holy that the good Hindoo peasant frescoes the walls of his hut with this refuse, and also constructs ornamental figures out of it for the gracing of his dirt floor. There were seated families, fearfully and wonderfully painted, who by attitude and grouping represented the families of certain great gods. There was a holy man who sat naked by the day and by the week on a cluster of iron spikes, and did not seem to mind it; and another holy man, who stood all day holding his withered arms motionless aloft, and was said to have been doing it for years. All of these performers have a cloth on the ground beside them for the reception of contributions, and even the poorest of the people give a trifle and hope that the sacrifice will be blessed to him. At last came a procession of naked holy people marching by and chanting, and I wrenched myself away.

At least the Brahmin and the scooter will be able to take me right into the middle of the religious festival that is the mighty Mela. To be with a Brahmin is to have an Access All Areas pass; to ride on a scooter is to be able to access all those areas. This year we have a Magh Mela, one of the most significant Hindu festivals, and one held every year at the very spot where Brahma created the world all those billions of years ago. Then every twelve years, in accordance with Vedic astrological significance,[35] they hold the Kumbh Mela. Twain was lucky enough to have stumbled into the big Mela, the Kumbh Mela. The difference?

This year's Magh Mela will attract two million pilgrims; the last Kumbh Mela, held ten years ago, had seventy million pilgrims and in 2013 they are expecting eighty million pilgrims. It was and will be the largest human gathering anywhere on earth, clearly visible from space orbiters. The Kumbh Mela that Mark Twain saw one hundred and fifteen years ago had two million pilgrims, the same as today's Magh Mela.

For a few moments I am enthusing about the mathematics as much as about the festival. As we have been wandering around the great mass of souls in northern India these past three weeks I have often found myself wondering what it must have been like for Twain, density of population-wise. Now I have at least one answer: eighty million to two million; forty to one. I started the mental calculations: take away thirty-nine houses from that bundle of buildings over there; lose thirty-nine of that line of forty cars; how would those forty loafers look if there were thirty-nine fewer of them? India becomes a sort of instant imaginary paradise, full of all the good parts, the color, the vitality, the energy, the chaos, the charm, the good humor—but now on a human rather than an overwhelming scale.

Uniquely, the number of Indians he saw Mela-ing then I saw Mela-ing now, Kumbhs and Maghs notwithstanding; we had reached some kind of numerical equivalency. We both saw two million orange-clad Hindus, mostly Brahmins and Sadhus, moving to and from the shore, laughing, dipping in and out the holy Ganges, re-wrapping themselves, having themselves one massive great dipping party; having fun; and, as was becoming clearer day by day, the doing of Hinduism is fun.

*

Rajesh stops the scooter on the higher ground just below the fort and asks me how it looks. Music festivals and recipes come to mind:

Take one Glastonbury or Summerfest and magnify it a few times; about five square miles should hold most of it.

Extend the duration from a long weekend to six weeks.

Change the multicolored tents to a uniform UN refugee dust-green, provided by the "organizers".

---

35 The Kumbh Mela takes place only when Jupiter enters Aquarius and the Sun enters Aries.

Change the mud to dirt-dust.

Fly red spectrum pennants from every tent, each shade showing a different home location or Brahmin variation.

Change the music from electric to flutes and drums, harmonia, bells and chanting.

Move the music from the stages into the tent-villages.

Keep the wood smoke but intensify by constant cooking and still air—and heat.

Substitute early morning mist for sun-smoke.

Re-jig *Desolation Row* to *Beggars Alley*. At either end have change-wallahs with one-rupee coins (two cents).

Re-jig *Field of Avalon* to *Sadhu City*. Dozens of Sadhus sit and pose for photos with Indian tourists (no Westerners seen except your correspondent). The more orange-clad, haystack-haired, bearded and beaded, barefooted, coconut shell-begging bowled they look the more the Indian tourists pay to squat beside them. (Beware, the more ragged ones are fake fakirs in fancy frocks. Winner of the Fullest Bowl Competition: one Mana Saah from Lucknow, five feet tall (approx), six-foot beard (red), seven-foot hair (henna), one pair thick old spectacles (angled, upside down), one over-turban (Tibetan lookalike lingo), one shawl (gold), one handkerchief (orange, about his person), one pair feet (leather-bare), fingernails (ten, long, curled, for the use of). Even I gave him ten (rupees).

Cancel all Portaloos and similar. Men and children just pee where they stand as always. Women go behind screens. No queues at all.

Keep the rows of palmists, astrologers, healers, soothsayers, peace paint artists and yogis, but add volume tenfold and color accordingly.

Keep the rows of food stalls, but ignore the health and safety regulations and fry, fry, fry.

Cancel all garbage collection contracts and sub out to gaudily decorated cows.

Keep the rows of souvenir stalls but reduce usefulness of objects to old clock parts, old string and old kettle elements.

Change drug of choice to *bhang*. *Bhang*—a preparation made from the cannabis plant—is bought from one of the government-approved *bhang* stalls. Take one measure in a scrap of old newspaper to a *lassi* shop. *Lassi*—a preparation made from yoghurt—when given enough sugar hides the earthy taste of the *bhang*. Your correspondent declined due to possible pillion balancing problems but from previous experience can report similarities to horse tranquilizer: a chirpy enough giddy-up followed by a rather rapid whoa and a good week's sleep.

And here the Glastonbury/Summerfest similarities must end for the pilgrimage is about meeting your favorite gods, not seeing your favorite acts, about wiping your karmic slate clean by immersing yourself—and by extension your Self—in water (you can see where John the Baptist got the idea a few thousand years later), not getting shit-faced and the lights going out—and it all revolves around dipping in three holy rivers, one of which is mythological and anyway subterranean—and there ain't any of those in Wisconsin or Somerset, England.

As we leave the site we pass countless other pilgrims hustling this or that, generally hobbling along. The last one is a well-dressed luminous yo-yo salesman standing in the middle of a roundabout with hundreds of decibels of horns blaring incessantly all around him. Now a roundabout here isn't a system of unidirectional traffic flow but a multidirectional series of corners. In the ten minutes it takes us to cover the ten yards to pass him he didn't sell any. The ten minutes also gave ample to time to ask "why?" on any number of levels about the yo-yo wallah and the great dip-in down on the river below.

*

Back at the horrible Ada Hotel (the Harsh has yet to open and secular tourism has yet to arrive in Allahabad) we compare notes. Gillian and Sita have made a remarkable discovery, a new Hindu god, Richard Sahib.[36]

They had been wandering around the park and near Company Bagh, the old East India Company headquarters, had seen a well-kept grave protected by equally well-kept railings. Anything well-kept immediately arouses interest and they walked over to investigate. Around the headstone were placed offerings of tobacco and alcohol, *bidis* and toddy. The original epitaph on the headstone had faded with time but someone had over-inscribed it, with great care, with all the letters of the Sanskrit alphabet. I had seen this before—in Roman letters—on an unknown soldier's World War 1 grave in Flanders; from the letters can be made any name that has ever existed.

Sita asked a gardener about the significance of this grave-site. The person

---

[36] Sahib means "sir" or "master" (mem'sahib means "madam" or "mistress").

buried there is known as Richard Sahib. He was a high-ranking British artillery officer who during the Sepoy Uprising sided with the Indians. One night he slipped out of the cantonment and found the local leader and told him to move his troops down towards the river. The leader noted how Richard Sahib drank and smoked a lot. That night there was a terrific electrical storm and the mutineers' previous headquarters—now empty—was struck by lightning.

Richard Sahib was hung for treason by the British and buried next to Company Bagh. One night, at the height of another electrical storm, he was seen risen from the grave dressed in an immaculate red and white uniform. The gardener who saw him was told to avoid rabid dogs and the next day another gardener, who didn't see the risen Richard, was bitten by one and died. Now whenever there is a downpour the gardeners gather under Company Bagh's shelter and wait for his good council. Sometimes he appears as himself and sometimes disguised as his avatar, a duck.

Gillian asks Rajesh what a good Brahmin makes of this story. He advises against looking for facts in the case of the god Richard Sahib. Five years ago a Canadian student included the Richard Sahib story in his thesis on Hindu mythology. He determined that Richard wasn't his name, he wasn't British let alone an army officer and traitor, and that he died before the Sepoy Uprising. According to the Canadian, the grave belonged to a Belgian missionary who died of an unknown disease. Never mind, Rajesh advised further; to the gardeners Richard Sahib is a local god who gives good advice and surely these are facts enough in themselves.

"Yes, I see," says Gillian, "but what about the duck?"

"Every god must have an avatar, that's how gods work," Rajesh replies patiently.

We may have looked a bit nonplussed but that was because we had yet to visit Benares, where the mysteries of Hindu mythology are born, sustained and destroyed—as indeed are we all.

5. BENARES

FROM ALLAHABAD TO Benares is only sixty miles, a quick, by Indian standards, train journey of two hours. In 1896 one joined the main Delhi to Calcutta line until Moghul Serai and then took a branch line to Benares. The combination of soot from the steam engine and dust through the open windows made the journey, wrote Mark Twain, "admirably dusty. The dust settled upon you in a thick ashy layer and turned you into a fakeer, with nothing lacking to the role but the cow manure and the sense of holiness."

Train journeys across India are the quintessential tourist experience and ones not quickly forgotten. For many, Twain and the writer included, the real joy is to be found not on the trains but on the platforms. Verily, there is no spot on earth more captivating than a random Indian Railways platform. And random is exactly what is unfolding in front of you; anything can happen.

We both had an enforced delay in our journeys to Benares. "There was a change of cars about mid-afternoon at Moghul-Serai—and a wait of two hours there for the Benares train." Our train was two hours late arriving at Allahabad.[37] Both circumstances encouraged sitting back and watching Planet Platform whirl its orbit around us.

> In other countries a long wait at a station is a dull thing and tedious, but one has no right to have that feeling in India. You have the monster crowd of bejeweled natives, the stir, the bustle, the confusion, the shifting splendors of the costumes—dear me, the delight of it, the charm of it are beyond speech.

> The two-hour wait was over too soon. Among other satisfying things to look at was a minor native prince from the backwoods somewhere, with his guard of honor, a ragged but wonderfully gaudy gang of fifty dark barbarians armed with rusty flint-lock muskets. The general show came so near to exhausting variety that one would have said that no addition to it could be conspicuous, but when this Falstaff and his

[37] Indian Railways timekeeping is as random as the life on its platform. All one can say is that they tend to leave the starting terminus on time—but further down the line... Later at Muzaffarpur we came across one that was 34 hours late. There is even a website devoted to averaging delays, www.indiarailinfo.com

motleys marched through it one saw that that seeming impossibility had happened.

I too would not have missed a moment. I make an armchair from my large and small wheely-bags, pitch camp in a corner discreet and watch and wonder. Where *are* they all going? How long has that extended family of twenty been lying there? Why do they always sleep wrapped with their heads covered and their bare feet sticking out? Who do those goats belong to? Is that geyser water safe to drink? Why is he hawking a puppet that just makes a horrid noise? Don't the throw-away clay cups cost more than the tea? Why is that Sadhu covered in costume jewelry? Why are the coolies[38] playing cards just when a train is arriving? Why are they jumping off the train when it's still at trotting speed? Why does no one lying around move out of the way of the new hordes? How do they make the sarees so bright? Good God, there's a peacock on that roof. How many of those useless trinkets can that wallah sell? How can he make a living? Who on earth would want to buy one? How come each train sits at the platform for twenty minutes? How young is that boy sweeping the carriages? Why is the Vegetarian Tea Stall only selling tea? Why is that cow walking between the tracks? Why is that man walking around with a bicycle horn in his hand, and why is he blowing it? Oh look, that must be the goatherd. But why are he and his goats here? Why is he holding a blue flag and she a green one? Why is she begging, I've seen a lot ropier than that? Why is she selling fruit directly from the platform when there's an empty basket nearby? What is he putting in that primus stove? What can that crow possibly want with that pencil-end? How can that coolie balance those sacks on his head? Why is she wearing odd shoes? Are those chickens with that family? Why are those two men holding hands? Why is he selling wind-up helicopters that don't fly? Is that a Sadhu or a fakir? Why is the Upper Class Waiting Room locked? How many watches is he selling from each arm? Is there a word for "slow bustle"? I wonder what that monkey eats? How come the announcer sounds like the queen: "Any inconvenience caused is *deeply* regretted"? No thanks, I don't want a taxi; no, nor an auto-rickshaw. I should be paying a license fee—or having to view ads—to be watching such a fandango.

*

---

[38] "Coolie" sounds like a rather condescending way of describing a porter but it is what they call themselves, as in "coolie, sahib, coolie, very cheap".

If you find the *Lonely Planet* guide to Syria and then look under Damascus you will see that chapter opens with a Mark Twain quote from *The Innocents Abroad*; a quote derived from his visit there in early 1869. In my book about his Grand Tour of the Holy Land, *Innocence and War*, I suggested that having read many other guide books and memoirs about Damascus, Twain's description still deserves to open the batting for *Lonely Planet*.

I would suggest the same is true of the holy ground that in 1896 was called Benares and is now—mostly—called Varanasi. I have forwarded the following extract from *Following the Equator*—without Twain's permission but I know he'd be delighted—to the Lonely Planet editors for their consideration:

> Benares was not a disappointment; it justified its reputation as a curiosity. It is older than history, older than tradition, older even than legend, and looks twice as old as all of them put together.
>
> It is on high ground, and overhangs a grand curve of the Ganges. It is a vast mass of building, compactly crusting a hill, and is cloven in all directions by an intricate confusion of cracks which stand for streets. Tall, slim minarets and beflagged temple-spires rise out of it and give it picturesqueness. The city is as busy as an ant-hill, and the hurly-burly of human life swarms along the web of narrow streets. The sacred cow swarms along, too, and goes whither she pleases, and takes toll of the grain-shops, and is very much in the way, and is a good deal of a nuisance, since she must not be molested.
>
> Benares is a religious Vesuvius. In its bowels the theological forces have been heaving and tossing, rumbling, thundering and quaking, boiling, and weltering and flaming and smoking for ages. There are Hindu temples without number—these quaintly shaped and elaborately sculptured little stone jugs crowd all the lanes. The Ganges itself and every individual drop of water in it are temples.
>
> The Ganges front is its supreme show-place. Its tall bluffs are solidly caked from water to summit, along a stretch of three miles, with a splendid jumble of massive and picturesque masonry, a bewildering and beautiful confusion of stone platforms, temples, stair-flights, rich and stately palaces—nowhere a break, nowhere a glimpse of the

bluff itself; all the long face of it is compactly walled from sight by
this crammed perspective of platforms, soaring stairways, sculptured
temples, majestic palaces, softening away into the distances; and there is
movement, motion, human life everywhere, and brilliantly costumed—
streaming in rainbows up and down the lofty stairways, and massed
in metaphorical flower-gardens on the miles of great platforms at the
river's edge.

Benares is the core of Hinduism, the powerhouse of its myths and practices and
I suppose in the grand scheme of things I'm a bit of an old Benares hand. Mark
Twain and I are about the same age, early sixties, on our visits to Benares. He
left here a hundred and fifteen years ago; I left here for the first time forty years
ago. Photographs and memoirs show that the Benares of the early 1970s was a
lot closer to the Benares of the late 1890s than to the Varanasi of the early 2010s
in everything except years; and in this city of living mythology time is anyway
something that only the clocks keep. I've been back here four times since that
first visit, the last time with my son five years ago. He still says they were the four
weirdest days of his life. It was for me too until this visit these five years later.
Mark Twain felt the same. If the India section of *Following the Equator* took up
a disproportionately large section of the book, then the Benares section took up
a disproportionately large section of the India section of the book. In fact one
could say that it is the only time writing about his world tour that he reverted to
his reportage roots. In two-dozen dazzling pages—the standout pages from what
is in truth at times rather a tired book—he shows that the journalist in him was
merely stowing away; it just took two days in Benares to bring him out on deck.

The biggest difference between the Benares of the 1890s (and the 1970s)
and the Varanasi of the 2010s is the sheer volume and density of the population
and its newly manic activity. When Twain came here the population was well
under half a million; by the time of my first visit it had rounded up to half a
million; now, although no one is sure let alone counting, it is nearly a million
and a half. It's not just that the numbers have trebled but that their activity has
trebled again, making them Mark Twain-era dense by a factor of nine. Twain
may have thought it "as busy as an ant-hill" but the ants now have aroused
ambition and internal combustion engines and have lost any semblance they
might have had of ant-patience or ant-discipline. What was a sleepy town on a
holy river, where the spirit and presence could walk in peace and reflect where
they stood, has become a bustling, jangling city where any attempt to walk in

peace will be met by a blare of furious horns from buses, cars, motor bikes or auto-rickshaws and any attempt to reflect where you stand will attract swarms of touts and hustlers selling you just about anything that you didn't know you didn't want. Varanasi now is just like the rest of India—only more so; an India without the high levels of organized predictability.

There is no opportunity for all these busy bustling horn-tooting newcomers and their attendant army of suppliants to spread out, even into shanties, as they have in every other city. Varanasi lies on only the west bank of the Ganges for the very sound reason that to have the misfortune to die on the east bank will hasten your return as a donkey. Twain thought this rather unfair on donkeys: "The Hindoo has a childish and unreasoning aversion to being turned into an ass. He would gain much—release from his slavery to two million gods and twenty million priests, fakirs, holy mendicants, and other sacred bacilli; he would escape the Hindoo hell; he would also escape the Hindoo heaven. These are advantages which the Hindoo ought to consider; then he would go over and die on the other side."

So far no Indians have taken Twain's advice and the million and a half inhabitants are squeezed into the west bank and further squeezed because the agricultural land around the city is highly fertile and vote-buying farming subsidies mean it is worth more as farm land than shanty land, which would otherwise be its fate. The result is that the one million and a half plus souls crammed into the mythological wonderland of the Benares of old India spend all day, every day, as busy as those ants in an ant-hill in the economic chaosocracy of the Varanasi of new India.

*

Now we are in Benares we should take the Mark Twain tour, to see what made such an impression on him then—and see if we can improve the tour, make it a bit easier on the nerves as we move around the myths.

Twain was shown around the sights of Benares by an American missionary, the Rev. Parker, who had also written his "Guide to Benares". One assumes the Rev. Parker had at best a tentative grip on Hindu mythology; one suspects all those idols and lingams quite gave him the vapors. As Twain said, "If Vishnu had foreseen what his town was going to be, he would have called it Idolville or Lingamburg."

They visited eleven holy sites together. Twain later added a twelfth attraction and re-ordered them into a kind of tongue-in-cheek pilgrimage narrative for logical Westerners. He wrote:

> I do not claim that the pilgrims do their acts of worship in the order and sequence charted out in this itinerary of mine, but I think logic suggests that they ought to do so. Instead of a helter-skelter worship, we then have a definite starting-place, and a march which carries the pilgrim steadily forward by reasoned and logical progression to a definite goal.

I should recall that a *ghat* is series of steps leading from a temple to a river, in this case the holy Ganges. I paraphrase the Twain-a-tour thus:

1. A dip in the Ganges in the early morning to purify the soul and give the body an appetite.

2. At the Cow Temple kiss the cow-tails and remove that hunger.

3. Visit the Dalbhyeswar Temple for some words with the god Shiva— albeit under another alias—to bring prosperity, and as an unavoidable by-product, rain—for he is in charge of both. Unfortunately the rain brings on a fever, so repair pronto to the...

4. Kedar Ghat, and "find a long flight of stone steps leading down to the river. Half way down is a tank filled with sewage. Drink as much of it as you want. It is for fever."

5. The fever is cured but brings on smallpox; time to visit temple of Sitala, goddess of smallpox.

6. Wishing to know how *that* is going to turn out, visit the Dandpan Temple and look down the Well of Fate.

7. The indicators being positive, head for the Briddhkal Temple and "secure Youth and Long Life by bathing in a puddle of leper-pus".

8. Having been granted a stay of execution, it's time for some fun, so it's off to see Shiva, in his Lord of Desires alias, at the Kameshwar Temple.

9. Although ready to live it up, better hedge your bets at the Well of the

Earring, the Holy of Holies.

10. To be doubly certain, better do some redemption and take a 44-mile walk around the city limits stopping at auspicious spots along the way.

11. Register your trek, "get your redemption recorded" at the Sakhi Binayak Temple.

12. Just to round it off go to the Well of the Knowledge of Salvation and bask for a while in the certainty that having done the rounds Salvation, and the Knowledge thereof, is at hand.

Now, just in case an alien arrives from outer space, dives into a bookstore and buys *Following the Equator* thinking it's a new travel guide… for the benefit of this great mass of alienated readers I have followed Mark Twain's advice and visited them in the order he rather mischievously later contrived. For the further benefit of the aforementioned aliens I have re-ordered them into a more practical route which minimizes dealing with the murderous traffic—as well as adding a more Hindu-centric sequence to the tour. It also happens to be a good one-day city tour which takes in all the major sites. This tour I can recommend to aliens and earthlings alike.

Firstly any visitor to Benares should take a guide for two reasons: the tour's first three sights are in the Chowk area, and if you thought Marrakesh's or Damascus' souks were a little complicated to find your way around you have yet to delve into the labyrinthine, squashed-up, cow-run back lanes of Benares. Then we are going to be ducking in and out of temples and a Hindu guide, while not essential, certainly eases one's way around the equally labyrinthine temple etiquette, where on the one hand anything goes yet on the other anything has to go in a prescribed manner. This, of course, implies that the guide will be a Hindu but I would recommend going one better and making sure he's a Brahmin—or even better a Pandit, from which word we derive pundit, a Brahminical scholar. Guides can be sourced from tourist offices and hotels; in India expect the pay to be about US$15 a day—a day being about six hours.

At a reception a month ago at the American Center in Mumbai, sorry Bombay, Sita and I had met a Sanskrit scholar, archaeologist and Benares resident, Mr. Shailesh Tripathy. He was interested in the project and offered to show us around once we had reached Benares.

"But you must know that I am not a qualified guide," he said, sipping the local, sickly Omar Kayyham (sic) sparkling wine.

"Good. Unless I insist otherwise before setting off, I find guides in India mainly want to guide me to their cousin's souvenir shop," I replied, sipping the slightly less disgusting Sula Sauvignon Blanc option.

"No danger of that, all my cousins are professional people," he replied rather haughtily.

"I'm sure you will be much better that the American missionary, the Reverend Parker."

"Who is he?"

I explain and Sita later emails him a fuller version of Twain's itinerary as above. We all agree it would be suicidal (literally) to take a 44-mile walk around the city's roads and so scrub no. 10.

I have an additional request. "For Mark Twain's no. 1, the Ganges dip, Gillian and I don't want to be downstream of any of the cremation *ghats*."

"And you?" he asks Sita.

"I'm not going anywhere near it, thank you very much," she replies flatly.

Shailesh harrumphs and gives me what I take to be an old-fashioned Indian look. "We should properly take the waters at the main ghat, Dasaswamedh. It won't be authentic otherwise. The body ashes from Harishchandra Ghat should be washed away to midstream by then."

"Well, maybe," I reply. "That's the first problem. I tell you swimming with the ashes is going to give me the willies. Second problem is the main *ghat* is crowded. I've only got my gay blue swimming trunks and I'm going to feel like an idiot prancing around in them in public. And Gillian's not too keen on swimming publicly in a saree."

"That's a far better reason," Shailesh says. "We'll start outside your friend's house[39] on Tulsi Ghat." And, a month later, we do.

Except we don't; well, he does and we don't. You would think Twain's instruction—"At sunrise you must go down to the Ganges and bathe, pray, and drink some of the water. This is for your general purification"—would be the easy part: a simple early morning dip, all the way, full immersion, no slackers, in the holy river. Not that he himself would have done it.

---

[39] We are staying at my agent's half-brother's Ganges palace on the edge of town.

Faith can certainly do wonders, and this is an instance of it. Those people were not drinking that fearful stuff to assuage thirst, but in order to purify their souls and the interior of their bodies. According to their creed, the Ganges water makes everything pure that it touches— instantly and utterly pure. The sewer water was not an offence to them, the corpse did not revolt them; the sacred water had touched both, and both were now snow-pure, and could defile no one. The memory of that sight will always stay by me; but not by request.

I try my luck. Bottom half sporting the gay blue trunks, top half wrapped in a shawl from the market in Baroda, Gillian and Sita cheering derisively from the shoreline, I waddle down the Tulsi Ghat to the river edge. Soon there are two problems, and the second relieves the first. First, in the back of the mind is the thought that this is a pretty filthy piece of water. And I saw a snake slithering along in it last night. If you've been brought up to feel it is holy and that nothing can pollute it—no corpses of man or beast, no sewage, no chemicals from Kanpur or detritus from Allahabad upriver or fertilizers flowing in from the Indo-Gangetic prairies, you have the advantage. If you've been brought up to suspect it just might be an ill-flowing cesspit of amphibious and vengeful e-coli sleepers just waiting to pounce, you have the disadvantage. Still, the in-built contrarian argues, one looks around and sees plenty of bodies bobbing up and down and they all seem pretty much alive. Shawl-free one wanders to the edge and dips a toe in the water: second problem. It's f-f-f-freezing. Feeling rather sheepish, surrounded by skinny-dipping skinny Indians, many of a venerable age, one retreats without too much decorum.

Shailesh, who is even older than me, is splashing around like a good 'un, dipping up and down and I can only look on enviously as his iffy karma is washed away—but not enviously enough to catch pneumonia and heaven knows what else besides.

"Come on in, why don't you?" he suggests, "it's invigorating."

"Well you invigor all you like. I'll try washing my karmic slate clean in a hot shower later."

"It won't work," he gloats splashing back up to the *ghat* steps.

I have a feeling he may be right karma-wise as in spite of a deluge of hot showers there has been no discernible karmic improvement.

The winter waters here were recently Himalayan snow and the chilliness is only to be expected; not so the state of the Ganges. The pollution is now causing concern to even the most convinced Hindu. The problems are many: the government has dammed the river several times before it reaches Benares and interrupted its flow—and it was the sheer flow which washed away the filth, down towards Calcutta, where it would be lost in the morass, before; the massive population growth all along the river has caused a corresponding sewage outbreak, as has the industrial growth caused a chemical and wastage problem; corruption means that any controls are simply bought off as it's far cheaper to pay a bribe than treat the problem; the farmlands leading into Benares are more productive than ever thanks to agricultural chemicals, which of course also wash off into the Ganges; and lastly Benares itself has grown to be a pounding city of a million and a half souls all going about their business, business of one kind or another which deposits its remains straight into the now barely moving holy river that defines the holy city.

Everyone agrees that the state of the river is just getting worse and worse. I wouldn't be surprised to see it spontaneously combust into holy blue flames. In a bad dream I see them sending out a fire-boat—as if!—which high-pressure hoses the flames with more toxic water and the gods decree that the whole city explodes in a massive cosmic act of retaliation against the filthy earthlings. Hmmm, I feel a Hindu myth coming on.

*

Off we go on our Re-Tour. There's no chance to talk with Shailesh as there isn't room for two abreast in the alleys, so we follow him crocodile file, left, right, half right, quick left, bit of a straight, left again, right at the junction and he stops. All around are brightly lit stalls selling brightly lit bangles, bracelets and anklets; we are in the bangles, bracelets and anklets area, having just followed him through the henna and dyestuffs area and before that the slippers and sandals stalls, opposite the pirated perfume stalls.

"None of this would have been here in 1896," explains Shailesh.

"The shops?"

"That's right," he says. "You can see they have all been carved out of ground floors. In 1900 there would have been more than enough stalls in the streets. Now India has so many new people and so many new shops. There's not really room for everybody." Right on cue a cow waddles past the other way, followed by a motorbike, horn blowing as usual. The cow, I'm pleased to report, pays no attention at all.

"Why are we starting here?" I ask.

"Because this temple, Sakhi Binayak, is dedicated to the god Ganesha, the god of prosperity and good luck, so every new venture starts with a visit to Ganesha. We are touring the temples, that's a new venture, so we should start here. Everyone can worship Ganesha and everyone does."

I look at my notes and say, "Mark Twain came here to have his redemption recorded after the 44-mile pilgrimage he didn't—and we won't—be making. Could that be right?"

"No, I think he was joking," Shailesh replies.

"Then Twain says; 'you will see a Brahmin who will attend to the matter and take the money. If he should forget to collect the money, you can remind him.'"

Shailesh smiles and agrees some things never change. We turn left and walk through a row of tacky, shiny shops selling glitzy gluck. Ganesha has now found himself in the back of a shop. He has clearly answered all those pleas for prosperity but in doing so has lost his pride of place—and his fee-collecting Brahmin.

Shailesh rings the bell above our heads as we enter and touches the base of the god's pedestal. "Ganesha is simple to pray with," he says, "he doesn't need a lot of offerings. So I say, 'Oh Ganesha, bless this tour of the temples. Show me how to show them. Make our day happy and fruitful.'"

"Am I right in thinking that you are in effect giving yourself a pep talk, wishing yourself well—as our guide?" I ask.

"In a sense, yes. Ganesha himself doesn't have the power to make our tour happy, only we can do that—but he can show me the example of how to make our tour enjoyable. He is, you see, a god, the god within me that needs bringing out. I do it by what we call *darshana* or looking, seeing. Inspiration is coming to be the best in myself, if you will."

Shailesh inspired—and Gillian, Sita and I enthused—on we press. As we shuffle along the back alleys and side alleys beyond the Sakhi Binayak Temple we see more and more dull-brown uniformed, heavily armed policemen. Young and eager they look too. Now after leaving Sakhi Binayak they are more and more in evidence lining the tiny alleys so we have to pass the larger soldiers crab-style. We must be nearing our second stop, in theory Benares' most famous site, the Golden Temple.

In practice it is little visited by foreigners these days since the bombings and the subsequent security siege. The whole section of the Chowk around

71

the Golden Temple and the Aurangzeb Mosque was sealed off after a number of bomb blasts across Varanasi in 2006 and 2010, supposedly—and it is unproven—sent with the blessings of the Muslims from the neighboring mosque, the self-styled Indian Mujahadeen. The "problem" is that the whole site was originally a Hindu temple until it was sacked, along with the rest of the city, by the Moghul Emperor Aurangzeb six hundred years ago. As the Afghan Moghuls were replaced by Indian Moghuls and then the East India Company, the Hindus felt confident enough to rebuild their temple on its original site next to the Aurangzeb Mosque. "Next to" was a bit too close for the Muslims, who have tried to bomb their point of view across. There is no security at all entering the Aurangzeb Mosque; the mosque is exquisite, its followers somewhat less so: the terror traffic is strictly one-way.

And very effectively sealed off it is too. There is double frisking to enter into the Golden Temple complex—it's a sort of self-contained shrine-village—and then double frisking again to enter the temple itself. Those who have been frisked before delving around the holy sites of Jerusalem will feel equally safe around the Golden Temple. In theory non-Hindus are not allowed but in practice that means non-Muslims; Shailesh and Sita have to show their ID and their name will reveal their religions, Hindu and Christian respectively; foreigners will have to show their passports and a small gesture—twenty rupees is recommended—in the security donation box is much appreciated. Again, with a Hindu guide life becomes a lot less complicated.

Once inside, we are looking for the Well of the Knowledge of Salvation. It hasn't changed for many a year, and certainly not since Twain's visit:

> There you will see, sculptured out of a single piece of black marble, a bull which is much larger than any living bull you have ever seen, and yet is not a good likeness after all. And there also you will see a very uncommon thing—an image of Shiva. You have seen his lingam fifty thousand times already, but this is Shiva himself, and said to be a good likeness.

> The well is covered by a fine canopy of stone supported by forty pillars and around it you will find what you have already seen at almost every shrine you have visited in Benares, a mob of devout and eager pilgrims. The sacred water is being ladled out to them; with it comes to them the knowledge, clear, thrilling, absolute, that they are saved; and you

can see by their faces that there is one happiness in this world which
is supreme, and to which no other joy is comparable. You receive your
water, you make your deposit, and now what more would you have?
Gold, diamonds, power, fame? All in a single moment these things have
withered to dirt, dust, ashes. The world has nothing to give you now.
For you it is bankrupt.

An uncannily accurate description of what one finds there now with one,
overwhelming exception: monkeys—and yet more monkeys, hundreds of them,
squabbling, stealing, frightening and out of control numerically and behaviorally.
If one finds the Venetian pigeons are ruining St. Mark's Square the same can be
said of the Indian monkeys in the Golden Temple.

Elsewhere in Benares too Twain found that "There are plenty of monkeys
about the place. Being sacred, they make themselves very free, and scramble
around wherever they please." Again true, but now much more so. Most animals
we humans meet day to day are afraid of us. Not the Indian monkey; as they
have become more and more numerous and confident they can see we are more
afraid of them than they of us. They must think we are just another breed of
monkey—and let's face it we must look as much like monkeys to them as they
do to us—some of us more so than others.

The breeding rate of these urban monkeys is now far outstripping the human
rate and the Hindus will do nothing about it, for not only are the monkeys
alive and therefore sacred but each time a Hindu sees one he is reminded of
Hanuman, the monkey god, the most accessible god of all and to kill—or even
interfere with—a likeness to a god is simply unthinkable.

Here in the Golden Temple I ask Shailesh what can be done about them.

"Nothing, it has really become their temple. We call it the Monkey Temple
in Hindi. Every time a worshiper brings an offering he is, at second hand, just
feeding the monkeys. They are in paradise but you wouldn't think so by the
racket they make squabbling with each other. I'm told that about fifty years ago
they contracted a plague of sorts and most of them died."

"Not that I wish them any harm, but…"

"Bring back the plague," Sita suggests.

"Well, the Indian way is not to persecute them but then not to help them,
just to leave them alone," says Shailesh.

"So no vets come the plague?" asks Gillian.

"No vets come the plague," he confirms

As one monkey flies across my face and three tiny monkettes scamper around my feet we head for the exit, and then through more frisking coming out. Looking back into the temple—and in spite of the reality of ape terror and the threat of Islamic terror—one has to be impressed by all the outpourings of gold that give the temple its name. Like a local population census, no-one is at all sure of the exact weight but something like eighteen hundredweight of pure gold went onto the temple roofs. It was donated by the Maharaja of Lahore, now in Pakistan, an ironic twist to the terror tactics against the object of his largesse.

It's a relief to be back in the unpoliced alleys, twisting and turning this way and that, dodging the cows and stepping around their pats as we make our way to Twain's next stop, the Kameshwar Temple. It's only about a minute away but that minute in the eccentricities of the Benares Chowk provides the usual hour's worth of entertainment.

This temple is the very opposite of the Golden Temple, being no more than extension of someone's ramshackle house. It's the shabbiest temple we have seen in all our time here, but then the immediate area all around it is equally shabby, including the old Honda motorbike parked right up close to Shiva's gate.

A lovely old man, wrinkled and stooped and dusty-orange-robed, emerges from the adjoining house and shows us around while Sita translates Mark Twain's notes to him: this temple was to Shiva in his guise of the Lord of Desires and one should, "Arrange for yours there. And if you like to look at idols among the pack and jam of temples, there you will find desires enough to stock a museum."

The temple and garden are indeed packed with the pantheon in miniature I am almost expecting a garden gnome to be in there somewhere. We take *chai* with the temple keeper, make a small donation to keep Shiva in desire fulfillment generosity and move on.

We now leave the press of the Chowk alleys and suddenly walk into bright light—and a thick haze of flesh-tinged wood smoke. We are above and looking down on Manikarnika Ghat, the main cremation *ghat* and the most auspicious place for rich or high-caste Hindus to be sent on their way to the next incarnation. We shall return to this fascinating, gruesome, unstoppable-watchable site later on, as Twain did, with an even better view from the river, so we turn inland and there find the Well of the Earring, where as he noted, one can find "Temporary Cleansing from Sin".

As we have seen and will see again, holy sites fall in and out of fashion and fashion has rather shunned the Well of the Earring of late. Shailesh confirmed

Twain's view that at the time it was "unutterably sacred. It is, indeed, the most sacred place in Benares, the very Holy of Holies, in the estimation of the people." It is still "a railed tank, with stone stairways leading down to the water. The water is not clean". But whereas he saw "people always bathing in it. As long as you choose to stand and look, you will see the files of sinners descending and ascending—descending soiled with sin, ascending purged from it", now it looks like an empty and unloved municipal swimming pool out of season. One really needs a Japanese-style face-mask to descend the steps and peer into the stagnant bathing pool which is so filthy and trash-strewn that even the most unquestioning devotee must think twice before dipping into this particular sin-cleansing bath.

Shailesh sees I am verging on the horrified and says, "It's not always this bad. In the rainy season the tank fills from below and some people swim in it."

"Some people?"

"A few."

"But surely it must just back up with sewage?"

"It's a question of faith," he says and shrugs.

It's now time to leave the Chowk and into the heart of the new Varanasi town. The smart move is to stay on the river and walk north along by the *ghats*. Most tourists—and Indians—go no further north than Manikarnika Ghat and the cremation show there. As one walks north the population thins and the *ghats* are no less interesting than the ones to the south—if you like that sort of thing. After an amble of twenty minutes one comes to Gaya Ghat and a quick turn inland brings one to the main road for a short assault on the eardrums in a rickshaw to the main post office. A hundred yards to its north and south respectively are our next two stops, the Dandpan Temple and the Briddhkal Temple; the former houses the Well of Fate and the latter the Well of Long Life.

In many ways I find this diversion into new Varanasi the most interesting part of the tour, away from the obvious tourism and into scenes of day-to-day life for Varanasi's day-to-day citizens: human, primate, bovine, canine and avian. The buildings are newer, certainly newer than Twain would have seen, but are already decaying; the open sewers either side of the road are as he would have seen them, albeit less foul.

The back road to the Dandpan Temple is also the main thoroughfare for motorcycles and water buffalo and it makes for an amusing spectacle to see the competing road users go about their business: the water buffalo sway serenely along impervious to all the chaos around them; the dogs just sleep where they feel like it, knowing that somehow the water buffalo and the motorcyclists will not step on or run over them; the motorcyclists weave in and out of the bovine and canine chicanes, the horns on the bikes as permanent as the horns on the buffalos; the humans survive as best they can, pressed up against a wall or sidestepping buff-pats or sometimes both at the same time, all done with endless patience and good humor.

Opposite the Dandpan Temple are stalls selling temple offerings: garlands, leaves, petals and small clay urns of Ganges water. Shailesh takes us through the dense crowd shuffling and pushing for position near the sacred tank which has replaced the sacred well. We see an evolution of Twain's ceremony. He "bent over the Well and looked. If the fates are propitious, you will see your face pictured in the water far down in the well. If matters have been otherwise ordered, a sudden cloud will mask the sun and you will see nothing, not a good sign." Now we see a Brahmin conduct a highly complicated routine of Ganges water management, whereby he pours Shailesh's watery offerings into a tank full of soaking garlands, leaves and petals and ladles some of it back into Shailesh's cupped hands. Shailesh in turn pours it back into the tank and then touches his wet palms onto his forehead; this is repeated three times to ensure that the fates are positive. I ask Shailesh how he feels, fate-wise; he shrugs fatalistically and says "only time will tell".

We now head back past the post office to our next temple, what Twain called "the mouldering and venerable Briddhkal Temple, which is one of the oldest in Benares, the home of the Well of Long Life". The good news—practical news rather than divine—is that I've learnt how to cope with the traffic in the interconnecting thoroughfare; one walks between a pair of water buffalo. Wits are needed: too close to the one behind might mean a shove in the bum, too close to one in front might mean… well, yes. The motorcyclists aren't too happy as one has spoilt their slalom course but overall it works and at a pleasant, stately pace to which one can soon adjust one's gait.

Thus promenading we arrive at the main road next to post office. The water buffalo, to a beast and for reasons known only to themselves, all turn left and join in that particular melee. We need to dodge death across the road and soon find ourselves in another sewageway and then promptly upon the Briddhkal Temple and its Well of Long Life.

Shailesh leans low to squeeze under the lintel and rings the bell above his head. Gillian, Sita and I kick off our shoes and follow close behind. Unlike the Dandpan of twenty minutes ago the Briddhkal is empty. The Brahmin in here is decidedly grumpy, whether the cause or the effect of the emptiness is unclear. Shailesh is a little sheepish admitting that he has never been here ("but you see there are over 11,000 temples here") and receives his instructions from Mr. Grumpy Brahmin.

Inside the entrance is the well. Everything is painted orange: the well itself, the grating over it, the pail that goes down it and the wheel around which the rope revolves. Shailesh lifts up the grating, lowers the empty pail, raises the full pail and hands it to the Brahmin. The latter takes a small swig and hands it to Shailesh who takes a longer draught. Only then are we allowed to look down the well at the water far below. God knows what's in it.

Outside I say to Shailesh, "Well you got off lightly."

"What do you mean?"

"You only had to drink it, not bathe in it too."

"Mark Twain, I suppose? Go on, what happened?"

I read from *Following the Equator*: "In here you will find a shallow pool of stagnant sewage. It smells like the best limburger cheese, and is filthy with the washings of rotting lepers, but that is nothing, bathe in it; bathe in it gratefully and worshipfully, for this is the Fountain of Youth; these are the Waters of Long Life."

He says he'll let me know and, brave face and saving face, doesn't say much else for a while.

Again we take the least traffic option and head back south along the *ghats* until we reach the midway Dasaswamedh or Main Ghat. This is split into two adjoining *ghats* and we want the second or southerly one—the site of the latest Islamic bomb in only December 2010.

It is also Sadhu Central. Sita insists they are all phony. "Not that there aren't real Sadhus. Of course there are but they are out wandering around teaching and learning as they should be—not sitting here posing and smoking hashish all day long," she shudders.

It's clear from the number of gullible young Westerners who think they are the real thing that a Sadhu franchise along the river front is not such a bad thing to have. Nothing much has changed there: "A good stand is worth a world of money. The holy proprietor of it sits under his grand spectacular umbrella and blesses people all his life, and collects his commission, and grows fat and rich;

and the stand passes from father to son, down and down and down through the ages, and remains a permanent and lucrative estate in the family."

Here, at our next stop, we are in for a nice surprise.

The temple Twain described is, or rather was, "Dalbhyeswar, on the bluff overlooking the Ganges, so you must go back to the river." It has since been washed away in one of the floods and has now become a kind of unofficial wedding *ghat* and if you are lucky—and the bride and groom need an astrologically auspicious day to marry—you will see a constant colorful procession of splendidly dressed young Indians go to and from the water's edge. In a ceremony with the Brahmin standing in the Ganges and the couple just in front of him on the shore, surrounded by the newly extended family, they bow and scoop up the Ganges water, pouring it over the hands and face and yes, drinking some of it too.

It is quite a sight. Indian women always dress as well as funds allow and in their wedding sarees they glitter and shimmer in a dazzling display of extravagance and finery. They accessorize with a vengeance too as a matter of course and for high days and weddings replace the trinkets with costume or real jewelry that leaves barely an inch of skin unadorned. The grooms look equally splendid with dress turbans and sequined long coats and trousers, bottomed off with inlaid *khussa* shoes.

Feeling full of good cheer we now climb the steep steps up to the nearest temple just a touch further south, the Sitala Temple. The bells will guide you there; there are dozens of them and most of them seem to ring most of the time. Shoes off and in we go. Ding dong ding dong. It's quite a racket, as loud as the horns heard in the back of a rickshaw, and I head back out more or less immediately counter-clockwise against the flow. Twain reckoned it wise to pray "in the temple sacred to Sitala, goddess of smallpox. Her under-study is there—a rude human figure behind a brass screen." Looking back in through the bars I can see a figure there but he's not very rude—in fact he's downright handsome and certainly has seen no smallpox. A few minutes later the others reappear, having done the circuit. They all look a bit bell-shocked but don't seem to have caught the pox, small or other wise.

Our last stops are two in one, both at the next *ghat* to the south, Kedar. First we climb up the red and white striped steps to the red and white striped South Indian Kedar Temple that Twain called the "Cow Temple". Shailesh feels sure that by "cow" he means Nandi, Shiva's bull vehicle and to which then and now the Hindus pray for relief from hunger.

It is not quite so atmospheric now as it was then. "The temple is a grim and stenchy place, for it is populous with sacred cows and with beggars. You will give something to the beggars, and reverently kiss the tails of such cows as pass along, for these cows are peculiarly holy, and this act of worship will secure you from hunger for the day."

Inside today there are no beggars; they are outside, more than a dozen of them in various stages of desperation. You give accordingly and enter what resembles a rather shabby Turkish bath with cracked tiles for decoration but without the steam for relaxation and cleansing—and by now, several hours of the dusty, farmyard tour later, a bit of cleansing would do no harm. The priests inside are less supine than the beggars outside, crying "give rupees, give rupees" as you wander around from manger to manger. There are no cows or bulls now but there clearly have been; Shailesh reckons they overnight here. Stenchy it is too so maybe the lack of steam isn't such a bad idea. Eventually one see the great Nandi himself, Bull One, covered in garlands. The devout do kiss his tail and none of them looks too hungry as a result. It's time to leave; this has been the least agreeable temple, even if one of the more eccentric.

A quick trot down the *ghat* steps brings us close to the river where "half way down is a tank filled with sewage. Drink as much of it as you want. It is for fever."

The tank, and it is a tank, is empty now but when the river floods it fills back up and when the water reaches the rim people do indeed bathe in it. Sita holds her nose and pulls a funny face. I know what she means: bathing in sewage to ward off fever does seem a hostage to fortune—but then at least three out of the four of us don't have the benefit of faith and I feel our Pandit is just playing along for our benefit.

*

The day is moving into the afternoon and as we only have Shailesh for the day I am going to suggest a variation on the usual tourist itinerary. It is standard practice—and quite rightly so—to take the dawn boat trip down the Ganges. In fact one doesn't need a guide at all for this transcendent, wordless scene as the pink, then golden, dawn rays from the empty plains across the river fall horizontally onto the venerable old waterfront. The *ghats* and the temples glow and reflect timelessly back upon the river and the early morning dippers' ripples deflect the reflections. "We made the usual trip up and down the river, seated in chairs under an awning on the deck of the usual commodious hand-propelled ark; for, of course, the palaces and temples would grow more and more beautiful every time one saw them, for that happens with all such things; also, I think one would not get tired of the bathers, nor their costumes, nor of their ingenuities in getting out of them and into them again without exposing too much bronze, nor of their devotional gesticulations and absorbed bead-tellings."

Most of the "commodious arks" are still "hand-propelled" but I suppose it was just a matter of time until someone discovered the joys of the internal combustion engine. Of course they don't fit some nice quiet, well-insulated, catalytic converted Japanese or Swedish diesel engine but an old outdoor thump-thump ex-generator you hear everywhere when there's a power cut. The first time I heard one—and I was in the safety of our palace—I thought there was about to be a crash landing from the Indian Air Force. Steadily, inexorably the hand-propelled arcs are becoming the propeller-propelled—and pretty soon I suppose they'll all have horns.

All that will wait for tomorrow's dawn. Today though we will walk ten minutes further south, to beyond the second cremation ground at Harishchandra Ghat and then take an afternoon boat back down to Manikarnika Ghat to see the main cremation site from the river and then turn around back down south again in the twilight to see the nightly evening *son-et-lumière* at the midway Dasaswamedh Ghat.

Benares is the most auspicious place for Hindus to die and the holy Ganges the most auspicious river on which their ashes can be laid. After squeezing past the overcrowding in the alleys and flinching at the decibels on the roads the newcomer to Benares next notices the markedly aged population. One could say that death keeps the city alive: not only do the nearly-dead come here in anticipation of their demise but the recently widowed or widowered stay behind and await their turn. A large part of the mounds of litter in the streets and on the river is the detritus of death. With its "God's waiting room" clientele it could easily be twinned with Venice, Florida or Eastbourne, Sussex but here the attitude to death is so completely different that comparisons soon wither in the smoke haze. Death here is not the end of *the* life but an end of *a* life—and ending this life here is a sensible precaution towards a better next life.

For better or worse, the cremation *ghats* hold an irresistible attraction for tourists. We foreigners can go for as long as our lives have been so far and never see a dead body and yet here within the space of an hour see a dozen—and in various stages of vaporization. They die here according to their means. I don't mean to be flippant about death and dying, but here in Benares one can break down the Ganges-bound into four classes—almost into four castes—which Shailesh explains as we take the gruesome, unstoppable-watchable tour down-*ghat*.

The A-listers are cremated at Manikarnika Ghat. Piles of size-sorted logs sit on the *ghat* steps waiting their turn on the pyre. Reinforcements are piled high in barges tied up under the *ghats*. The pyres are laid out, half a dozen at a time, on two layers of stone ledges leading down to the water. Smoke drifts and billows in the sunlight, swirling around the temple spires. Hot cinders fly forth like confused fireflies. Teams of the low-caste *doms* bring a steady roster of bodies down to the shore on bamboos litters. The bodies are wrapped in brightly colored paper and ribbons, not unlike Christmas presents. Next the body, still on its litter, is shown the water's edge, not for total immersion but for the relatives to splash the Ganges water onto the corpse. The body is then taken onto the pyre, the latter arranged in cross-stitch pattern about a dozen logs deep. The eldest son then undoes the many layers of shrouding to reach the bare face and then pours some urnfuls of Ganges water onto it. The male members of the family then walk seven times[40] around the pyre, sprinkle various seeds and ointments on it and then the eldest son lights the metaphorical blue touch paper and they all retire.

Photographing all this is a sensitive subject. On the one hand the family mourners all whisk out their mobile phones to photograph the open, watered face one last time immediately prior to—and then during—the lighting ceremony; on the other hand any tourist seen photographing the scene is swiftly told not to do so. It happens to me thus:

"No photo, no photo."

"Oh, OK. But, why not? They photo…"

"Photo negative dead man's soul no good."

"Ah, but there is no negative, it's digital."

"No photo, no photo."

I can see the point—it is a bit like gawping—but it's hard not to photograph what, for us, is such an extraordinary yet matter-of-fact scene. Apart from the burning bodies and the attendant relatives and the busy, rag-wearing, dark *doms* there is the usual Indian farmyard pageant standing by: cows wander around the

---

[40] To awaken the seven safe havens for the soul to visit.

pyres grazing on discarded garlands, goats chomp on the trash, dogs sleep just feet away from the burning bodies, monkeys scratch and fidget, water buffalo wallow just upstream, crows fly and croak in and out, kite-hawks hover in and out of the spiraling smoke, dom children wander around barefoot in the smoldering ash and cowpats, puppies play with each other—all this as though death was the most natural thing in the world—which of course it is.

The same squeamishness about photography applies to looking and staring. I mean, how close is it polite to stand near a body-draped pyre, near somebody's late mother, somebody's late son? The Japanese tourists, who always wear face-masks in India anyway, have no compunction about walking right up to a pyre, practically to within prodding distance. The photography issue goes away when one is photographing from a boat, by the way, as it seems quite in order to stand up on board and snap away from the river. Shailesh says that is because the river is holy and so everything that happens on it is instantly forgiven. And, the heathen reflects, you get much better shots.

There is no mourning at the cremation as that has already taken place immediately after death and it is considered bad luck, reincarnation-wise, to mourn overtly at the time of cremation. After the fire is lit the family disperses

and only the *doms* with their long and blackened bamboo poles remain to hasten the burning of the remains, prodding various limbs back into the fire and poking the fire to keep it going. Still, it takes a surprisingly long time—about two hours—until the ashes of flesh and wood are ready to be scooped up and emptied (nothing as ceremonial as scattered) into the river or, as Shailesh explains, back to the source, back to from whence we all came.

This A-list *ghat* is a big budget operation; it costs ten thousand rupees, about US$200, to be cremated here. It is run with seamless efficiency; in fact the unkind might suggest it is one of the very few efficient Indian undertakings. And like the undertakers back home the *doms* know how to charge. They say it needs nearly eight hundredweight of wood to be burned, whereas, as we shall see in the B-list *ghat*, it needs nothing like that. Then they have invented a story that sandalwood is the most auspicious wood and so of course that is extra. And then there's the fire, as Twain noted: "The fire used is sacred, of course—for there is money in it. Ordinary fire is forbidden; there is no money in it. I was told that this sacred fire is all furnished by one person, and that he has a monopoly of it and charges a good price for it. Sometimes a rich mourner pays a thousand rupees for it. To get to paradise from India is an expensive thing. Every detail connected with the matter costs something, and helps to fatten a priest. I suppose it is quite safe to conclude that that fire-bug is in holy orders."

The whole scene we see now is exactly as he would have seen it then. Actually I am surprised that he found the whole affair as distasteful as he did since, as we have seen, at the time he was a great champion of cremation.

It is a dismal business. The stokers did not sit down in idleness, but moved briskly about, punching up the fires with long poles, and now and then adding fuel. Sometimes they hoisted the half of a skeleton into the air, then slammed it down and beat it with the pole, breaking it up so that it would burn better. They hoisted skulls up in the same way and banged and battered them.

The sight was hard to bear; it would have been harder if the mourners had stayed to witness it. I had but a moderate desire to see a cremation, so it was soon satisfied. For sanitary reasons it would be well if cremation were universal; but this form is revolting, and not to be recommended. In all I saw nine corpses burned. I should not wish to see any more of it, unless I might select the parties.

83

Sita is as blasé as only the young can be but neither Gillian nor I find it nearly so gruesome as did our earlier visitor, and given an understanding of Hinduism and Shailesh's running commentary it seems like a good inter-life career move for a rich and righteous Indian to take, given all the other options. I must admit my main concern is ecological as the tons of trees—and the wonton waste of wood built into the charging system—that must have to be chopped down to keep the pyres burning and the subsequent smoke arising is plainly too wasteful for a withered world. It sets one to thinking that there must be some kind of microwave version of cremation that could do the job just as well—and there is, just down river to where we heading.

So that's the A-listers; the B-listers are cremated at Harishchandra Ghat near to where we started this rather ghoulish boat ride. As one is hand-propelled up river and up-*ghat* one is conscious for the first time that the smoke that one has been coming across for the last few days contains remnants of old flesh and bones too.

Drifting off Harishchandra Ghat it is immediately apparent that this is a far more low-key affair. There are no stone ledges, just banks of mud. Like Manikarnika, they cremate half a dozen at a time but the *doms* are also B-list, shuffling around aimlessly. The ceremonies at the water's edge and on the pyres are haphazard—as are the corpses, some once loved in poverty and others as unloved in life as they now are in death. The farmyard contingent is lackluster too; there just aren't the lavish pickings to be found here and so only the B-list

cows and B-list goats clear the detritus and without much enthusiasm; the others don't even bother to show. Shailesh reckons this is a thousand-rupee cremation and agrees with my assessment that there is room in the market, or along the *ghats*, for a middle way, for an A- or B+ cremation.

But if the gap between death's smart *ghat* and death's scruffy *ghat* seems too large we now see the same between the B- and the C-listers' options. It's all close by. Right behind the smoldering Harishchandra Ghat is a large, modern, shoddy circular construction on concrete stilts. It's not designed to fit into the ancient surroundings and seems uncaring and bare-bricked in its duty as a municipal human incinerator, for that is what it is. A large sign on the back announces that this is the 200-rupee option. Shailesh says it is known locally as the Electric Ghat. It only runs once a day at dusk. There is a long ramp up to an open door. Corpses are taken up on bamboo litters and dumped in a bowl. You can tell it's low-budget because here the bamboo is reused and doesn't form part of the pyre. Come the time a switch is thrown, immense heat is generated, the extractor fans whirl and while the bodies vaporize dark grey smoke puffs out of the long galvanized chimney. The following morning at dusk when the remnants have cooled down in the night, *doms* empty the bowl from below and deposit the collective ashes in the holy river. Again, one can't help feeling the gap in indignity is too large and that there should be B- and C+ options to more accurately reflect the cremation grading of the dead with the caste grading of the living.

Lastly come the D-listers who aren't cremated at all but soaked and drowned into the next life. It all happens at Harishchandra Ghat, and Twain saw then what we see now: "They do not burn fakirs—those revered mendicants. They are so holy that they can get to their place without that sacrament, provided they be consigned to the consecrating river. We saw one carried to mid-stream and thrown overboard. He was sandwiched between two great slabs of stone." Exactly that, except it's not just fakirs these days but any destitute person, the unknown and the homeless. Here the *doms* wrap the corpse in left-over shrouds and tie a loop-knot around the neck. One then rows a boat out to mid-stream while another sits on the stern with his hand through the loop-knot, towing the still-floating corpse through the water like a reluctant water-skier. A slab of stone, tied onto the loop knot, sits on the stern and when the time is nigh the stern rider chucks the slab overboard and the corpse sinks, leaving behind only the a few lonely bubbles in exchange for a lonely life.

THE INDIAN EQUATOR

*

All this death is giving us a thirst and after we take our place among the flotilla watching the *son-et-lumière,* Golap, our highly skilled hand-propellist, leaps off the bow of our commodious ark and brings back some beer. Shailesh, being a good Pandit, declines—and he has seen it all before. Sita prefers Bollywood and heads off to find a cinema.

We say good-bye; it has been quite a day. We both doze off before the show ends but from what little I see I'm sure it is well done. The last memory is of Twain's quote in *The Calcutta Patriot* two weeks later: "I think Benares is one of the most wonderful places I have ever seen. It struck me that a Westerner feels in Benares very much as an Oriental must feel when he is planted down in the middle of London. Everything is so strange, so utterly unlike the whole of one's previous experience."

6. HINDUISM

IT IS A TRUISM that foreigners either love India or loathe it. This is not a country from which one returns and tells friends: "Oh, I suppose it was *alright*." Whether you love it or loathe it depends on how you react to chaos—and farmyards. Mark Twain and I clearly love it, and yet I can quite see why an equal number of people head screaming for the nearest airport, or in his case seaport; what to one person is happy, crazy, freewheeling, maximized, anarchic chaos is to another a gigantic urban-farmyard-cum-uncleaned-lavatory-cum-garbage dump where the animals have taken over and the chain doesn't pull. India is not for the faint of heart nor mild of spirit nor weak of mind nor dull of sense nor correct of politic; it is a concurrent explosion of energy, contradictions, spontaneity, degradation, opportunity, hopelessness and vitality, a country without padding where a few hundred million have grabbed the twenty-first century by the whiskers and many more hundred million still tuck the nineteenth century into bed at night.

On one point though the love-it and loathe-it brigades agree—or at least they ask the same question. How can India, as a society, put up with itself? Anywhere else 1.2 plus billion people living cheek-by-jowl would be thinking of new ways to lay waste to each other and yet they all seem to rub along quite happily together. Why, when four of the ten richest people in the world are Indian, when the intermediary *nouveaux riches* are uniformly vulgarian and flauntatious and think the Indian tradition of philanthropy is a fancy word for extra-curricular leg-over, when the mass of the *hoi polloi* are destined to live in acute poverty, and many in down-dirty squalor, why with all this blatant injustice isn't there a revolution? How come any of us can walk home at night, stepping over bodies sleeping on the sidewalks, knowing that even that thing around our wrist is worth enough to keep any of them going for six months, and do so without any fear of a dispossessed vagrant taking a pop at us? Why, given the sophistication and urbanity of the elite, are all the politicians in the world's biggest democracy tribal embezzlers at best and outright gangsters at worst. How on earth do they put up with it all—and with each other?

The answer is that mainstay of Indian life, Hinduism. I carefully avoided putting the word "religion" in front of Hinduism as I sensed several thousand pedants reaching for their quills—and strictly speaking the pedants are right: Hinduism is not a religion in the sense that it has an all-powerful, all-knowing superhuman figure its followers must worship and obey. The problem is that there is no single word in English to describe what the Oxford dictionary has as a "diverse family of devotional and ascetic cults and philosophical schools, all sharing a belief in reincarnation and involving the worship of one or more of a large pantheon of gods and goddesses". Fair enough, although "large" is a bit of an understatement but we'll come to that later. In fact we are swimming in gloomy waters trying to define Hinduism in words at all as the whole point of the practice of treating with the pantheon is to take us beyond the limitation of words, beyond the subsequent differentiating formulation of subject/verb/object which affects our whole way of thinking, beyond our mental concepts restricted by time and space and into a transcendent sphere where we realize the godhead within us—and equally within all of us—and within everything we perceive.

And this surely is the answer to the foreigners' question. These 1.2 billion souls living on top of each other are not 1.2 billion egos but 1.2 billion aspects of the same Consciousness. To harm one aspect-holder is to harm all aspect-holders, including oneself as a fellow aspect-holder.

For us foreigners the best-known part of Hinduism is karma which we have allied, philosophically, to the Golden Rule. In Hinduism karma goes further than that as it is an integral part of re-incarnation and to live by the laws of karma becomes simple common sense; man is not punished for his sins but by his sins. To sin is simply counterproductive, the spiritual equivalent of banging your head against a brick wall.

∗

Like most visitors to India Mark Twain thought he should learn about Hinduism and like most visitors he made the mistake of trying to learn it as a series of facts—as we would learn the names and dates of the presidents or state capitals. I made the same mistake: I found something like "The Complete Idiot's Guide to Hinduism" and got as far as page 5 before reaching for the drinks cabinet. We came to the same conclusion:

> I should have been glad to acquire some sort of idea of Hindoo theology, but the difficulties were too great; the matter was too intricate. Even the mere A, B, C of it is baffling.

There is a trinity—Brahma, Shiva, and Vishnu—independent powers, apparently, though one cannot feel quite sure of that, because in one of the temples there is an image where an attempt has been made to concentrate the three in one person. The three have other names and plenty of them, and this makes confusion in one's mind. The three have wives and the wives have several names, and this increases the confusion. There are children, the children have many names, and thus the confusion goes on and on. It is not worth while to try to get any grip upon the cloud of minor gods, there are too many of them."

That is absolutely right; the Western, conditioned adult mind is soon way out of its depth. Apart from the 330 million gods and goddesses there are different god-teams and then different god-days, -weeks and -months. The next day Twain noted with some frustration that "The great god Vishnu has 108 names—108 special ones—108 peculiarly holy names and just for Sunday use only." Someone forgot to tell him that Vishnu has at least 892 other names as do all the other major gods

and goddesses, and their respective consorts and incarnations-as-children have thousands of names as well. Multilimbing as well as multinaming is the norm.

Then there are the chariots. The gods and goddesses each need a vehicle to transport them around the imagination. This is seldom what one would expect, so that Ganesha, part-man part-elephant, has for his transport not as one would expect a mammoth or juggernaut (another offshoot of Indian mythology) but

89

a... mouse. One's instinct is to look for parallels in our own classical mythology where gods are also omnipotent and immortal, but Hindu mythology is so convoluted by the fantastical that it makes the goings on of the Greek gods and demigods seem as simplistic as Robin Hood. It is truly—and truly meant to be—beyond the limitations of the day-to-day mind.

Unfortunately today the word "myth" has come to mean something that is untrue. The "Mythbusters", claiming to unearth misconceptions, is a popular TV series; the phrase "urban myth" has come to mean a story that is widely held to be true but is actually untrue; myths are ripe for "debunking". Exposed politicians and crooked bankers cry "It's a myth!" when caught red-handed. A myth, as it was understood from the beginnings of knowledge until the Age of Reason, meant a story that helped explain the inexplicable. A myth by its very nature could not be, did not claim to be, "true", as a fact is true; a myth only started where facts and emotions could not be explained. As Karl Gustav Jung discovered in his search for the soul, myths have always used deliberately fictitious motifs and like all good fiction have asked those "what-if?" questions that take us beyond what we like to think of as "ourselves" and gives us a glimpse of the Self in all.

Thanks to the work of Jung and Joseph Campbell and Karen Armstrong and others, the Western world is now re-evaluating the significance of mythology and Varanasi is a fine place to see mythology in action; and as they all point out, it needs to be in action to have any meaning. As Mark Twain and I discovered, mythology is not a psychology that the can be studied in the hope of reaching an intellectual conclusion. It needs *doing* —and from an early age so that it is just another part of life, a part of life that doesn't see itself as myth at all. *Doing* it has advantages for the myth—it keeps it alive and evolving—and for the partakers of myth—it keeps them actively involved in the unexplained world, the very opposite to the fatalism of which the Indians are sometimes so wrongly accused.

I had the advantage of homestaying with an Indian family in Benares and could see all this where it was meant to be seen, in action. In the palace grounds were two temples, a large one to Shiva and a smaller one in the courtyard to Kali.

"Kali wards off the evil spirits," explains my host Kashi, a 33-year-old Western-educated Bengali.

"A spirit guard dog," I suggest.

"Yes, and a burglar guard dog too. If a thief enters the house and sees Kali looking at him he will run away. She is not to be upset," he grins knowingly.

One can see how Kali—and Shiva in the larger temple—fit into family life. Kashi, his wife Bullbullee and two daughters, Kashica, five, and Misti, three, talk to them and about them as family members throughout the day.

"Don't shout, Kali is resting."

"Kashica, give some of that to Kali."

"I'm leaving at three, Kali."

"Sweep out around Shiva too."

"We all hate the monsoon, Kali especially. So sweaty."

"Kashica, light these for Shiva."

They don't have to stray far to feel the godly incarnations. The house behind has become a Buddhist[41] meditation and study centre. At the end of the alley is a house where Ganesha, using a broken tusk as a pen, took down dictation from Shiva and gave us the Ramayana. There is a temple to Ganesha outside the house and we see him fully decorated with red paint and yellow garlands, his ten arms arrayed in an arc behind his Buddha-style pot belly. The house where it all happened is right there/probably right there/possibly somewhere near/ well, quite close, close enough that every year they have a 48-hour chantalong. There is a relay of two singers and a harmonium and tabla players; shifts change every... well whenever anyone new shows up. The whole neighborhood becomes involved in ferrying supplies back and forth and general encouragement. The lyricist had an easy time of it: the couplet "Sita Rama; Sita Rama" is just repeated over and over again for the two days alternating between the two singers. They have thoughtfully mounted a loudspeaker outside the front door so all around can join in the celebrations. Anywhere else in the world one would call time on the neighbors from hell, file for a restraining order, but here one somehow goes native—and it doesn't seem to matter much any more.

At night various cows and goats stop by and chomp on discarded garlands. Thank heavens on the second day there is a power cut and I'm sure that, like me, all the neighbors rush to bed to catch up on their sleep with "Sita Rama; Sita Rama" still much on their minds.

Then every morning somewhere around 5.30 the house wakes up to the full hoopla from the communal Shiva temple just behind it. What a fantastic racket: bells of various hues, drums of various beats and chants of various prayers all ring together for ten minutes of early morning chaos; happy chaos—a state in which the worshippers, along with most of India, will spend the rest of the day. The

---

[41] The Buddha is the ninth incarnation of Vishnu.

temple has a regular turnover of worshippers throughout the day; most drop in for a few minutes, ring the bell, have a few words with Shiva and continue the day fortified by god-to-god contact.

For the last three hours there has been another party with what sounds like a *mariachi* band. Lots of bells and chanting; weeping and wailing and gnashing of teeth this ain't. I pop round to have a look-see. Twin four-year-old Brahmin boys are having their heads shaved, one of their rites of passage. They are all from Bombay but the uncle works in Delhi for Coca-Cola; "headquarters in Atlanta," he says with pride. "My brother, their father, works for Electrolux in Mysore." And they've come here to this Shiva temple hundreds of miles away for the birthday? "Yes, this is a special Shiva temple for Brahmins. And it's not actually the boys' birthday but the day nearest it which is astrologically auspicious, you see."

All around the temple all day long is a market selling bits of bright cotton and string and scarves, bells, straw mats, coconut shells, incense and rice for the temple guests to buy as offerings. Worshipping—still not really the right word but pointing in the right direction—is lighthearted and joyful. By making the gods happy they are making themselves happy, for after all, are they not the same? Fun is the right word; and after a week of total immersion in Hinduism I would say above all the practice of it is fun, fun for family, fun for the nation, which brings us back to why they are not all at each others' throats.

∗

Time, methinks, to join in the fun. Accepting that the adult Western mind will never understand the theory of Hinduism it seems the best way forward is to join in the practice, to *do* the myth. My host Kashi leads me by the nose.

"You are a writer, isn't it?" he asks.

"It's kind of you to say so."

"No, I mean that's what you do. If I was a writer I would become friends with the goddess Saraswati."

"Saraswati?"

"Saraswati, the goddess of wisdom and knowledge. And writers. And learning. At primary school in Bengal we used to start each day with incantations to Saraswati. In Bengal we also see her as Ganesha's half brother. In Buddhism she is a guardian angel."

"But I thought you said earlier that Ganesha was the god of writers."

"No, he's the god of writ*ing* not writ*ers*. Ganesha is a scribe."

"Like a secretary?

"Yes, Saraswati is the creative force. She invented words."

"And how will I know her?"

"That's easy. She is white skinned and wears white clothes. She sits on a white water lily and besides her is always her vehicle, a white swan."

"A vision in whiteness?"

"Yes. That's also one of the reasons Hindu widows wear white, not black as yours do. They want wisdom in their older years. Normally she has four arms, one hand for a book of palm leaves for learning, another hand for a string of pearls or a vase for the love of giving wisdom. The other two hands are for a sitar. Sometimes each hand is for a Veda. That's when she has eight arms. She is the goddess of all the arts."

"And her consort?"

"Her consort is Brahma, the creator."

"So she was consorted well?"

"Very well!"

A few moments later we are at a nearby temple to Saraswati. On the way over Kashi explained the rules of *puja*, the Hindu ritual in the temple. It wasn't a long lecture; there are no rules. In fact you don't even have to be in a temple. Sometimes you can talk to the Absolute through Saraswati directly, sometimes you may prefer to use a temple Brahmin. You can stay in the temple for one minute or sixty or all day. You can offer her gifts or keep your hands in your metaphorical pockets. You can talk to her, *with* her would be more accurate, silently or in a mumble or right out loud.

What is common practice though is to ring a bell suspended near the door as you enter the temple. This is to take the mind off the external sounds and help it turn inwards; like a sort of instant *mantra*. Kashi now lights some incense and waves it in front of the gilt-framed image of the goddess. The frame has copious amounts of garlands of marigolds draped over it. Around it lie random petals, rice grains, coconut shell shards, old incense sticks, camphor butts, orange slices, an unopened apple, boiled sweets (unwrapped) and a dozen lit candles.

Kashi says—and I repeat: "O goddess, O Saraswati, consort of creation, knower of the Vedas and fountain of knowledge, show us the powers we share, show us wisdom and true knowledge of the Absolute, find it in me and I will find it in you, we are as one with the One, unlimited, beyond conception. I will write as you will write, with creation and truth and love. Bless us together as one, O goddess, O Saraswati."

*

I will leave it to readers to decide if Saraswati and I are working well together as future chapters unfold. We three musketeers are off to Calcutta in a couple of days and I will seek out a Saraswati temple and repeat the incantation; and also in Darjeeling after that. I just liked being brought out of "my" self, to make place for the "other".

The last word—for now—on the "other" should rest with Albert Einstein: "To know that what is impenetrable to us really exists, manifesting itself to us as the highest wisdom and the most radiant beauty, which our dull faculties can comprehend only in their most primitive forms—this knowledge, this feeling is at the centre of true religiousness. In this sense, and in this sense only, I belong to the ranks of the devoutly religious."

*

Before leaving Benares Mark Twain had an important engagement, arranged with some difficulty by the Rev. Parker: they were to meet one of India's most renowned gurus of the time, Swami Sri Bhaskarananda Saraswati, as Twain said "a living god". He held court in a small park now known as Anand Bagh, near Assi Ghat. The old ashram where they met still stands, now as a large, open-fronted, wooden and fluted columned shelter along the north side of the park. People use it to rest and enjoy the shade.

Twain was impressed:

Then Sri Saraswati came, and I saw him—that object of the worship of millions. We got along very well together, and I found him a most pleasant and friendly deity. Meeting him was a strange sensation, and thrilling. I wish I could feel it stream through my veins again.

He was tall and slender, indeed emaciated. He had a clean-cut and conspicuously intellectual face, and a deep and kindly eye. He looked many years older than he really was, but much study and meditation and fasting and prayer, with the arid life he had led as hermit and beggar, could account for that. He is wholly nude when he receives natives, of whatever rank they may be, but he had white cloth around his loins now, a concession to Mr. Parker's European prejudices, no doubt.

He has attained what among the Hindoos is called the "state of perfection". It is a state which other Hindoos reach by being born again and again, and over and over again into this world, through one re-incarnation after another—a tiresome long job covering centuries and decades of centuries. But in reaching perfection, he has escaped all that. He is no longer a part or a feature of this world; his substance has changed, all earthiness has departed out of it; he is utterly holy, utterly pure; nothing can desecrate this holiness or stain this purity; he is no longer of the earth, its concerns are matters foreign to him, its pains and griefs and troubles cannot reach him. When he dies, Nirvana is his; he will be absorbed into the substance of the Supreme Deity and be at peace forever. Throughout the long course he was perfecting himself in holy learning, and writing commentaries upon the sacred books. He was also meditating upon Brahma, and he does that now.

This god is comfortably housed, and yet modestly, all things considered, for if he wanted to live in a palace he would only need to speak and his worshipers would gladly build it. Rank is nothing to him, he being a god. To him all men are alike. He sees whom he pleases and denies himself to whom he pleases. Sometimes he sees a prince and denies himself to a pauper; at other times he receives the pauper and turns the prince away. However, he does not receive many of either class. He has to husband his time for his meditations.

They exchanged signed copies of their books. "I gave him a copy of *Huckleberry Finn*. I thought it might rest him up a little to mix it in along with his meditations on Brahma, for he looked tired, and I knew that if it didn't do him any good it wouldn't do him any harm."[42]

*

Actually Mark Twain would have been somewhat familiar with Vedanta philosophy due to his knowledge of Ralph Waldo Emerson's essays on the

---

[42] In the weekly *English Courier* Twain said: "We traded autographs. I said I had heard of him, and he said he had heard of me. Gods lie sometimes, I suspect."

Bhagavad-Gita and the Transcendentalist movement. Emerson wrote that:

> What is popularly called Transcendentalism among us, is Idealism. As thinkers, mankind have ever divided into two sects, Materialists and Idealists; the first class founding on experience, the second on consciousness; the first class beginning to think from the data of the senses, the second class perceive that the senses are not final, and say, the senses give us representations of things, but what are the things themselves, they cannot tell.

> The materialist insists on facts, on history, on the force of circumstances, and the animal wants of man; the idealist on the power of Thought and of Will, on inspiration, on miracle, on individual culture. These two modes of thinking are both natural, but the idealist contends that his way of thinking is in higher nature. He concedes all that the other affirms, admits the impressions of sense, admits their coherency, their use and beauty, and then asks the materialist for his grounds of assurance that things are as his senses represent them. But I, he says, affirm facts not affected by the illusions of sense, facts which are of the same nature as the faculty which reports them, and not liable to doubt; facts which in their first appearance to us assume a native superiority to material facts, degrading these into a language by which the first are to be spoken; facts which it only needs a retirement from the senses to discern. Every materialist will be an idealist; but an idealist can never go backward to be a materialist.

> The idealist, in speaking of events, sees them as spirits. He does not deny the sensuous fact: by no means; but he will not see that alone. He does not deny the presence of this table, this chair, and the walls of this room, but he looks at these things as the reverse side of the tapestry, as the *other end*, each being a sequel or completion of a spiritual fact. This manner of looking at things, transfers every object in nature from an independent and anomalous position without there, into the consciousness that is everywhere.

*

On the train to Calcutta I ask Sita about another aspect of Hinduism that doesn't immediately make sense, Hindu extremism.[43]

She looks rather blank and Gillian mentions the word "oxymoron".

"I know," I say, "like Calvinistic licentiousness or Catholic austerity."

"Or Islamic broadmindedness or Judaic self-doubt," she suggests.

I remind Sita that, as far as I know, Mahatma Gandhi was assassinated by a Hindu extremist.[39]

"We learned at school he was an extremist who happened to be a Hindu—of sorts—rather than a Hindu extremist. You can't be a Hindu extremist. Have you heard of Hindutva?"

"No."

"It's a kind of Indian fascism but instead of being political it is religious. It's a Brahmin thing. They think they are a race apart and want to legalize the caste system and make everyone speak Sanskrit."

"And are there many of them?" asks Gillian.

"No, I've never seen any," says Sita. "They are in the papers but who isn't? Like the Saffron Terror."

The idea of Saffron Terror has been much in the news in India recently as it is mentioned in WikiLeaks. In July 2009 Indian Prime Minister Manmohan Singh was hosting a lunch for Hilary Clinton and the US Ambassador Timothy Roemer. Clinton was told that "there may be a counter threat (to Pakistani-backed terrorism) from radicalized Hindu groups". Somehow the term Saffron Terror crept into the conversation but as far as anyone knows it has crept no further.

"I never think about it," says Sita, "but there are a billion plus people out there. Bound to be some scallies."

---

[43] Gandhi was assassinated in January 1948 as he was about to address a prayer meeting. The assassin, Nathuram Godse, was a Hindu nationalist who held Gandhi responsible for weakening India by "supporting" the existence of Pakistan.

A CAB SUBSTITUTE.

7. CALCUTTA

IN 1887 MARK Twain's friend Rudyard Kipling wrote of Calcutta:

> Once, two hundred years ago, the trader came meek and tame.
> Where his timid foot first halted, there he stayed,
> Till mere trade
> Grew to Empire, and he sent his armies forth,
> South and North,
> Till the country from Peshawar to Ceylon
> Was his own.
> Thus the midday halt of Charnock[44]—more's the pity!—
> Grew a City
> As the fungus sprouts chaotic from its bed
> So it spread
> Chance-directed, chance-erected, laid and built
> On the silt
> Palace, byre, hovel—poverty and pride
> Side by side
> And above the packed and pestilential town
> Death looked down.

*

"A comfortable railway journey of seventeen and a half hours brought us to the capital of India, which is likewise the capital of Bengal, Calcutta." I assume they must have traveled on the 13152 Sealdah Express which is supposed to take fourteen hours—although yesterday it took sixteen hours.

The Twain party's journey was not just comfortable but held some amusement. Twain and Smythe were evidently in a four-berth male compartment, with Livy

---

[44] Job Charnock worked for the East India Company and is usually regarded as the founder of Calcutta on the east bank of the Hooghly river. In 1690 he persuaded the Company that this was the place to establish its Bengal headquarters because of its defensible position and its deep-water anchorage. The Company received permission from the Great Mughal in Delhi to build a factory in Bengal, and Charnock set up his headquarters near a hamlet on the Hooghly.

and Clara in their own female compartment further down the first-class carriage. "Mr. Smythe and I got out at a station to walk up and down, and when we came back Smythe's bed was in the hanging shelf above and an English cavalry officer was in bed on the sofa which Smythe had lately been occupying."

> It was mean to be glad about it, but it is the way we are made; I could not have been gladder if it had been my enemy that had suffered this misfortune. We all like to see people in trouble, if it doesn't cost us anything. I was so happy over Mr. Smythe's chagrin that I couldn't go to sleep for thinking of it and enjoying it. I knew he supposed the officer had committed the robbery himself, whereas without a doubt the officer's servant had done it without his knowledge. Mr. Smythe kept this incident warm in his heart, and longed for a chance to get even with somebody for it.

*

Many Mark Twain enthusiasts have commented on his life-long dislike of imperialism and the resultant puffed-up vanity of colonialism. The one exception to this rule was the jewel in the crown of imperialism, the British Raj reign of India. Not only did he forgive the British for their incursion but on numerous occasions pointed out how beneficial it was to the natives; how lucky they were to have the British to rule over them.[45] Around then he wrote of Warren Hastings that "he saved to England the Indian Empire, and that was the best service that was ever done to the Indians themselves, those wretched heirs of a hundred centuries of pitiless oppression and abuse." His point was—and one easily forgotten these hundred plus years later—that before the Raj the Indians were more oppressed than they were under the Raj. The British had at least, he felt, lifted the stone and let in some light around the edges. The British themselves felt that if they had not made a Raj in India someone else would have done— and they would not have made such a good job of it. Certainly those who know about the cruelties the Dutch inflicted on Indonesia, the piracy the Portuguese

---

[45] He felt something similar about the British treatment of Indians closer to home. In Johannesburg, South Africa, he said: "Look at the difference between the position of the Canadian Indians and the Indians with whom the United States government has to deal. In Canada the Indians are peaceful and contented enough. In the United States there are continual rows with the government, which invariably ends in the red man being shot down."

dispensed around their seaborne empire, the savagery of French colonialism in Africa or the tribal genocide of the Spanish in their *Novus Orbis* would agree, if only on a lesser evil basis; and don't even consider the activities of the Belgians in the "dark continent". (The American annexation of the Philippines was then still two years hence and his opposition to this move would cause him to be an important figure in the American Anti-Imperialist League.)

The years have put enough space between India's colonial era and now for an open-minded view of the benefits—or otherwise—of the British period to be seen objectively, and perhaps there is no better place than the Calcutta of Mark Twain's time and the Kolkata of today to stand back and take stock.

Calcutta was a British creation; Kolkata, as Calcutta has become, is an Indian evolution of that creation. The political classes may not like this but the facts are too self-evident for them to be ignored. There is sensitivity in even proposing this locally: while Indians in general don't like being reminded they have been ruled for most of the last 500 years by the Afghans and British, with smatterings of French and Portuguese sovereignty around the edges, this is especially so in proud Bengal.

Rudyard Kipling's famous quip about Job Charnock's lunchtime halt becoming an empire's capital only works as a quip because it is so obviously true. What were three tiny hamlets on the east bank of the Hooghly river—one which was called Kalikata[46]—grew into the great Calcutta through the initiative of British traders and administrators, helped increasingly as time passed by Indian princes and powerbrokers, and by whole swathes from the merchant and warrior castes acting out of self-interest. Twain recognized that not only was Calcutta a British invention but a triumphant and tolerant one—at least it was to him in 1896; no doubt later events would have tempered his enthusiasm. "The handful of English in India govern the Indian myriads with apparent ease, and without noticeable friction, through tact, training, and distinguished administrative ability, reinforced by just and liberal laws—and by keeping their word to the native whenever they give it."

He may not have known the care the British took to make sure that this was so. All of India was actually run, executively, by at most 1,300 members of the India Civil Service. Standards of recruitment were exceptionally high, mostly from Oxford or Cambridge and always with a first-class degree, preferably with

---

[46] Nicknamed by the British "Golgotha" as the climate was so unhealthy in the bug-ridden bogs and swamps.

honors. After graduation they had to study for a further year the root language of Sanskrit and a vernacular language such as Urdu, Hindi, Punjabi or Bengali as well as attend an intensive course on "something of the history of India and the law".[47]

The next layer of civil servants, although less exalted educationally, were no disgrace to good governance either. Almost exclusively privately educated—and so toughened up by the deprivations of that nineteenth-century penal colony, the British boys boarding school—and often having forbears with Indian government experience, they epitomized what Kipling referred to as the "white man's burden". Young men from sheltered backgrounds but classically educated would be sent out to outlying areas, often days' hard traveling away, to settle disputes, collect taxes, oversee projects or mend diplomatic fences. They may not have had much experience of life but they had learnt all about *Pax Romana*, the rules of which they now applied to *Pax Britannica*. This is not so much to defend the colonialism that Twain admired as, like him, to admire it for what is was at the time (and to reflect how very much worse it could have been).

*

There is no better way to see the Calcutta he saw then and compare it with what we see now than to walk between two magnificent Raj buildings: the Victoria Memorial built just after his visit, then a walk across the two-mile-long central park, the Maidan, and at the far end of the park Government House, now called Raj Bhavan, from where the viceroy ruled the sub-continent. After that we will visit all the sites the Twain party saw between 7-14 February, a busy week: the Royal Theatre where he lectured, the *Statesman* offices where we were both interviewed, what was the Belvedere stately home and is now the National Library, the monuments to the Black Hole and Ochterlony and the Indian Museum.

But first we both need to check in to our hotels. Ours is straightforward enough: the Bengal Club is a reciprocal of the Royal Bombay Yacht Club and thus able to accommodate us. It's not exactly what it was, the Bengal Club, and now one scurries into what would have been the servants' quarters at the

---

[47] Even more remarkable was the Sudan Political Service. It recruited only unmarried men between the ages of 21 and 25, almost all from public schools, one-third of them the sons of Anglican clergy. Yet it was so well run that it enabled 140 men to have charge of nine million people.

back of the building; the front, with its grand entrance, ballrooms, withdrawing rooms, book-lined corridors and uninterrupted views of the Maidan was sold as European membership declined after Independence. Still, Gillian and I as honorary members have a suite of sorts out back but Sita, as a guest, has to make do with a bit of a cupboard. Madam remains unamused. I plug in and find a message from our www.marktwainindia.com website that *The Times of India* wants to run my Hinduism blog[48] in the "How others see us" column.

The Twain party took suites in the newly opened Continental Hotel on 9 Chowringhee Road, the best hotel address in town. A series of announcements about the Continental appearing in *The Statesman* give us a flavor of what it must have been like. On opening we learn that the owners, the Boscolo brothers, had built "extensive premises which are in every way suited to the Requirements of a First Class Hotel which will cater for the Public as heretofore under the style and title of the Hotel Continental". Further announcements claimed that "Patrons, Constituents and the Public generally are hereby informed that the extensive additions are now complete and form the most Recherche [sic] and Comfortable Residents for families and Bachelors in Calcutta." Later we read that "special attention has been paid to Improvements of the new Private Tiffin Rooms" and further that "on Wednesdays and Saturdays an Italian orchestra will be in Attendance during dinner hours". Several years later an advertisement claimed that "among important guests have been Mark Twain and Winston Churchill".

After the Twain party's visit the Continental spread from 9 Chowringhee Road to nos. 10, 11 and 12 and bordered the equally illustrious Grand Hotel. They all closed in the 1930s when six guests died of food poisoning—rumored to have been caused by a dead cat found later in the shared water tank. The hotels emptied, guests cancelled bookings and the hotels never recovered.

As memories faded nos. 11 and 12 re-opened as the Ritz Continental and when that failed were torn down and rebuilt in the 1970s as the Peerless Inn as stands today; a typically ghastly blob of concrete in a ubiquitous style Gillian defines as Sub-Continental Hideous. The remains of the Grand were rescued by an ambitious 25-year-old Armenian jeweler, Arathoon Oberoi Stephen, and today the Oberoi Grand is *the* five-star hotel in town—although it too could do with a lick of paint.

No. 9, where the Twain party stayed, is still standing—just about.

---

[48] A first draft version of the last chapter.

Chowringhee Road is now supposed to be called JJ Nehru Road, but of course everyone still calls it Chowringhee Road. No. 9 is in a desperate state of disrepair and the landlords have put signs up everywhere warning people to stay away:

> Pursuant to the Direction given by the Honourable High Court of Calcutta, dated 13th August 2008, Notice is Hereby Given to the Unauthorised Occupants for the exercising of Abundant Caution that

> this Building at 9, Chowringhee Road, Calcutta is in very Dilapidated Condition and may Collapse at any point of time. As such the Landlord, the Life Insurance Corporation of India has begged the Honourable High Court of Calcutta for Permission to Demolish this dangerous Structure. Therefore, in the Event of any Untoward Incident, the Owner, the Life Insurance Corporation of India, will not be held not be responsible.

Of course, just like the equally condemned Watson's Hotel in Bombay, the building is full of offices. The chance of free accommodation on Chowringhee Road is well worth the risk of no. 9 falling down on top of you. Whereas Watson's

Hotel was full of lawyers, the Continental is a microcosm of Indian enterprise. The ground floor is a series of stalls selling everything from stiff collars to flutes to string vests to pirated DVDs. Upstairs the professional classes hold sway. Under a spaghetti cluster of exposed, improvised wiring one climbs up dust-carpeted stairs with wobbly banisters and whole treads missing.

On the second floor, surrounded by moldy, peeling walls lie the premises of Drs. Smith Bros, Dental Surgeons; In Attendance, Dr. S. K. Basu. Opposite the dentist, a doctor of a different sort, a pen doctor: The Pen Hospital, managed by the Central Pen Corporation of India Ltd. Above them we find the Calcutta Institution for Further Education and opposite them The Calcutta Serological Institute Laboratory (P) Ltd. On the top floor, where the Twain party had their suites, is—in unintentional posthumous honor of Smythe—Messrs. Carpenter & Sons, Theatrical Impresarios & Film Distributors. Theirs is the corner office with the hole in the wall; from the street one can see straight through to the ceiling. Across the passage is an unnamed accountancy firm, which should be called Charles Dickens Accountancy Practitioners Ltd., with, unbelievably, an Underwood typewriter on the desk and still in use.

Vijay Muni, of the accountancy with the Underwood, told me the backstory to no. 9. Like many owners of historic buildings in Calcutta, the landlords are caught in a bind. On the one hand the authorities of the Archaeological Survey of India[49] are demanding these buildings' preservation and even restoration, while on the other the Marxist local government of Calcutta, which before being voted out in 2011 had been in power for 34 years, had long since imposed a rent freeze. The owners retaliated by refusing to pay property tax knowing the Marxists would not want to take it over as they would then have pay their own taxes and then deal with the rent controlled tenants who refused to pay rent due the state of building, a state caused by the Marxists' policy in the first place.

I tell him of grander times and the letter from Mark Twain to the proprietors, the Boscolo brothers: "Continental Hotel, Calcutta. 18 February 1896. I am glad to be able to say that my ten days' stay in those houses with my family has been exceedingly comfortable and satisfactory."

So let the Re-Tour commence with visits to the Victoria Memorial and the Raj Bhavan. Our main purpose in visiting the Victoria Memorial was to spend some time in the Calcutta Gallery which traces the history of the city from

---

[49] A famously inept and corrupt QUANGO whose dead hand pervades the India it is meant to protect.

hamlet to capital. It is a superb exhibition, full of wonderful images with factual comments but without the usual burden of political correctness. My only gripe would be that the exhibits are poorly lit and at child height, so that one spends lot of time peering closely, bent double. A better way to see it would be from a wheelchair with a flashlight.

Twain described Calcutta thus:

> It has a population of nearly a million natives and a small gathering of white people. It is a huge city and fine, and is called the City of Palaces. It is rich in historical memories; rich in British achievement—military, political, commercial; rich in the results of the miracles done by that brace of mighty magicians, Clive and Hastings'

The paintings are all by European artists and of the colonial, central, empty, elegant part of the city—the famed City of Palaces around the giant Maidan park—and of the sprinkling of white people as Twain mentioned. All but a few of the native million are kept off canvas, and no doubt conditions for the local Bengalis were just as grim then as they are now but without the comfort of statehood. We see Calcutta in its prime, still the capital of India, the Maidan with a large racecourse (still the largest in Asia) in one corner of it, a full golf course in another, palaces along its side and the imposing Government House at it head. The park is clean and mown, the palaces clean and sentried, the boulevards clean and lightly trafficked. On them *tongas* ride hither and thither; no one seems to be walking, as Twain frequently pointed out. From time to time an Indian prince sweeps through the Maidan with an enormous train of men and beasts—and not without a spare man to pick up the mishaps of the beasts.

Although Twain never saw the Victoria Memorial[50] it would be wrong to leave it without a brief description. Guide books refer to it as "Kolkata's Taj Mahal" or the "Raj Mahal" and there certainly are similarities. Both are magnificent buildings built to honor the death of a female royal; in fact the Victoria Memorial's architect, Sir William Emerson,[51] was inspired directly by the Taj Mahal.[52] Both are the only two buildings in India whose lawns, lakes, shrubbery and herbaceous borders are beautiful sculpted and free from litter.

---

[50] Construction started before her Diamond Jubilee in 1901 and it was opened twenty years later.

[51] Also responsible for All Saints Cathedral in Allahabad and the Gothic Crawford Market in Bombay.

Both are seen at their most evocative with a full moon lighting the white marble. Both are perfectly symmetrical and built to a scale that inspires awe yet remains relatable.

Others will disagree but to my eyes the Taj Mahal is perfect while the Victoria Memorial is merely glorious, beautiful, magnificent but ultimately it is just a tad too fussy—it's just one ornate, one faux minaret, one Renaissance hint too many. The former is like a sculpture, the whole is formed from the whole; the latter is like a construction, built from the inside out. The former is transcendent, reduced by description; the latter needs description to define it.

Yet there is something more. The Taj Mahal was conceived in grief by the heart-broken ruler Shah Jahan as a mausoleum for his third wife Mumtaz Mahal, whom he considered to have been the perfect wife and mother. The Victoria Memorial was conceived in imperial triumph by Lord Curzon as a memorial for his empress, Queen Victoria. However much he might have admired her powers of wifery and motherhood it was her imperial prowess that he thought should be remembered. And there is a subliminal political consideration too: the fact that it was built as a memorial for not just a dead old white empress but for her whole extended royal family—in fact in praise of the whole concept of imperial monarchy—rather than as a mausoleum for a beautiful young Indian princess will always set the memorial at a disadvantage.

(Lord Curzon, to whom history has been less than kind, keeps an eye on you at the entrance, then passes you on to the suspicious gaze of an overlarge Lord Clive once inside. Warren Hastings and Lord Cornwallis, for reasons obvious yet obscure are dressed as Roman emperors—at least I assume that is why they are togged up in togas. The Empress Queen herself is around every corner: at her coronation, her marriage, her children's baptism, her first and second jubilees and so on. An inscription from Curzon sets the tone, saying the Memorial is for the benefit of all native classes so they can better themselves by learning from the glorious British history.)

It would be unfair to blame the Maidan, Calcutta's Central Park, for the state into which it has fallen these past fifty years, post-Independence. In Twain's time Indians were not barred from using the park but they had no interest in doing so; the whole idea of a park was as alien to them as a temple compound and *ghats* were to Europeans. Nowadays the Maidan can at best be described as downtrodden. The race and golf courses are now separate fenced off areas and

---

52 We will visit the Taj Mahal in three weeks, Twain time.

both are still immaculate but the rest of the park has threadbare grass—if any—and a layer of scattered litter on it. The shrubbery has simply withered away through disrespect. Countless sports clubs have infringed on the Maidan's edges and no one stops the motorcycles and their inevitable horns using the crisscross lanes as shortcuts. However much it may have gone to the dogs aesthetically the Maidan still fulfils its purpose just as well now as it did then; the hundreds of thousands of Bengalis who enjoy the Maidan on a Sunday afternoon are now enjoying it just as much as the dozens of Europeans did back then.

As we complete our historical journey across the heart of old Calcutta and new Kolkata we see in front of us Government House that was, or Raj Bhavan that is; the offices and residence of the Viceroy of India and the Governor of Bengal respectively. Here we find an Anglo-Indian reversal: the seat of power is as grandiose as it ever was, but instead of being full of the viceregal household and a throng of administrators and assistant chief to the chief assistants it is now, more or less, believe it or not... empty.

What a beautiful building! Modeled on Robert Adam's 1759 Kedleston Hall in Derbyshire in the English Midlands, the ancestral home of the Curzon family (which other?) and built fifty years later, it features four wings connected by two segmentmentally curved corridors. From above it looks like a curved blade propeller-shaped to catch whatever breeze it could. Adam's original had a south front based on the Arch of Constantine in Rome and a Palladian north front dominated by a massive multi-columned Corinthian portico. The central block was designed solely for grand occasions. In Kedleston Hall's case there were only two wings, one for the family and one for the servants; not so much upstairs, downstairs, but east wing, west wing. Government House or Raj Bhavan is proportionately bigger all round and has two extra wings for the affairs of state. Lord Curzon, viceroy from 1899-1905, must have been in a permanent state of *déjà vu* all over again: he only had to add a row of urns along the roofline to transform Government House in India into Kedleston Hall back in Derbyshire.

But how to compare then and now? As a building, a pile of bricks and plaster sitting in 27 beautiful acres, it has seen no obvious signs of decay but its circumstances have changed entirely. The decline started in 1911 when the Raj decided to move the capital of India from here to New Delhi. Government House was no longer the home of the viceroy and the seat of power with dominion over three hundred million souls, one-fifth of the world's population; it was from then occupied by the Governor of Bengal with no more than ceremonial rights over a quarter of that number.

Since 1947 the newly named Raj Bhavan has remained the residence of the Governor of Bengal, albeit a much smaller Bengal and, as we shall see later, quite likely to become even smaller. And as we saw in Bombay, the governor's role is purely ceremonial and titular. As a result nearly all the lesser rooms are mothballed and the grand reception rooms used only once or twice a year and then for comparatively pettifogging occasions. In an evocative throwback, the fifteen- by ten-yard anteroom to the banqueting hall is still called the "little yellow breakfast room". The old debating chamber looks like a parliament in one of the Channel Islands or a Caribbean colony; it is well preserved but without debates has lost its soul. The Supreme Court, where Mark Twain sat in on a session when the viceroy Lord Elgin presided, is still there, ready and waiting for the accused, who here at least will always be innocent and never proved guilty.

There's no doubt that the governors and their ladies loved the palace and a history plaque shows how each incumbent added something to the whole we see today. Lord Hastings imported the gravel, Lord Ellenborough donated the startling Chinese cannon on the brass dragon at the entrance, Lord Northbrook installed hot water, Lord Hardinge replaced the front gates, Lady Amherst started the garden, Lady Bentinck tore that garden up (she thought flowers unwholesome) and started again, Lord Auckland dug the fish pond, Lady Mayo planted more trees, Lady Lytton built a swimming pool, while all Lady Dufferin could find left to do was install the tennis court.

The strangest part about Raj Bhavan is that it is not open to the public. I had to plead historical research to be allowed in but even that took Sita endless applications and patience. Even then she could only get permission for Gillian to enter without her cameras and me without my iPhone (aargh!); she, being a native, wasn't allowed in at all. Once inside I couldn't help asking the aide-de-camp why—if the White House and Buckingham Palace and now even the haughty Élysée Palace are open to the public—Raj Bhavan in all its magnificence was closed to its citizens. I wish I had a video of the three-second look of panic and incomprehension, followed by the two-second shudder at the mere suggestion of the concept I received in return, which summed up perfectly the political-cultural differences between Europe and Asia. It also prompted the heinous thought that if democracy is the world's least worst option, India has it solely thanks to the British example.

Talking of which… a round-up of Calcutta in Mark Twain's time and

Kolkata these days wouldn't be complete without mentioning the change in the British presence. Now that *has* changed. Where once there was the full pomp and regalia—and absolute power—of viceregal Government House, there is now a rather downtrodden two-story consulate that looks like a low security-risk prison. It houses a small staff led by the very energetic and well-informed Deputy High Commissioner, Sanjay Wadvani, who was kind enough to pop over to the Bengal Club to brief me. Sanjay now has to make do with a staff of only ten, five of whom are concerned with boosting Anglo-Indian trade and investment—worthy to be sure but hardly the stuff of diplomatic subtlety, let alone worthy of WikiLeaks tittle-tattle.

To rub salt in the wounds the long-running Marxists had changed the address from the Raj-inspired Harrington Street to Ho Chi Minh Street, no doubt to annoy the Americans who have their own much larger (although it's hard to think what they actually do) consulate a few doors down the block.

Our Re-Tour did, however, draw one blank, much to Sita's... and Gillian's.... and Ok, me too, my relief. Clara wrote to her friend Martha Pond that

> I went out this morning with a servant to a Durga temple to see a goat sacrificed and I assure you going to that place was like going into the very lowest parts of New York (I should think). One of their musical bands was playing, crowds of natives were yelling their prayers out, many were throwing flowers and fruits to the idol and all ready to fight for a few coppers.

> A young black priest offered to lead me through the crowd & the creatures in the demand for money hit the priest two or three times because he didn't encourage me to give them money & several attacked my servant with such violence that he had to scatter coppers all about himself in self- defense.

> I was naturally timid so we hurried along as quickly as possible to the sacrificing block were already 12 goats had been butchered. The pools of a brilliant blood was sickening & the stench enough to knock one down. As we stood there a man brought up a bleating lamb by the legs but I couldn't wait any longer, much as I adore horrors I fled from this one, it was a little too much.

*

The next morning we set off to follow Twain's route around the sites. "The mention of Calcutta infallibly brings up the Black Hole. And so, when that citizen finds himself in the capital of India he goes first of all to see the Black Hole of Calcutta—and is disappointed.

"The Black Hole was not preserved; it is gone, long, long ago. It is strange. Just as it stood, it was itself a monument; a ready-made one. It was finished, it was complete, its materials were strong and lasting, it needed no furbishing up, no repairs; it merely needed to be let alone.

"It was the first brick, the Foundation Stone, upon which was reared a mighty Empire—the Indian Empire of Great Britain. It was the ghastly episode of the Black Hole that maddened the British and brought Clive, that young military marvel, raging up from Madras; it was the seed from which sprung Plassey; and it was that extraordinary battle, whose like had not been seen in the earth since Agincourt, that laid deep and strong the foundations of England's colossal Indian sovereignty."

All true, but the fact is the memory of the Black Hole was an embarrassment even in colonial times, and is now not mentioned at all. Twain was shown instead an engraved monument outside what is now the landmark GPO[53] building with its high-domed roof and tall Ionic-Corinthian columns. Six years later Lord Curzon had a better memorial made and put it at a quiet road crossing; there's no such thing as a quiet road crossing any more and after the Marxists took power they encouraged their thugs to vandalize it. The Indians never like being reminded of colonial times and especially so in any incident where they are not shown in the customary heroic martyr guise. The monument has now been moved out-of-sight-out-of-mind to St. John's Cathedral, the main Anglican church built in 1784[54] and now barely able to muster half a dozen worshippers on a Sunday. Seldom can an event in history have been so ill-starred as the Black Hole of Calcutta in 1756.

What the names on the monument do bring to mind is the extraordinary spirit of adventure that enthused the Honourable East India Company. In the early, glory days they made the rules of up as they went along; they were there for commerce, not to spread a religion or impose a political creed. They soon found

[53] General Post Office.
[54] Looks familiar? It is modeled on the Church of St. Martin's in the Field in Trafalgar Square, London.

that good commerce needed good governance and with the help of some more than willing Indian co-operators the newly-rich British and the already-rich

Indians built the City of Palaces and the capital of British India. "John Company" sowed the seeds of its own destruction by greed further inland, but then it was greed that made it all happen in the first place. That ambition overreached itself in 1857, leading to the Sepoy Uprising and the end of Company rule and the halcyon days of unrestrained business. The names of the young hopefuls remind us that Britain's opportunities lay in its Wild East as much as America's did in its Wild West. Looking back over our shoulders at the scale and opulence of St. John's Cathedral, the lesser of Kolkata's two cathedrals at that, reminds us of the confidence that they must have felt that British rule was going to last forever.

Twain would have seen that same confidence in the building next to where the Black Hole monument stood. The Writers Building was not as he might have thought a building for ten thousand budding Mark Twains but for ten thousand "writers", which is how the East India Company termed its clerks. The massive eight-story Italianate Gothic building is a remarkable statement of optimism for a commercial company to build, spending far more than was necessary to house their clerks. Perhaps shareholders weren't so short-termist in those days. On the roof ledge are giant statues to the seven gods of enterprise: Justice, Education, Faith, Commerce, Agriculture, Charity and Navigation.

We now head back to the Maidan to see the Ochterlony Monument. In 1896 it dominated the Calcutta skyline, much to Twain's chagrin: he didn't approve of the "cloud kissing monument to one Ochterlony".

> Wherever you are, in Calcutta, and for miles around, you can see it; and always when you see it you think of Ochterlony. And so there is not an hour in the day that you do not think of Ochterlony and wonder who he was? It is good that Clive cannot come back, for he would think it was for Plassey; and then that great spirit would be wounded when the revelation came that it was not. Clive would find out that it was for Ochterlony; and he would think Ochterlony was a battle. And he would think it was a great one, too, and he would say, "With three thousand I whipped sixty thousand and founded the Empire—and there is no monument; this other soldier must have whipped a billion with a dozen and saved the world."

> But he would be mistaken. Ochterlony was a man, not a battle. And he did good and honorable service, too; as good and honorable service as has been done in India by seventy-five or a hundred other Englishmen of courage, rectitude, and distinguished capacity. For India has been a fertile breeding-ground of such men, and remains so; great men, both in war and in the civil service, and as modest as great.

> But they have no monuments, and were not expecting any. Ochterlony could not have been expecting one, and it is not at all likely that he desired one. There is a sort of unfairness about it all.

Sita has been swatting up and as we stand beside the cloud-kisser she tells us all about it. Sir David Ochterlony was an East India Company general who fought against the Kingdom of Nepal in 1828—and won.

In gratitude for this new trade route the Company offered to build him a monument. Fine, he said, I'll have a tower made with a Turkish dome supported by a Syrian column on an Egyptian plinth. When it was finished he opened it with his thirteen wives in attendance, many of them seated on his herd of elephants. As Gillian is snapping away she notices some confusion in the execution: the plinth is Syrian, the dome Egyptian and the column Turkish. Inside there is a staircase for viewing from a Moorish balcony under the dome but it had to be closed after several (post-Independence) suicides.

Also, after Independence it was renamed Shahid Minar after what the British called terrorists and the Indians call freedom fighters.[55] (The Kashmiri separatists fighting the Indians now are of course "terrorists" and no doubt after their independence will become posthumous freedom fighters.) Naturally everyone ignored the Marxists and still calls it the OM. On the Maidan ground next to the monument is a venue for political meetings, modeled philosophically on Speakers Corner in London. It's a busy place—Bengalis are political people—and the park there is now just scrubland and covered, inevitably, in trash.

Kolkata is not an early riser so the sightseer or history hound has a normally-populated city to explore until about 10.30 a.m. when the working day starts. After that you have to take your chances with the broad masses *en masse*, and boy, are they broad and *en masse*. There isn't one square piece of sidewalk that isn't being slept on by night or sold from by day—or used by rushing coolies with enormous bundles on their heads. That's quite a sight as they trot and shout their way through the crowds, a faster form of delivery than the seized solid roads.

It has to be said that both our visits to Calcutta were made much more pleasant by being in winter, in what is still called "the cold season". Of course it's no such thing, the temperature being ideally warm, neither hot nor cold. As Twain explained: "It was winter. We were of Kipling's 'hosts of tourists who travel up and down India in the cold weather showing how things ought to be managed.' It is a common expression there, 'the cold weather' and the people think there is such a thing. It is because they have lived there half a lifetime, and their perceptions have become blunted.

"In India 'cold weather' is merely a conventional phrase and has come into use through the necessity of having some way to distinguish between weather which will melt a brass door-knob and weather which will only make it mushy. It was observable that brass ones were in use while I was in Calcutta, showing that it was not yet time to change to porcelain; I was told the change to porcelain was not usually made until May."

---

[55] Likewise the city's main square was called Dalhousie Square and is now called BBD Bagh after the initials of the three yahoos who bungled an attempt to assassinate the then Lt. Governor, Lord Dalhousie.

We are on our way back to the Bengal Club when I notice it for the first time. It had to happen somewhere and here in Calcutta someone had the bright idea of fixing their horn to be on permanently. Quite often one would notice that your driver would spend so much time blowing his horn that it would be easier for him just to jam it on permanently. Now a motorcyclist here has done just that: he has replaced the horn button with a horn switch. It plays a "tune" of sorts, simple scales, all the time. Needless to say he is jammed solid and not actually going anywhere.

And next? Already buses have louder horns than cars—horns so loud that if you are riding a rickshaw and are at bus horn height (well, there is no "if", you are at bus horn height)—it hurts to hear it. These new perma-horns will surely up the ante and if I was a budding Indian entrepreneur, and let's face it there are 1.2 billion of them, I'd start making loud-loud-louder horns with an on/off switch instead of a button. In fact one could dispense with the "off part" of the switch altogether and just wire it into the car's ignition system. When you turn the engine on the horn starts at the same time and stays on until you turn the engine off again.

*

That evening we both have an engagement. Mark Twain had to give the first of his three At Home Talks at the Royal Theatre, a few minutes stroll along Chowringhee Road at no. 16. I had to give the same *Joy Unconfined!* Byron Talk[56] I gave to the Royal Bombay Yacht Club at the Oxford Book Store in Park Street.

Sita had not been able to find out too much about the Royal Theatre, except that it had burned down on 2 January 1911 and that it was in bad repair even on the At Home nights of 10, 12 and 13 February 1896. The site at 16 Chowringhee Road is just fifty yards from the Continental Hotel and is now part of the Oberoi Grand Hotel. I later found a theatre review by a Major Hobbs who reported that during a performance of Much Ado about Nothing a horse fell through the rotted wooden floorboards and "played the devil's tattoo with its hooves on the corrugated iron walls of the theatre during the remainder of the evening".

The Byron Talk at the Oxford Book Store seems to go well enough and they sell a few copies afterwards. In general, English bookstores in India have a great

---

[56] As I had rather presumptuously started to call my one hour audio-visual book-promoting presentation.

selection of titles but have them displayed without any obvious organization, a mild metaphor for India herself. Many a happy hour can be spent here in Park Street as to browse is to borrow: there's a lovely little coffee shop with home-made cakes upstairs. Next to the café is a row of armchairs in which one can read the books and then just put them back on any old shelf that comes to hand.

But here's a funny thing. All along the Park Street sidewalks either side of the Oxford Book Store are stalls selling pirated copies of the books randomly displayed in the store itself. The idea is that you find the book you want in the shop and then pop out and buy it at a fraction of the price from the sidewalk. Not only that, but one cannot help notice that the pirate sellers had their stock categorized better than the shop. I ask the manager, Sandeep Sharma, how such a thing can be allowed.

"The Marxists sympathize with them. We have complained many times but we are the big bad capitalists," he replies.

"But surely the pirates are just as much capitalists as you are—and not tax paying ones either?"

"Yes, but they have more votes. As for taxes, don't make me cry! Only the few shops pay taxes—and indirectly pay all the non-taxpayers' taxes too. The city is bankrupt, totally bankrupt."

"So I've heard. By the way, I couldn't find a copy of *Joy Unconfined!* on the pirate stalls."

"So?"

"I don't know whether to be pleased or displeased it's not being pirated. It's either vanity or greed being ruffled."

And here's another funny thing. The next morning at breakfast Gillian is reading the Calcutta edition of *Times of India* and notices a familiar face on page 3—a 1/8 page color photograph of your correspondent arguing with a politician at a public rally, and under the headline "British writer in GJM bust-up", a great big article about me disrupting the rally for Gorkhaland independence. It had indeed happened that the previous afternoon on the way back here from the Ochterlony Monument; while Gillian and Sita peeled off back to the Bengal Club and a ten-minute shower, I headed for an appointment with the editor of another newspaper, the venerable old *The Statesman*.

It's a timely story of today's interconnectedness and here is how it came about. About ten days ago I was in the public library-cum-cobweb-museum in Benares and started chatting to a young American. He is a freelance travel writer-cum-tour guide. He was interested in the Mark Twain in India story and later we had dinner and an interview about my trip and it appeared the next day on the web version of *In-Travel* magazine, with a reference to our strathcarrons-ahoy website. The next day there was an email off our website from the *Asian Age*, another of the Indian English-language papers: they had seen the *In-Travel* piece and could they do a telephone interview about the trip for a Sunday supplement? Yes, I replied, but check on our marktwainindia website to find out more first. They did—and then wanted to change from doing a telephone interview to repeating the Allahabad blog about the Magh Mela under a Friday feature called "Then & Now"—and would I mind if they took out some of the "more offensive" jokes? No problem—and I thought that was the end of it.

Meanwhile Sita had contacted *The Statesman* in Calcutta to ask if we could nosy around the archives[57] when we arrived from Varanasi the following week. *The Statesman* was very much the newspaper of record in India and they had an interview with Twain and some reviews of the At Home Talks in the 12-15 February 1896 editions. "No problem, give us a call when you arrive." Then the editor, Sudipto Das, emailed her back: just checked your marktwainindia website and can we do a features interview with Ian now as we did back with Mark Twain then?

So yesterday afternoon I arrived at what remains of their once mighty offices for the archive access chat and the interview.

The Statesman Building is a massive and imposing semi-circular structure in a prime location of downtown Calcutta. One goes through the vast portals gingerly, expecting inside to find scenes from *Citizen Kane* or the opening of *Scoop* but—nothing. Not only is it empty but destroyed. Outside a loudspeaker has started chants and yells which echo around the empty cavern that once housed the mighty *Statesman*. Up the helical stairwell to the first floor—even higher ceilings and grander rooms and even more desolation but this time with added wanton destruction. Second floor, same story. The newspaper office is now crouching on half of the top floor.

What had happened? A familiar tale. Calcutta's three-and-a-half-decade-old Marxist government was virulently anti-capitalist. Rents were and still are strictly controlled but property tax on occupied business premises is the very opposite—out of control.

---

[57] For the 8 February 1896 pre-Talk interview at the Continental Hotel and the 11 and 13 February At Home reviews.

In response the landlords just make the space unlivable and so untaxable, as can be seen on the piledriven floors below. Meanwhile new technology, freelancing and home working mean that they can run the paper from a few square feet in the attic—and pay minimal property taxes. As Sudipto says, "everybody loses but Marxist purity stays intact".

Anyway, pleasantries over, the editor is displeased; the *Asian Age* has got there first: there's a note on the bottom of yesterday's "Then & Now" column plugging my Allahabad story as next week's feature. I explain and apologize and suggest that instead we work together on an expanded Calcutta "then and now" piece using their archive and we agree to knock something up on Tuesday.

Meanwhile outside the loudspeakered yelling and chanting is reaching what one hopes will be a final crescendo.

"What's all that about?" I ask.

"It's the Gurkhas. They want an independent Gorkhaland. Don't blame them."

"Independence from India?"

"No, from Bengal. They are a different race from the Bengalis—they are Himalayan, like the Nepalese or the Tibetans. In fact they are Nepali. They want to become independent like Sikkim. And they hate the Marxists. I'm Bengali and I don't blame them. They've been on strike for two weeks, all of north Bengal is paralyzed."

That explains a lot. For the past two weeks no tourist has been able to reach Darjeeling—and worse, no tourist has been allowed to leave. We have booked an overnight train to leave late on Tuesday and arrive late on Wednesday. I called the hotel yesterday to find out what was happening. They were furious with the strikers.

"We only have two businesses here, tea and tourism. The GJM (the Independence party) won't let the tea out or the tourists in". Or out.

"It doesn't sound very clever to ruin the only businesses there are," I suggested.

"Exactly," said Sudipto, "why ruin your local support? They all want independence, but not if it means going bust."

Sudipto says goodbye until Tuesday, which I'm pleased to say has now turned into lunch as well, and I walk down through the wasted, deserted cathedral that once was alive with the rush and hubbub of messengers and subs and cubs, typesetters and expense fiddlers. Outside the noise from the loudspeakers is drowning out even the concerted horns of an Indian traffic jam. On the stage are an array of pretty, well-dressed Himalayan women. Behind the stage stand large posters of Bengali police atrocities. A spokesman is working the crowd, half in their local Nepali dialect and half in English. I'm the only foreigner and people look curiously in my direction. Someone asks if they can help me. Yes, I say, I would like to ask a question over the mike. Much debating, still all smiles. What's my name (this all on the loudspeakers)? "Mac" (I use this everywhere to make life easier). Where am I from? New Zealand (a recent innovation, no Kiwi imperial baggage—and they always beat them at cricket). What is my question?

"I would like to ask what is the benefit to the people of Darjeeling to stop the movement of tea and tourism? I have spoken to my hotelier who says everyone in Darjeeling is very upset that you are ruining their businesses."

I got some guff in reply about ends justifying means but meanwhile the whole incident had attracted quite an additional crowd. As I left a photographer from the *Times of India* gave me his card; I gave him mine; and five minutes later the phone rang. It was the Delhi desk asking for a telephone interview; I obliged. Needless to say they made large chunks of it up and it read like I was virulently anti-GJM and pro-Bengali. As I'm having lunch here tomorrow with the British Deputy High Commissioner, Sanjay Wadvani, this may be diplomatically inconvenient, even if far from the truth.

Meanwhile I have taken the precaution of emailing the spokesman of the GJM I met yesterday asking for a an interview with him in Darjeeling as I see parallels between his quest for Gurkha independence now and the Indian quest for independence in Mark Twain's time. I also thought an email from him would give me Safe Conduct through any GJM roadblocks on the way up there.

*

When Twain wasn't lecturing at the Royal Theatre he was enjoying the full pomp and pageant of a Calcutta that no longer exists.

> I saw the fort that Clive built[58]; and the place where Warren Hastings and the author of the Junius Letters fought their duel; and the great botanical gardens[59]; and the fashionable afternoon turnout in the Maidan[60]; and a grand review of the garrison in a great plain at sunrise;

---

[58] Fort William, now completely out of bounds, the HQ of the Indian Army's Eastern Command.

and a military tournament in which great bodies of native soldiery exhibited the perfection of their drill at all arms, a spectacular and beautiful show occupying several nights and closing with the mimic storming of a native fort which was as good as the reality for thrilling and accurate detail, and better than the reality for security and comfort; we had a pleasure excursion on the "Hoogly" by courtesy of friends, and devoted the rest of the time to social life.

There were two visits the Twain party made which I was anxious to see, first to the Indian Museum and second to Belvedere, then the residence of the Lt. Governor of Bengal and now the Indian National Library.

It would seem the Indian Museum is unchanged—at least if the dust and attendants are anything to judge by—since their visit there on 11 February, still housing the same extensive selection of natural history exhibits from around the Commonwealth. Many of the animals are stuffed and it is unclear whether or not they are better off than their counterparts still alive in the disgusting zoo nearby.

It is the ideal shape for a tropical museum, featuring a large square well-stocked garden with a working fountain as its centerpiece and around it the four-sided, two-story building with massively thick walls and high ceilinged colonnades and cloisters. Off each side are various rooms for anything that has ever flown, swum, burrowed, hunted or foraged. The catalogues list 35,000 exhibits; if one did nothing else for two months but spend a minute viewing each one there would still be a pinned butterfly or two that one had missed. Twain noted that: "One should spend a month in the museum, an enchanted palace of Indian antiquities. Indeed, a person might spend half a year among the beautiful and wonderful things without exhausting their interest." True enough, but from his notes we see he was only there for half an hour; quite enough for the Re-Tour too.

We were all looking forward to visiting what is now the National Library previously Belvedere. Our favorite work in the Calcutta Gallery at the Victoria Memorial is a wonderful painting by Smythson, RA, from 1845 of the viceroy's bodyguard in superb uniforms lining Belvedere's drive and steps. Between them Indian ladies in a dazzle of sarees and Indian gentlemen in elegant costumes

---

[59] Now an organic garbage dump on the Hooghly river spread around a 250-year-old banyan tree.

[60] A full-dress, colonial-tropical *passeggiata*.

mingle with drabber European guests. On the lawn are tents with pennants flying and magnificent marquees with uniformed waiters rushing about. Elephants sporting silver and gold inlaid howdahs wait patiently to one side, fully dressed horses with gleaming carriages on the other. It's a scene of color, light, splendor and pageant—a record of a colonial-tropical fantasy come to life.

It has to be said that even in its pomp Belvedere was never the prettiest stately home in the world, but still, a proper stately home it was and one with its own parkland to match. It was originally a "gift" from the Mir Jafar to the new rulers, the Company, on behalf of the outgoing Moghul Empire. Just before the Sepoy Uprising it became the official residence of the Lt. Governor of Bengal, as it was when the Twain party lunched there.[61] Fifteen years later, after the capital moved from Calcutta to Delhi, it ceased to have its former significance. All ranks moved up a notch: the viceroy from Governor's House/Raj Bhavan to Delhi and so the Governor of Bengal from Belvedere to Governor's House/Raj Bhavan. Belvedere's fortunes declined and it was used only occasionally by viceroys on their winter visits to the races and for gala parties and balls.

Lord Curzon took pity on it and declared part of it to be the site for the new Imperial Library. The aim was simple but typically, imperially grandiose, for it to house a copy of every book that had ever been written about India. Thus it continued until Independence when it was renamed the National Library, one of Jawaharlal Nehru's pet projects. Nehru said: "I do not want Belvedere for the mere purpose of stacking books. We want to convert it into a fine central library where large numbers of research students can work and have all the amenities of a modern library. The place must not be judged as something like the present Imperial Library—it is not merely a question of accommodation but of something much more."

Oh dear, poor old JJN would be horrified at the awful mess they've made of it since the lofty pronouncements. The building itself is in a terrible and decayed state, the neglect having worked its way through the first line of plaster defenses and now attacking the exposed brickwork. The gardens are a shambles and, as always, covered in litter. The parkland beyond has become a sort of freelance dump caused by people throwing junk over the perimeter walls.

Meanwhile the books have been moved out to new surrounding buildings, all done in the usual Sub-Continental Hideous style and all totally ignorant of what

---

[61] In a letter to her daughter Jean, Livy declared their lunch at the Belvedere was the finest meal they ate in India.

was and still could be the wonderful parkland in which they lie—and of course the stately home which they surround. The whole operation must have cost far, far more than maintaining the stout stately home, but as Sita points out, there's far more baksheesh to be had from building new horrors than maintaining old ladies. To add insult to injury, the Reference Library, the centerpoint of Nehru's vision, is now off limits to anyone without prior permission from an office in the Writers Building, which Sita says will take a week and the usual tea money.

It's a shame some of these incredibly newly-rich Indians we keep hearing about don't buy a few of India's own stately homes rather than buying them abroad. Presumably they can "find a way" past the dead hand of the Archaeological Survey of India, here too destroying what they are supposed to preserve. The Indian "piles" are not yet real piles and are still just about salvageable, but not for much longer. In the meantime lovers of the sublime can only remember Smythson's portrait and weep.

*

Time for us both to leave Calcutta/Kolkata for the Himalayas—but lastly we have to ask what Mark Twain would have made of the Kolkata we have lived through. I think he would have loved it for a short period, as we both had and as he loved the chaos and confusion of India, a free-for-all which this new Calcutta compresses and amplifies before hurling it right back.

8. DARJEELING

The Twain party made the twenty-four-hour train journey from Calcutta to Darjeeling from 14 to 15 February. It was a delightful trip, the first half through the beautiful fertile upper plains of Bengal and then the 6,000-foot climb up to Darjeeling on the toy train. We can see equally now what he saw then:

> The plain is perfectly level, and seems to stretch away and away and away, dimming and softening, to the uttermost bounds of nowhere.

> What a soaring, strenuous, gushing fountain spray of delicate greenery a bunch of bamboo is! As far as the eye can reach, these grand vegetable geysers grace the view, their spoutings refined to steam by distance. And there are fields of bananas, with the sunshine glancing from the varnished surface of their drooping vast leaves. And there are frequent groves of palm; and an effective accent is given to the landscape by isolated individuals of this picturesque family, towering, clean-stemmed, their plumes broken and hanging ragged, Nature's imitation of an umbrella that has been out to see what a cyclone is like and is trying not to look disappointed.

Smythe was feeling particularly gleeful, having some payback for being bounced out of his lower bunk by the English cavalry officer's servant on the way in to Calcutta:

> When we arrived, the usual immense turmoil and confusion of a great Indian station were in full blast. It was an immoderately long train, for all the natives of India were going by it somewhither, and the native officials were being pestered to frenzy by belated and anxious people. They didn't know where our car was, and couldn't remember having received any orders about it. Then Satan came running and said he had found a compartment with one shelf and one sofa unoccupied, and had made our beds and had stowed our baggage.

> The train started and Mr. Smythe's opportunity was come. His bedding, on the upper shelf, at once changed places with the bedding—a

stranger's—that was occupying the lower sofa that was opposite to mine. About ten o'clock we stopped somewhere, and a large Englishman of official military bearing stepped in. We pretended to be asleep. The lamps were covered, but there was light enough for us to note his look of surprise. He stood there, grand and fine, peering down at Smythe, and wondering in silence at the situation. After a bit be said:

"'Well!' And that was all.

But that was enough. It was easy to understand. It meant: "This is extraordinary. This is high-handed. I haven't had an experience like this before."

He sat down on his baggage, and for twenty minutes we watched him through our eyelashes, rocking and swaying there to the motion of the train. Then we came to a station, and he got up and went out, muttering: "I must find a lower berth, or wait over." His servant came presently and carried away his things.

Mr. Smythe's sore place was healed, his hunger for revenge was satisfied. But the next day the English gentleman asked to travel with us, and he did. A pleasant man, an infantry colonel; and doesn't know, yet, that Smythe robbed him of his berth, but thinks it was done by Satan without Smythe's knowledge. He was assisted in gathering this impression.

Livy too was enjoying the trip. She wrote to her youngest daughter Jean:

We are so royally treated everywhere we go that I cannot begin to command the time to write to you beloved ones at home about it. On the trip the railway company put the fares at ½ rate and gave us the director's carriage with a carriage attached for our servants. In the car were easy chairs & sofas & a good sized table &c &c.

We left Calcutta at 4.30 and at 5.30 there was sent into our carriage tea & bread & butter & cake &c &c and servants to serve us who remained standing behind our table until we had finished our tea.

At 8.30 we left this train and got into a boat to cross a river. The boat belongs to the same people. We were to be on the boat for about an hour. How I do wish you could have seen the pictures that presented themselves to us there. Natives in all the brilliant and pink dress costumes one could imagine, standing about the station and all the way down to the boat. On the boat was beautifully decorated and spread dinner table to receive us, where, as the guests of the president of the railroad we dined with him most sumptuously.

*

The *Darjeeling Mail* leaves Calcutta at 10 p.m. every night and terminates at New Jalpaiguri, or NJP, at 8 a.m. the following morning. It is one of the best trains in India, refurbished and with crisp sheets and pillowcases and thick blankets in the two-tier second-class sleeper. One would hope that the *Darjeeling Mail* would tie in with the toy train so that one steps off one and onto another, but no. The toy train should leave from another station, Siliguri, a few miles away, but doesn't. It should leave after 8 a.m. to enable Darjeeling-bound passengers to transfer, but is scheduled to leave at 7 a.m.—and then doesn't leave there then anyway. It is one's first experience of Darjeeling's current turmoil, man-made and sorrowful. Instead of taking the toy train from Siliguri one now has to take a shared jeep up the mountain, bouncing and banging over a terrible road on a journey that leaves one as uncharmed as the toy train would have left one charmed.

Before re-joining Mark Twain for a stiff recoverer at the bar at the charming Windamere Hotel in Darjeeling, where he stayed in one its early incarnations, your indulgence please for a quick look at why Darjeeling is going to the dogs.

*

As we have been following Twain's Grand Tour around India the political situation has been as stable for us now as it was for him then. India then had to contend with rule by the Raj but he was there at a peaceful point midway between the two great revolts, the Sepoy Uprising of 1857 and the post-World War 2 Gandhian Uprising that led to Independence in 1947. India now has to contend with rule by a particularly vile set of embezzling politicians, but if it is a scamocracy—as the equally corrupt Indian media insists on calling it—it is also a democracy in rude health.

The exception to this rule now is in the area around Darjeeling which

125

is seeking its own independence, not from India but from the state of West Bengal. Calling itself Gorkhaland to reflect the indigenous Nepalese Gurkha population and lying across the ridges and valleys of the Himalayan foothills, this famously beautiful area has been in turmoil—and a downward spiral— since 1986. What once proudly hailed itself the Queen of the Hills is now an unplanned, overgrown, shabby, ugly, poor and edgy spread of fear and doom. The tourists have mostly disappeared, frightened off by the uncertainty of the transport strikes and the crumbling infrastructure, taking their tourism to more welcoming and accommodating Himalayan destinations.

How did it come to this? In 1828 two British officers from the East India Company, surveying the uninhabited area with Gurkha guides, saw the Dorje Ling Buddhist monastery and decided to recommend the area for a sanatorium and military outpost. The land was nominally under the control of the King of Sikkim and a land-lease deal between him and the East India Company was soon arranged. By 1857, when control of India passed from the East India Company to the Raj, Darjeeling was a thriving town of 10,000 souls, mostly Gurkhas from Nepal brought in to man the new tea plantations and build the Scottish Highland-style colonial houses. Such was the new resort's popularity as a hill station from which to escape the Calcutta summer that twenty years later the British bought the Maharaja of Cooch Behar's summer palace to use as a Governor's House and the Governors-General in effect ruled India from Darjeeling from June to September for the next thirty five years, until the government moved to Delhi. By the time of Twain's off-season visit from 15 to 17 February 1896, Darjeeling was near its peak of prettiness and pleasantness and it was as a healing resort and summer hill station in spectacular yet reachable Himalayan surroundings that over the next fifty years its reputation was established. The fact that the best tea in the world was grown on nearby plantations did its reputation no harm either.

The cause of the rot was two bungled attempts by the British to partition Bengal, firstly in 1905 and secondly at Partition in 1947. The northeast of India is now a hotchpotch of states and territories: Assam, Arunachal Pradesh, Nagaland,[62] Manipur, Mizoram, Tripura and Meghalaya. (Sikkim, half-encircled by the Chinese in occupied Tibet, was its own kingdom until 1975, when it asked to be joined to India as its own state.) None of these states or territories has any greater connection to West Bengal than Darjeeling, whether historically,

---

[62] Nagaland wasn't even part of the Raj yet somehow woke up one morning to be told it was now Indian.

tribally, racially, linguistically, religiously, culturally or commonsensically. As a result there are now over forty separatist movements in the northeastern areas. West Bengali propaganda suggests that some or all of them are sponsored by mischief-making, neighboring China, a theory discounted by well-informed foreign observers. Of these movements the one based in Darjeeling for an independent Gorkhaland is the most conspicuous because it is the best known, and up to now most visited, by the outside world.

You can see the Gurkhas' point. Darjeeling is now, just as it always has been, a Nepalese town on Indian land. In the British era that wasn't important as Darjeeling was a small resort of only 35,000 at Independence and the Gurkhas and the British enjoyed mutual admiration and shared blood spilled in battle. Now under Bengali rule the Gurkhas are treated as Nepalese usurpers using up valuable Indian land. More to the point the Gurkhas look enviously at Sikkim just to the north: a separate state for separate people with allegiance directly to Delhi and the recipient of a substantial amount of Delhi largesse as well.

We will return to Twain's time here soon but let's see why his trip cannot be repeated today, why Darjeeling has slid down the proverbial mountain since the glory days of pre-Independence—and why matters will only become worse due to the lack of worldly-wisdom of the sinister separatist movement, the Gorkha Janmukti Morcha or GJM, who have taken a wonderful cause and somehow managed to alienate everyone who could help them achieve it.

Their first mistake was to take their example from Mahatma Gandhi and not, talking Gurkhas, from Joanna Lumley.[63] Gandhism led to Indian Independence through a policy of non-violence and non-co-operation. The GJM's policy of non-co-operation with West Bengal takes no account of the external circumstances that made Gandhism such a potent force. Britain had just finished an exhausting war and was tired of conflict—and tired of exchequer. India was a massive administrative burden and to restore it to its pre-war honey-pot status would be an enormous and unpopular undertaking. Furthermore, every Briton knew that India had played a gallant part in the Allied victory and the nation's sympathy was if not *with* Gandhi, certainly not against him. There was yet something bigger if less tangible afoot: a post-war change of the world order was in the air, a time for the United Nations made up of independent nations. India and its partition were ideas whose time had come; the sense of

---

[63] A well-loved British comedy actress who embraced the cause of Gurkha war veterans having British nationality.

inevitability made its achievement not so much "if" but "when".

The GJM are trying to apply this model to their dispute with West Bengal but cannot see that all the roles are reversed. Britain is small, India is huge; West Bengal is large, Gorkhaland is tiny. Britain was tired of dispute, India was in the mood for more; West Bengal is indifferent, Gorkhaland is desperate. Britain was broke, India could live on nothing; India is booming, Gorkhaland is throwing itself into poverty. Britain and India had emotional, institutional and military ties to each other: they cared for each other—personally—underneath the dispute; West Bengal couldn't care less if the foreigners in Gorkhaland self-destruct or not, in fact rather hopes for it sooner than later. There is no sense of inevitability, no "if" nor "when".

Then there is one further GJM variation on the Gandhi example of non-violence and non-co-operation. Gandhi would never use violence against his own people, whereas the GJM have terrorized the Gurkha opposition out of existence. The opposition leader was assassinated in May 2009, his throat cut by a Gurkha dagger at a public rally in the centre of town. One wanders around the back alleys and sees burned out houses, including the Tourist Office. People one meets as a travel writer—taxi drivers, hoteliers, shopkeepers, teachers, tour guides, librarians—are frightened into being seen to support the GJM; all of them support independence, far from all of them support the GJM's tactics.

Gandhi's non-co-operation was against the British not against his own people. Gorkhaland's only three businesses, tourism, tea and teaching, have been particular targets of the GJM. The endless and random strikes cut access to and from Darjeeling. The last one lasted for ten days and trekkers returning to base found they couldn't leave. Meanwhile word has spread around the travelers' forums and tourist operators: give Darjeeling a miss. The next target is the tea plantations, the area's biggest employers: the first flush crop is the most valuable and they've just been told it can't be transported. The new school term starts late February; students come from afar but now have to sit in untaught classrooms.

There are endless other stupidities: a mobile phone ban on under eighteens; result: teenage uproar, Gandhian style non-co-operation and a swift reversal. A six-month alcohol ban because alcohol taxes were going to West Bengal; result: disaster for the legal wine and beer shops, an instant black market for the racketeers and no drinker deprived. A decree that all cars should have Gorkhaland number plates; result: no one could drive in West Bengal so they had to have two number plates; result: another rebounded brainwave. The claiming of

Gorkhaland's boundaries not just for the foothills but also for pockets of land in the plains; result: an ideal excuse for West Bengali ridicule. The latest nonsense is a teaching ban; it's too soon to know the result but one wonders how many feet these people think they have in which to shoot themselves.

So one sees all this, sees the streets full of unemployed young men, sees the fear in people's eyes and thinks: why? Does the end justify the means—the rationale behind every dictatorship's hatred for humanity? One concludes that this nascent Pol Pot-ism is just plain stupid then one hears more. The policy of non-co-operation with West Bengal goes further than the symbolic. The world famous toy train can only complete the last section of its journey because of a landslide down-line three years ago. The toy train experience, as taken by the Twain party on 15 February, is a World Heritage Site and the West Bengal government and Indian Army have proposed clearing the landslide; the GJM has refused because it means taking West Bengal money. The road up to Darjeeling is in terrible condition and the road from Darjeeling to Tiger Hill is even worse, and will not be passable after this year's monsoon. There is a West Bengal budget to maintain the roads but the budget remains unsullied by GJM hands. The phone lines to the plains are too old to support broadband but upgrading would mean taking Indian technology so businesses and visitors cannot communicate commercially with the outside world. Then one thinks: this is something beyond stupidity, this is purity and thus rather admirable… and then one thinks again of Pol Pot and the vanity of purity. As my contact at the American Consulate in Calcutta said, the movement is run on a mixture of emotion and amateurism, a dangerous combination.

*

So, back to join Mark Twain at the bar at the Windamere, or Ada Villa as it was then. He tells me he had a very different trip to our harrowing four-hour bone-shaker through the potholes in a shared jeep.

> We changed from the regular train to one that skimmed along within a foot of the ground and seemed to be going fifty miles an hour when they were really making about twenty. Each car had seating capacity for half-a-dozen persons; and one was substantially out of doors, and could see everywhere, and get all the breeze, and be luxuriously comfortable. It was not a pleasure excursion in name only, but in fact.

129

After a while they stopped at a little wooden coop of a station just within the curtain of the somber jungle, a place with a deep and dense forest of great trees and scrub and vines all about it. The royal Bengal tiger is in great force there, and is very bold and unconventional. From this lonely little station a message once went to the railway manager in Calcutta: "Tiger eating station-master on front porch; telegraph instructions."

It was there that I had my first tiger hunt. I killed thirteen. We were presently away again, and the train began to climb the mountains. In one place seven wild elephants crossed the track, but two of them got away before I could overtake them. The railway journey up the mountain is forty miles, and it takes eight hours to make it. It is so wild and interesting and exciting and enchanting that it ought to take a week. As for the vegetation, it is a museum. The jungle seemed to contain samples of every rare and curious tree and bush that we had ever seen or heard of. It is from that museum, I think, that the globe must have been supplied with the trees and vines and shrubs that it holds precious.

The road is infinitely and charmingly crooked. It goes winding in and out under lofty cliffs that are smothered in vines and foliage, and around the edges of bottomless chasms; and all the way one glides by files of picturesque natives, some carrying burdens up, others going down from their work in the tea-gardens.

At an elevation of 6,000 feet we entered a thick cloud, and it shut out the world and kept it shut out. We climbed 1,000 feet higher, then began to descend, and presently got down to Darjeeling, which is 6,000 feet above the level of the Plains.

He is no less enthusiastic about the local people.

We had passed many a mountain village on the way up, and seen some new kinds of natives, among them many samples of the fighting Ghurkas. They are not large men, but they are strong and resolute. There are no better soldiers among Britain's native troops. And we had passed shoals of their women climbing the forty miles of steep road from the valley to their mountain homes, with tall baskets on their backs hitched to their foreheads by a band, and containing a freightage weighing—I will not say how many hundreds of pounds, for the sum is unbelievable.

These women porters[64] one can still see today using exactly the same carrying techniques as they did then. One whisked my suitcase out of the back of the jeep and ignoring the case's four wheels threw it over her shoulders, tied a haystack knot around its middle and attached the band Twain mentioned to her forehead. I know it was just over 55 pounds as I'd had to decant some books from my checked into my carry-on at the airport in Bombay. She then sherpa-ed up the steep hill alleys to the Windamere with your correspondent puffing and panting behind wheeling his distinctly light-weight carry-on and feeling distinctly ungallant.

Twain had a more exotic and unusual ride up to the hotel: "At the railway station you find plenty of cab-substitutes—open coffins, in which you sit, and are then borne on men's shoulders up the steep roads into the town." At the jeep stop there are now dozens of real cabs, little Japanese microbuses, so many dozen that they have jammed up the only road so that it is quicker to pant-trot along behind the mountain goat porters.

The railway station is at the lower level of the town and the hotels, clubs, smarter shops, temples and the town square are high up on the ridge. Mark Twain's party and their open coffin made the climb up the steep lanes and "Up there we found a fairly comfortable place, the property of an indiscriminate and incoherent landlord, who looks after nothing, but leaves everything to his army of Indian servants. No, he does look after the bill—to be just to him—and the tourist cannot do better than follow his example. I was told by a resident that the summit of Kinchinjunga is often hidden in the clouds, and that sometimes a tourist has waited twenty-two days and then been obliged to go away without a sight of it. And yet went not disappointed; for when he got his hotel bill he recognized that he was now seeing the highest thing in the Himalayas."

The old Ada Villa was really more of a boarding house than a hotel. One can only assume that the Darjeeling Club, popularly known as the Planters' Club and more typical of the sort of place they would have stayed was full—or at least

---

[64] No coolies in the Himalayas.

didn't have the three spare rooms the Twain party needed. The Ada Villa was transformed into the Windamere Hotel in 1939 and is now far more than "fairly comfortable" and the landlord the opposite of "indiscriminate and incoherent". In fact it takes less than ten minutes for it to be my favorite hotel in India. It feels like my perfectionist great aunt Fiona has said "borrow my country house for the week and invite your friends." It's not just that it is so comfortable in a familiar, chintzy, throwback sort of way but it makes the guests feel comfortable, chintzy and throwback too. I'm sure this is its secret, to make Victoriana work without ladling on nostalgia or applying a—dread word—theme. One wallows in the way things should be done but seldom are; a last pocket of resistance to the lowest common denominator. Staff are brisk and quiet and polite—and soothsayers for one's needs. The rooms are suites with proper baths and changing rooms. In the evenings the air is heated by coal fires and in the day the air is cleaned by throwing open the windows. The green telephones in the rooms have signs saying "When certain numbers are dialed the phones ring simultaneously in separate rooms, causing alarms to guests who value their repose. We have been keeping this deficiency in our intercom service under review and, meanwhile, crave your indulgence." In other words, they don't work. Then there's the notice

in the sitting room: "Visitors are respectfully requested not to move around furniture in this room in order that comfort may be shared in fair proportion by all. Also, visitors are requested not to take off their footwear or put their feet on the furniture, or lie supine on the hearth or sleep behind the settees lest unintended offence be given to others."

The hotel really doesn't deserve to have its business vandalized by the GJM. Ones senses that Agatha Christie is about to sweep into the dining room and say "ah, now I've got you all together" or Noel Coward will soon be jumping up to change the 78, or in my case that Mark Twain and I are sharing a snifter and cigar in the bar.

*

That night's At Home Talk was at the town hall at 9.30 p.m. It's just a short walk along the ridge. The town hall is still standing, just about, but no longer in use except as a ramshackle store house for… rams and shackles.

It was and is part of a sports club compound. In 1896 it was called the Amusements Club; in 1909 it changed its name to the Gymkhana Club, a name it still retains today. Back then there were eight tennis courts, a squash court, a skating rink and stables. A small racecourse used up all of the perimeter of a plateau below, encircling a compressed polo pitch. Numerous photographs survive of the equestrian life of members and mounts. Inside the club there were card rooms and billiards rooms. There were enough planters, soldiers, recuperators and administrators to keep both the Amusements or Gymkhana Club and the nearby Planters' Club, full and busy.

Nowadays the Gymkhana Club has been taken over by the GJM as its unofficial headquarters and visitors are met with suspicious stares—at Sita even more than at Gillian and me. The secretary has to find someone for permission to show us even the outside of the town hall. Sullen stares follow us round. There's not much else to see: the eight tennis courts have become two and they are as potholed as the roads. The squash court and skating rink have not been used for years. Inside the card rooms are in use but not for cards. Maybe this is the room where they dream up all their stupid schemes.

Talking of which, right opposite the Gymkhana Club stands a mighty handsome eight-story white building in stone and marble. It is visible from around the upper levels and is really most eye-catching, clearly not the work of the Indian school of architecture. It is the new auditorium-cum-communal hall, or should be, but since it was commissioned by a previous separatist grouping the GJM has declared it politically unacceptable and banned its use apart from the occasional two-day hunger strike. The monkeys aren't so fussy and now troupes of them have made themselves at home in the best address in town. Nor is upkeep allowed and now the first tell-tale signs of damp and decay are starting to appear in its details. The great white building is becoming a great white elephant. It is ironical that the one and only handsome new building we have seen in India is barred from use.

And talking of which, the spread of ugliness down the slopes of Darjeeling is even more noticeable than elsewhere because of the setting. One needs to stay high. Heading along the upper level, the ridge, from the White Elephant past the Gymkhana Club and the Windamere one enters the large square, Chowrasta. This is most attractively laid out with a golden statue and temple at one end and in-scale and period shops along the side. Tibetan monks swirl by, ponies take laughing children for a ride, old Himalayan faces sit on park benches and smile the day away. Above it is Observatory Hill, topped by a dazzling Sikkimese temple where Buddhism and Hinduism are practiced side by side. All this is for pedestrians only and on the opposite side of Chowrasta is the start of The Mall, the main shopping street full of Tibetan tit-tat and English tea shops. Half way along higher up on the left is the Planters' Club. One reaches the end of The Mall and the horning traffic starts again and then one sees the ugliest new building in a country of ugly new buildings: the orange-ochre and monsooned-concrete colored Telecommunications Building; the safe haven of higher Darjeeling is over and one is back in India.

*

Early next morning Livy and Clara rose at first light to see sunrise over the high peaks to the north and west. At first I had assumed that like every visitor today they had taken themselves up to the viewing station on Tiger Hill, but having made that half hour journey by car and pothole realize they must have seen the spectacle more closely, probably from the viewing point on the far side of Observatory Hill. As Livy wrote to Jean: "Look on the map, and try to realize that we who belong to you are away up here in the Himalayas on the border of Thibet [sic]. I cannot think that it can be true."

We got up at 5:30 to see the view. I went out in the rickshaw with two men pulling and one pushing. Clara and a gentleman went on horseback and Mr. Smythe walked. Papa we left in the dressing down by the window, as he had decided to get his view from there. He got the view and the most glorious when it was.

In his notes Mark Twain wrote:

While my party rode away to a distant point where Kinchinjunga and Mount Everest show up best, I stayed at home for a private view. I got a pipe and a few blankets and sat for two hours at the window, and saw the sun drive away the veiling gray and touch up the snow-peaks one after another with pale pink splashes and delicate washes of gold, and finally flood the whole mighty convulsion of snow-mountains with a deluge of rich splendors.

Kinchinjunga's peak was but fitfully visible, but in the between times it was vividly clear against the sky—away up there in the blue dome more than 28,000 feet above sea level—the loftiest land I had ever seen, by 12,000 feet or more. It was 45 miles away. Mount Everest is a thousand feet higher, but it was not a part of that sea of mountains piled up there before me, so I did not see it; but I did not care, because I think that mountains that are as high as that are disagreeable.

Today the trip up to Tiger Hill from base camp Darjeeling is a more or less compulsory tourist rite of passage. I was there at the same time of year as Twain's party and clambered out into pre-dawn at much the same time of morning, 5 a.m., as Livy and Clara. The road up to Tiger Hill is now in terrible condition and it takes well over half an hour to complete the six-mile climb through the potholes and open sores that level out at 8,500 feet. In the spring and autumn viewing seasons two hundred cars a day batter the track. In the summer the monsoon washes chunks of foundation away. In the winter ice widens the cracks. I imagine it will be Shanks's Pony only pretty soon.

We are not alone as people come from all around to take their chances of a clear view. Luckily there are *chai* and coffee sellers aplenty to help us wake up. Everyone has had early alarm calls and a rough ride to the viewing summit; everyone chatters teeth and words excitedly, bashing themselves to keep warm. Then the clamor subsides as the first change in the sky's hue shows to the east.

The spectacle starts with an easing of the dark into grey, then a hint of cayenne and as the gods turn the brightness up and inch by inch, billion mile by billion mile, the golden apple slips free of the horizon. The only sound is clicking cameras, Gillian's more than most, and whispered oohs and aahs. All eyes now turn left to the north and west as the peaks and slopes of the range around the Kanchenjunga massif glow in turn, timelessly, first Venetian pink, then fresh flaxen before settling down to virgin white and another day of snow, as old as the world, freezing and melting and freezing in the sunlight.

Everyone now wants to see Everest hiding between other, seemingly higher, peaks one hundred miles away across the earth's curve. Usually she is coy and is so again for us earthlings this morning. By 6 a.m. the night-time mist below dissolves and clouds wrap themselves around the peaks but for ten minutes back there nature and consciousness share a transcendent experience of the change and constancy of beauty, of the one without a second.

I have no idea if the breakfast at Ada Villa was as good as the one at the Windamere Hotel is now but feel it would be impossible for it to be so. The secret of making porridge—the only meal I know how to make apart from toast—is to forget water and the microwave and use a significant saucepan, politically incorrect full-bore milk and slow stirring. No need for further milk, but a dollop of honey doesn't go amiss. There's obviously been some industrial espionage as the Windamere chef has pinched my formula but with a warm stomach on this cold high Himalaya morning all is forgiven.

*

Meanwhile Mark Twain was busy watching the world go by.

> I changed from the back to the front of the house and spent the rest of the morning there, watching the swarthy strange tribes flock by from their far homes in the Himalayas. All ages and both sexes were represented, and the breeds were quite new to me, though the costumes of the Tibetans made them look a good deal like Chinamen. The prayer-wheel was a frequent feature. It brought me near to these people, and made them seem kinfolk of mine. Through our preacher we do much of our praying by proxy. We do not whirl him around a stick, as they do, but that is merely a detail.

> The swarm swung briskly by, hour after hour, a strange and striking

136

pageant. It was wasted there, and it seemed a pity. It should have been sent streaming through the cities of Europe or America, to refresh eyes weary of the pale monotonies of the circus-pageant. These people were bound for the bazaar, with things to sell. We went down there, later, and saw that novel congress of the wild peoples, and ploughed here and there through it, and concluded that it would be worth coming from Calcutta to see, even if there were no Kinchinjunga and Everest.

The bazaar, now called Chowk Bazaar, spreads down from The Mall and is still the scene of colorful chaos it was then. Only the size has changed—along with the rest of Darjeeling which now has over 300,000 souls, a twenty fold increase since Twain's time. It is not only the size that has changed: traffic has arrived and with it Indian driving manners and so in an area that cries out to be pedestrianized one's amusement is somewhat curtailed by having to squeeze up against the walls and find respite from the blaring horns. The trading from the stalls is almost exclusively local as there's not much for foreigners to buy unless they are self-catering or have lost their luggage. Most of the souvenir shops—and the more interesting Tibetan artifact shops—are up in the peace and quiet, and no doubt extra expense, of The Mall.

At midday Twain ambled down to the Planters' Club. *The Standard* reported that "he had a peg,[65] was genial and entertaining, and kept the billiard-room so jolly, that, though it was full of members, no one could play." He himself remembered that "It was a comfortable place. It is loftily situated, and looks out over a vast spread of scenery; from it you can see where the boundaries of three countries come together, some thirty miles away; Tibet is one of them, Nepal another, and I think Herzegovina was the other." Well, I suppose Sikkim does sound a bit like Herzegovina after a couple of pegs.

Today the famous Planters' Club still exists but as a shadow of its former self; the unkind might dismiss it as a metaphor for Darjeeling. It no longer has any members; that is to say there is no membership scheme. The public rooms are still there, the bar and lounge and dining room, but they are only open in the day and don't serve anything to eat or drink. Heads and antlers of dead members of the *cervidae* family look down disapprovingly at the threadbare carpets and damp-patched walls; they prefer the good old days of pegs and billiards, joshing

---

[65] Or "tincture"—a shot and a mixer, in this case brandy and soda. A chotapeg was a single; a burrapeg a double. I can't see Twain bothering much with the former.

sahibs and flirting *mem'sahibs*. From dusk the whole place is shut down. Upstairs there are nineteen bedrooms which are more tired than the most tired of guests; it has in effect become a two-star hotel with three-star prices trading on four-star cachet.

In spite of being run-down its position and renown make it still highly salvageable. The great white planters have long gone, replaced by here-today gone-tomorrow managers for multinationals. The officers and gentlemen of the Indian Army are higher up the Himalayas towards the border with China and the movers and shakers are broking power down in Calcutta, but if the GJM sees sense it has all the makings of a wonderful counterpoint to the Windamere; not competitively but complementarily.

Later that night Livy and Clara left; Twain and Smythe left the next morning. It is not clear why they split up, presumably a shortage of space on the railroad.

This next morning they had a much finer view of the massif and Twain told Smythe: "I intended to tell the many people in Calcutta, who told me of the grandeur of the snows, that I had seen them, whether I had or not. I am glad to be saved the pain of telling a lie."

And so for Mark Twain's famous adventure down the mountain in the brake car, unfortunately now impossible to recreate due to the GJM's ransacking of the route and the brake car having been disbanded—and in the museum.

If one visits the toy train museum at Ghoom, the highest railway station in the world, one sees this plaque with a Twain misquote and misspelling: "The most enjoyeable day I've spent on earth is of mixed ecstasy of deadly fright and unimagineable joy."

But he did have the time of his life and wouldn't have begrudged the botched citation one iota:

> We changed to a little canvas-canopied hand-car for the 35-mile descent. It was the size of a sleigh, it had six seats and was so low that it seemed to rest on the ground. It had no engine or other propelling power, and needed none to help it fly down those steep inclines. It only needed a strong brake, to modify its flight, and it had that. Mr. Barnard, the chief engineer, was to take personal charge of our car, and he had been down the mountain in it many a time.

> Everything looked safe. Indeed, there was but one questionable detail left: the regular train was to follow us as soon as we should start, and it

might run over us. Privately, I thought it would.

We started, like an arrow from a bow, and before I could get out of the car we were gone. The sensation was pleasurable—intensely so; it was a sudden and immense exaltation, a mixed ecstasy of deadly fright and unimaginable joy. I believe that this combination makes the perfection of human delight.

The pilot car's flight down the mountain suggested the swoop of a swallow that is skimming the ground, so swiftly and smoothly and gracefully it swept down the long straight reaches and soared in and out of the bends and around the corners. We played with the train behind us. We often got out to gather flowers or sit on a precipice and look at the scenery, then presently we would hear a dull and growing roar, and the long coils of the train would come into sight behind and above us; but we did not need to start till the locomotive was close down upon us—then we soon left it far behind. It had to stop at every station, therefore it was not an embarrassment to us. Our brake was a good piece of machinery; it could bring the car to a standstill on a slope as steep as a house-roof.

A few miles down the mountain we stopped half an hour to see a Tibetan dramatic performance. It was in the open air on the hillside. The audience was composed of Tibetans, Ghurkas, and other unusual people. The costumes of the actors were in the last degree outlandish, and the performance was in keeping with the clothes.

To an accompaniment of barbarous noises the actors stepped out one after another and began to spin around with immense swiftness and vigor and violence, chanting the while, and soon the whole troupe would be spinning and chanting and raising the dust.

And so, presently we took to the hand-car and went flying down the mountain again; flying and stopping, flying and stopping, till at last we were in the plain once more and stowed for Calcutta in the regular train.

That was the most enjoyable day I have spent in the earth. For rousing, tingling, rapturous pleasure there is no holiday trip that approaches the bird-flight down the Himalayas in a hand-car. It has no fault, no blemish, no lack, except that there are only thirty-five miles of it instead of five hundred.

PART FOUR
BADLANDS, BAD TIMES

A RAILWAY STATION.

9. MUZAFFARPUR

TO SAY THAT Muzaffarpur is the back of beyond is to give beyond slightly more recognition than it deserves. It's not at all certain why Mark Twain chose to lecture here at all, apart from the fact that Smythe must have rounded up a good fee from the local planters. A lonely old life it must have been for them stuck out here too.

Twain's twenty-seven hours journey here was circuitous and inconvenient and it meant splitting the family up and meeting *en route* westwards two days later. Not much has changed; the 15609 *Avadh Assam Express* is not one of the more glamorous routes that Indian Railways ply, and the rickety old train clangs along in its own time, fours hours later than the fifteen hours promised. To add to the grimness we are shoveled into a compartment from hell. Opposite Gillian, Sita and me is a family on an outing from perdition: he farting brazenly, she making an intermittent funny high-pitched squeak for no apparent reason and two children bored and being fed on fizzy drinks and boiled sweets.

At least the train rattles along so slowly that one can get a good look at the poorest state of India, Bihar, known to Sita and her compatriots as the Badlands of India. It is still recognizable from Twain's description:

> There is nothing pretty about a mud Indian village. It is a little bunch of dirt-colored mud hovels jammed together within a mud wall. As a rule, the rains had beaten down parts of some of the houses, and this gave the village the aspect of a mouldering and hoary ruin. I believe the cattle and the vermin live inside the wall; for I saw cattle coming out and cattle going in; and whenever I saw a villager, he was scratching. This last is only circumstantial evidence, but I think it has value. The village has a battered little temple or two, big enough to hold an idol, and with custom enough to fat-up a priest and keep him comfortable.

The scene inside the train is as otherworldly as the one unfolding outside in the plains—and on the open dormitories and farmyards otherwise known as platforms. The hawkers are on corridor patrol selling an astonishing variety of brightly colored plastic knick-knackery. In quick succession we see brightly colored plastic blister packs of small racing cars, brightly colored plastic revolvers, brightly colored plastic flip-flops, brightly colored plastic mugs, brightly colored plastic combs, brightly colored plastic banana guards, brightly colored plastic rattles, brightly colored plastic thermos flasks, brightly colored plastic toothpicks, brightly colored plastic ping-pong ball shooters, brightly colored plastic zip pullers, brightly colored disposable plates—these the last things India needs one might have thought. Sita's favorite is a small brightly colored plastic tube of ear spray boasting the motto "made in Germany". Gillian is rather partial to the brightly colored plastic lipstick holder bandoleer; I am keener on the brightly colored plastic anti-rabid dog water-pistol. This must be like life before the shopping channels.

Relief failed to arrive with disembarkation; we checked into an appalling dump called the Chandralok Hotel, supposedly the best hotel in town and the only one claiming two stars (from whom is uncertain). Over dinner of an insipid curry, remixed chutney and the last of our Darjeeling wine we looked back wistfully at the joys of our compartment on the 15609 *Avadh Assam Express*.

*

Muzaffarpur, in the state of Bihar, was as much of a backwater then as now but at least then there were far fewer people with whom to share the experience—and an empty backwater is far less trying than a full one. Now it is as crowded as anywhere else, possibly more so as the farmland around was famously fickle, suffering from the scandalously hot mid-plain summer and then not knowing how much damage the floods would bring. The plainsfolk flocked to the towns, making at least some sort of self-generated economy—and thus improvement over their poor benighted life chances in the Bihar badlands.

Twain arrived at Muzaffarpur Junction at midday and stayed at a bungalow belonging to a an indigo planter called Mr. Hall, a member of the Muzaffarpur Club founded eleven years earlier. Twain slept all afternoon, changed into his tuxedo and was entertained to a private dinner for twelve in the Muzaffarpur Club. He then gave an At Home there from 9.30 to 11 p.m. Later, no doubt after a couple of convivial pegs at the bar, he and Smythe would have been pulled by a rickshaw-wallah to the station for the 1 a.m. connection to meet Livy and Clara at Dinapore on the Ganges and then all together onto Benares.

Today it is as if the Muzaffarpur Club froze the clocks at 11.30 p.m. on 20 February 1896 and have yet to thaw them out. If India in general is prone to avoiding change for change's sake, Muzaffarpur turns the whole avoidance exercise into its *raison d'être*.

We arrive unannounced as the phones in Muzaffarpur aren't working and are ushered in to see the secretary, Sanjay T. G. Sharma (Col. Rtd.). He is nearly as old as the club and just as courteous. He speaks that wonderful old Indian Army clipped English I've heard at clubs so many times before. His office has rows of dusty box files up against one wall and old calendars strung up on the other. The flip calendars all show December for that year. The walls are a color I can only describe as faded. He sits behind a massive old stately desk, which he later tells me is made from oak and came with the club. On it are lying four piles of beribboned files and two empty inkwells. The floor is dust swept, cracked tiled and matches the walls. An ancient retainer in a dhoti and worn out, shuffling flip-flops brings us *chai*. I explain my mission. The colonel says all this is possible but it might take some time to find the records and do I mind waiting. I say, no, I've got all day. He gives me a look which says he wasn't used to dealing with such urgency.

"Come with me," he says, "and we will tour the premises." He lifts himself up with surprising agility. On the way out he barks to his clerk in the Indian fashion. From the Anglo-Hindi I can pick out "1896" and assume the clerk is about to get even dustier in the vaults.

We enter a large T-shaped area. "The lecture would have certainly been in here," the colonel says. We are in a miniature aircraft hangar. I look up and up and up to a corrugated iron roof. A dozen fans hang motionless just above head height. A very dusty bookcase sits near one corner. None of the spines have survived. "All from the English time," Sanjay says and sees me looking up, up, up. "That's for the summer. It's toasting in here. How many did he lecture to?"

"I don't know. There's no newspaper record for here and he doesn't say. But it was usually to all the members," I reply, "There wasn't a lot of entertainment. How many members are there now?"

"Two hundred and fifty. Same as then. The constitution has not changed."

"At all?"

"At all."

"Presumably there are no planter members now."

"Oh no, our members are the Muzaffarpur elite. People like your father," he gleams at Sita. "Not any old Tom and Jerry can get in here. Joining fee is one hundred thousand rupees [US$2,000 or £1,500]. We have white balls and black balls as before. It's a two black ball regime here. Mostly they are senior members of the IAS [Indian Administrative Service, the successor to the colonial elite ICS, Indian Civil Service], doctors, leading lawyers. We have a four-year backlog. Dead man's shoes, we say."

He leads me into a room off the hangar, much smaller with a lower ceiling and tawny yellow walls. There are no windows but rusty iron meshes. It hasn't been used for years. "This was the dining room," the colonel says.

"So it was," I reply. "He said he had a private dinner for twelve. I can just see them sitting here now. And the kitchen?"

"It was an English kitchen in the cookhouse. It still has English tiles on the roof. But we have not eaten here since many years. I'll show you the other room."

On the opposite side of the hangar is an identical sized room to the dining room. It was once white instead of the yellow it has become. "This was the billiard room. Look." Sanjay shows me the raised bench with withered upholstery and the scoreboard on the wall. It could only ever have been a billiard room. In the middle is a ping-pong table with a dark grey surface. It hasn't been dusted for years. In fact nothing seems to have changed at all since the last British member left, including the dust.

"Where is the billiard table?" I ask.

"We keep it in another room. It isn't used. It is English too, bought new in 1895."

We wander back through the hangar. I'm trying hard not to be rude or insensitive when I ask Sanjay why the members are members as there don't seem to be any facilities.

"For the veranda," he replies. "Come." We go back through the remains of the dining room and from a side door enter into what might be another club. Ahead of us stretches a long, clean space with cane sofas and occasional tables on one side and eight columns on the other. The walls are freshly whitewashed—the first I've seen in India—and the floor clean and quarry tiled, not unique but unusual. Mosquito net rolls hang ready to drop from between the columns. Even the wiring is tucked into place—mostly.

Beyond the columns Indian grass grows down to a small lake. There is hardly any litter. "It's delightful," I say, "you could almost call it the Veranda Club."

"Every Saturday afternoon and evening the members gather. We serve beer and hire in the food. Some bring their own whisky. It's always fullish."

"I can see why."

We drop into a couple of cane chairs and look down to the river. I say, "In

Mark Twain's notebook he drew a sketch of Mr. Hall's farm. He said it was on the Ganges but that must have been a mistake."

"Yes, he would have meant the Bodhi Ganduk. That's a tributary of the Ganges. Runs past Muzaffarpur about two kilometers from here."

"And Hall had a steamer to cross it to reach here, apparently."

"That's quite likely," says Sanjay. "The lake down there probably was a bulge in the river. You can see it's all silted up over that side."

"And from what I've read the planters were a pretty eccentric, hard living lot. Not badly rewarded either: Hall told Smythe that taking good years and bad they made a return of fifteen percent. Quite likely to have his own steamboat. And a still. What happened to them after Independence?"

"The planters? It was an English thing really, indigo. The Indians have lots of small farms. Family farms, not big spreads like the English had. Even if they stayed the politicians would have given their land away. Can I see the sketch?"

Back in his office Gillian digs out the sketch. A fresh—in the sense of recently deposited rather than newly made—bound book sits on the edge of the desk: the 1894-1897 Visitors Book.

The colonel looks at the sketch. "Apart from the river name it's pretty clear.

146

The windmill is the clue. I think that will be on north side opposite. There's a narrow road bridge over it now. We can take a look later." He barks another order to the clerk. This time the common word is rickshaw.

"Is the address Andrews Fields helpful?"

"Not really, but the windmill in the sketch is."

I stand over his shoulder as he opens the ancient tome. He flicks through to find the entry for 20 February 1896. The pages are semi-stuck together, but dryly. At first he turns them too roughly and some parts get left behind. He soon has the knack of separating them, easing in an old steel inches ruler. There it is: Member: R. K. Hall, Andrews Fields. Guests: M. Twain & C. Smythe. Hall has signed RKH in the Member column, Smythe has signed CGS in the Guest column. Well, well, one of those lovely moments when our paths re-cross.

A quick *chai* more and the colonel and I clamber into one rickshaw, Gillian and Sita another. Ours has 1913 painted on the back; the driver looks even older than that. I'm not light and neither is the colonel. I suggest we take three rickshaws or spread the load with Gillian or Sita; he will have none of it.

Bihar is not only the poorest state in India but the one with the worst reputation for dacoitery,[66] caste killings, the most thuggish police force, the most corrupt and gangsterish politicians and general backwardness—really the Badlands of India. Two minutes with eyes on stalks in the back of the 1913 rickshaw is enough to confirm at least the latter; a further three minutes talking to the colonel confirms the remainder.

"It's very underdeveloped. There has been so much money sent here from central funds over the years but the politicians have stolen it. This is the part of India most like the one that Mark Twain would have seen—I mean it would all have been like this. Now these of course. You see these everywhere"—he is pointing to an engine on the back of a converted rickshaw—"generators, as there are so many power cuts."

We pass slowly by shop after shop—actually more like shack after shack, stall after stall, shed after shed, lean-to after lean-to. Sometimes there's not even that, just a person practicing his trade on the sidewalk: a shoe-fixer here, a barber there, a metal grinder here, a tailor there. Tailors have practically died out in the big cities, but here nearly every clothes stand has one. I've never seen so many stands. No one seems to be doing any business and some of the stock looks as

---

[66] From *dacoit*, originally a highway robber but now often used for any sort of robber.

tired as the rickshaw. Sanjay explains they don't need to do much business. They sleep in the stall and pay no rent because no one owns the sidewalks. "But they'll pay a bit for protection, that's for sure. When the election comes they'll get that back for their vote. The gangsters are politicians, or *vice versa*; they take and give back."

"What's the point?" I ask, "if they end up even."

"Ties them all in. The politicians get free votes. The stall holders can't do anything about it. It's the system."

Now we are upon the old British road bridge over the Bodhi Ganduk. It is just wide enough for two-way traffic and built before there was much of any traffic. Now it is a seething mass of impatience, a smothering mass of still-air pollution, a total impossibility of movement beyond the speed of the slowest hand-pushed cargo-rickshaw. There is no space between the opposing flows but that doesn't stop the motorcycles and pushbikes competing for it. The noise from the horns behind, in front, all around is—must be—a danger to the eardrums, especially in an open rickshaw at horn height. I jump off and tell Sanjay I'm walking across because it's quicker and my ears and nerves can't take the decibels and bedlam. He sits tight and doesn't see it as anything more than an inconvenience. I say I'll wait for him on the other side down-road from the subsequent pent-up overtaking maneuvers and the accompanying horn blasts. As I wait an elephant and three camels head onto the bridge in the opposite direction. Oh, boy.

"We've gone past it," Sanjay says disapprovingly from the height of the rickshaw when we meet again.

"Gone past what?"

"The windmill opposite. What's left of it. We'll do a few lefts and see if we can get back."

We do—and we do. We pass more shops, stalls, lean-tos, shacks, stands and sheds, and it seems that many of them are also factories, cottage industries. If you want a saucepan you go to a saucepan maker, if you want shoes a shoemaker, shirts a *kurta* maker. A new wheel? There are spoke makers. A new dynamo? There are dynamo rebuilders. New specs? There are spec makers, but you choose the two arms and the lenses from an ancient pile. Want a smoke? Buy one at a time. Want a basket? Go to the weaver. Something woolen? The fleecer is outside, the knitter inside. A new saddle, no, but here's someone who will rebuild your old one. Want a pee? Right where you stand, or squat.

Eventually we come close to the river. On Twain's sketch there is sand marked next to river, as there is now at this same time of year. "Of course in the monsoon all this floods up to the level of the shacks," says the colonel. We look over at the stump of the windmill. I say it looks like a large Shiva lingam, and it does.

"It was around here, Hall's farm, Andrews Fields," says Sanjay. It's almost impossible to think of this as an orderly Europe indigo farm with a steamboat on the end of a jetty. In front of us is a large expanse of greenery, undulating and unkempt. A few cows graze here, a few goats nibble there. A few men sleep randomly on the grass. Small circles of men sit around, playing cards or talking. They look up and wave as we pass. They all, men asleep and men at large, cows and goats, seem to be quite happy in the Indian fashion. On our left are the new villages, all piled in together. Hall's bungalow may well be in there somewhere but it would take a while wading through the overgrowth of frond huts and bamboo and fertilizer sack shacks to find it. The colonel suggests it would be better not to find it. "There will be whole families in each room, an open fire in the middle, the usual Indian peasant invasion, I'm afraid."

I ask if there's a way back without going over the Indian Styx. There isn't and I'm still in therapy. Sanjay Sharma aside—no doubt like Mark Twain with Roger Hall aside—I can't wait to get out of the depressing morass of dust-dirt and shed-shacks that calls itself Muzaffarpur. Neither can my companions.

10. LUCKNOW

BREAKFAST AT THE Mohamed Bagh Club in the cantonment area of Lucknow is as much a sumptuous unhurried Anglo-Indian affair for us now as it was for the Twain party a hundred and fifteen years ago and probably exactly the same fare too: papaya with yoghurt and honey followed by a massala omelette on paratha and real coffee (unusual in Nescafé India). As is the wont in Indian clubs everything is just as it was—and so is just as it should be—but here there has been a striking addition to the breakfast room[67] since Mark Twain's mornings here of 22, 23 and 24 February 1896: a panel of six one yard square black and white photographs along one wall, each panel going to make up a panorama of Lucknow as she looked in all her splendor in 1923.

A closer look reveals Lucknow much as he would have would seen her, the Lucknow that had just recovered from its first disaster, the Sepoy Uprising of 1857 and was yet to know of its second disaster, the Partition of India of 1947. Before the first disaster Lucknow was the epicenter of the highly evolved Indo-Islamic civilization, a unique post-Moghul center of fine art, poetry, high Urdu and gracious manners. This first disaster, the Sepoy Uprising, was primarily caused by the greed of the East India Company, which after many years snipping away at the edges of the Kingdom of Oudh decided to annex it all, including of course its capital Lucknow. The consequence of the British "victory" in the uprising was that what passed for India was to be run directly by the Crown rather than by the East India Company; the consequence for Lucknow was that by the time of Twain's visit the pre-uprising glory had returned to the city but the power had not—and, as we know, glory without power soon becomes effete and pantomimic.

*

Apart from both of us enjoying the hospitality at the Mohamed Bagh Club and visiting Lucknow fifty years after one its two disasters, Twain and I were both under the care of the resident army: Twain the British and myself the Indian. Twain's Grand Tour was to a large extent a tour of the Raj rather than a tour of

---

[67] In Indian clubs always a distinct, dedicated area.

India and in following his footsteps my Re-Tour often meets the Raj's successors, that particularly British institution, the Indian Army.

The Mohamed Bagh Club, like all the other Indian clubs in which we stay, is in the cantonment—the best day-to-day reminder of the Raj. Apart from the obvious military bearing of the area it is the "maintained" aspect that sets it apart; whereas almost all old buildings in Indian cities are left to crumble and decay, in the cantonments the old military maxim "if it moves salute it, if it doesn't paint it" holds sway to the good. In the cantonments the roadside trees are painted, the streets are swept clean and there are even pavements. Cantonments also link one back to the loosely populated India of Twain's time; there are no shops or stalls or rickshaw stands or shantytowns and so none of the teeming mass of humanity and their assorted animal outriders that the towns hold today.

The secretaries at most Indian clubs are ex-military and the Mohamed Bagh Club is no exception. I was lucky that Lt. Col. Amrind G. K. Nazeer was not only generous and hospitable but a historian and an anglophile. Phone calls must have been made while I was admiring the breakfast room panels for at 09.15 hours prompt an olive green military jeep with the EME Regimental Association flag on the starboard wing and a young Sikh lieutenant with a violet turban as its driver pulls up outside the freshly painted club entrance portico. In the fluent hybrid of Hindi-English intermingle spoken by the Indian Army I can make out the words "Residency for certain", "at his disposal", "other sites extant", "Mark Twain", "townside", "lunch or tiffin" and "sixteen hundred hours".

Young Udham Singh asks me, "Where first, sir?" I pull out my Mark Twain Lucknow notes and say, "First the Residency, please. Then the Imambara complex, then Chatter Manzil—the Umbrella Palace, and lastly La Martiniere."

First we have to leave the cantonment and re-enter Indian India. Wham! Crowds; bustle; joggle; shuffle. We had arrived in Lucknow just before midnight by train and the city was sleeping, but now it is wide awake and stopping and starting and stopping and starting, inch by inch, so densely jammed, so nasty-noisy, so polluted everywhere in sight, so incoherent in its shambles, so unable to support reflection that one wonders at which point the one point two billion Indian psyches will collectively scream "Enough! There's no more room on the India bus!"

Elsewhere one soon gets used to the overcrowding in India, helped immeasurably by the good nature of the Indians themselves who seem to be so used to being squished and squashed up together that they take it as just another part of life. Transport the rickshaw driver pedaling away in front of us to Alice Springs and he would spooked out by the emptiness and pedal that rickshaw to the nearest city for a nice bit of snuggled-up overcrowding. But Lucknow, even by Indian standards, raises the density bar and for the first time in India I see signs of road rage and bad temper that would have flared up long ago anywhere else in the world but here has yet to gain a foothold—and you'd have to have pretty small feet to gain any sort of foothold around here.

People talk of the population time bomb, not just in India but everywhere bounded by the tropics—but I have the feeling that here on the subcontinent the bomb has already exploded and we are living with the aftermath. In Kenya or Nigeria for example, or in Southeast Asia (apart from *dirigiste* Singapore and Malaya) one can see quite clearly that large parts of the population are children and certainly half the country is under twenty-five. In Palestine and Israel too teenagers abound, but there the alarm is tempered by the hope that it will be the next generations that settle for peace and prosperity as the old warmongers on both sides die off. But here in India the evidence of the eyes is different. They take a census every ten years and the last one was nine years ago—and the census takers are the first to admit to hopeful guessing and willful rounding-up—but nine years ago they suggested thirty percent of the population were under fifteen (with the male/female split suggesting that dowry-prevention daughter killing is still horrifying high). It is nothing like thirty percent now; the US Bureau of Census put the under-fifteen guestimate at eighteen percent as the demographic bulge ages upwards.

*

Sorry for the digression, and back to Mark Twain's tour. The Great Imambara complex, centered around the late eighteenth-century mausoleum, is at the heart of the Indo-Islamic city and civilization that Twain saw when it was still alive and we now see as a needless wreck, a neglected monument to past Islamic colonial glories that seem at best like an irrelevance and at worst an embarrassment to modern Hindu India.

But what a sight it must have been! The skyline of gilded domes and sculptured whitewashed cupolas and confident minarets were all on a grand, sweeping scale; one is reminded of Constantinople. Spread out between them were the formal gardens and watercourses, not unlike Versailles in scope and design. To the side were square lakes and wallowing palaces, not unlike Udaipur.

It was a unique civilization born out of the heart of the disintegrating Moghul Empire moving east and absorbing Hindu influences as it did so, an attempt by the principalities to be more Moghul than the Moghuls. They called them the days of gold and silver: Islamic rule being the gold and Hindu influences being the silver, the best of all worlds.

That was then; this is now. Old Lucknow lies abandoned, caught in the crossfire of Muslim and Hindu rivalries that left Islamic Lucknow abandoned to its Hindu fate after Partition. The skyline is still there but has not been cleaned or painted for fifty years. The gardens are littered with old plastic bags and bottles. The watercourses have dried up and become secondary garbage dumps. The lakes are fetid, fluid rubbish tanks, the palaces dying of neglect.

Lucknow and its principality of Oudh or Awadh, like most of northern India, has for the last seven hundred years been the Poland of Asia, invaded by empires as they swept this way and that. This only came to an end with Indian Independence in 1947. The Muslim elite which had ruled Lucknow for three hundred years left for Karachi in Pakistan, their places being taken by simpler Hindu Punjabis heading the other way. Lucknow has only been Indian for the last 65 years and—heaven knows, understandably enough—the Indian government feels it has better things to spend its money on than maintaining reminders of imperial Islamic magnificence.

What is less clear is why some of the oil-rich Islamic countries—or companies or individuals--don't step into the breach. Here, after all, is Islamic culture at its most refined, open to the new and admirable to all. The buildings (not a word to do their splendor justice) are still only a few hundred years old and built to last for several hundred more. The old gardens may be covered in new litter but are still easily salvageable. The attempt at just keeping the paint inside the palaces up to scratch is pathetic: it only reaches up to stretch height and no effort to match the colors has been made at all. Faced with such imaginary Arab largesse, even the Indian government might feel honor-bound to move the Punjabi junk stalls out of the central enclave that divides the palace grounds and whose presence there completely ruins the effect the architects intended and the visitor hopes for.

The Saudis spend freely enough promoting Islam but the sad fact is that the kind of conservative, fundamental Islam promoted by the Saudis, Wahhabism, is a far cry from the liberal, poetic and cultural Islam practiced by the Nawabs here even up to sixty five years ago. For a fraction of what they spend building madrasahs in Pakistan to teach children the Koran by rote in Arabic they could really show a skeptical world that Islam isn't just synonymous with terrorism. They won't, but there's no reason not to hope that more enlightened Gulf Muslim states or companies might pay for a lick of paint and a dozen gardeners.

Walking back to the jeep, seeing Indian hovels leaning against the arches and walls under the stucco explosion above, seeing the garbage piled up in the moats which once were home to crocodiles, seeing souvenirs shops in the gateways selling tack and tat, seeing the zenana complex that once held the Nawab's eight hundred wives rotting from within and without, seeing around the site not domes and minarets but already-decaying-yet-still-unfinished tower blocks, one has an idea what a visitor to Rome must have felt like in 450 AD, a generation after Alaric and his Visigoths had sacked the city.

*

Mark Twain's next stop was the Chattar Manzil, the famous Umbrella Palace, so-called because of the brolly-shaped dome that sits on top of it. Twain lectured there, hosted by the United Services Club who used it as their headquarters. Udham Singh and his passengers were not detained there long; we got no nearer than the main gate and were turned away; the old palace is now the Central Drug Research Centre and out of bounds to anyone without the required swipe card.

The photograph panel in the breakfast room showed that Twain's main point of interest in Lucknow, the Residency—the scene of the heroic British resistance for five hot and horrible months to the Sepoy Uprising—was a *tonga* ride through open country from the Great Imambara. Not so now; after a nerve-racking hour-long walk through the obstacle course and race track of the new Lucknow we arrive at the Baillie Gate, the starting point then and now of the tour of the Residency.

The word "Residency" sounds like a single grand building with some matching grounds but actually it describes half a dozen grand buildings lying around a 65-acre park. It has been left exactly as it was at the end of the five-month siege, a series of shelled out or even razed buildings with only the size of the foundations to indicate their previous grandeur. It is today a perfectly tasteful monument to all those who died in the Sepoy Uprising, British and Indians alike—and, of course, many more loyal Indian natives died for the British cause than did British natives on this foreign soil. There was death and desperation in equal measure.

Twain's description is as good as I've read:

In Lucknow there was a great garrison, composed of about 7,000 native troops and between 700 and 800 whites. These white soldiers and their families were probably the only people of their race there; at their elbow was that swarming population of warlike natives, a race of born soldiers, brave, daring, and fond of fighting.

The natives established themselves in houses close at hand and began to rain bullets and cannon-balls into the Residency; and this they kept up, night and day, during four months and a half, the little garrison industriously replying all the time. The women and children soon became so used to the roar of the guns that it ceased to disturb their sleep. The defense was kept up week after week, with stubborn fortitude, in the midst of death, which came in many forms—by bullet, small-pox, cholera, and by various diseases induced by unpalatable and insufficient food, by the long hours of wearying and exhausting overwork in the daily and nightly battle in the oppressive Indian heat, and by the broken rest caused by the intolerable pest of mosquitoes, flies, mice, rats, and fleas.

Six weeks after the beginning of the siege more than one-half of the original force of white soldiers was dead, and close upon three-fifths of the original native force. But the fighting went on just the same. Both sides fought with energy and industry.

The exhausted garrison fought doggedly on all through the next month October. Then, November 2nd, news came Sir Colin Campbell's relieving force would soon be on its way from Cawnpore. On the 12th the boom of his guns was heard. On the 13th the sounds came nearer—he was slowly, but steadily, cutting his way through, storming one stronghold after another and the long siege of Lucknow was ended.

The last eight or ten miles of Sir Colin Campbell's march was through seas of blood. The weapon mainly used was the bayonet, the fighting was desperate. Neither side asked for quarter, and neither gave it. At the Secundrabagh, where nearly two thousand of the enemy occupied a great stone house in a garden, the work of slaughter was continued until every man was killed. That is a sample of the character of that devastating march.

*

But there is an interesting dynamic going on here. Just before arriving at the Residency entrance one walks past an old Nawab palace and garden, presumably abandoned in 1947. The palace is small, as palaces go, and the garden the width of the palace façade, say twenty yards, and about a hundred yards long. The building itself is now a filthy, crumbling squat and the garden an urban scrub farm with goats nibbling at what they can, chickens pecking at this and that and some squat shacks and grubby hovels along the edges. Of course, litter is everywhere. In other words this rather charming ensemble, which would have made a fine museum or art gallery and ornamental garden, or even a boutique hotel or government office, has been left to rot. As we enter the Residency compound five minutes later, however, we see another old structure in ruins— and meant to be in ruins—yet these ruins are maintained to a particularly high

standard. Thus in Twain's time, "The Residency ruins are draped with flowering vines, and are impressive and beautiful. They and the grounds are sacred now, and will suffer no neglect nor be profaned by any sordid or commercial use while the British remain masters of India. Within the grounds are buried the dead who gave up their lives there in the long siege."

The answer lies in national pride, or rather lack of national embarrassment. All the Nawab splendor is a reminder of Islamic subjugation, and no matter how enlightened the rulers were they can still be viewed as foreign rulers who ruled over a supine people. The Residency on the other hand—even when it stood— was a far, far less impressive symbol of civilization than the Indo-Islamic pieces that surround it. Yet it does represent a Hindu fightback against foreign rule; even though the Sepoy Uprising was ultimately unsuccessful it did succeed in proving that British rule was not invincible or inevitable.

There is little to see in the Residency complex but it's a lovely space in which to escape from the mayhem of new Lucknow surrounding it. The 65-acre park has some beautiful old banyan and palm trees and some recently planted tamarind and Indian elm. A small team sweeps up the leaves and litter; another team tends the flowers. For the first time since leaving the cantonment one can just sit quietly doing nothing, unmolested, and hear birds that aren't crows—and birds that are crows. The usual touts and hustlers are kept out by the 100-rupee entrance fee and the imposing uniformed guards on the gate.

Most visitors would seem to be canoodling couples, mostly with a chaperone. The couples find a quiet alcove or ledge or bench away from the main paths. They sit side by side, the man with his arm draped across her shoulders while she talks incessantly. The chaperone—in English a neutral word but in most languages feminine, and in India actually always feminine—sits quietly out of earshot or strolls, seemingly aimlessly, nearby. Sometimes two chaperones meet and chat and forget their supervisory obligations.

It is not documented that Twain visited the extraordinary pile known as La Martiniere, but as it is so close to the Residency and the Mohamed Bagh Club and as it played such an important role in the Sepoy Uprising it is hard to imagine that he passed it by.

It was built by an equally extraordinary Frenchman who eventually became Major General Claude Martin of the East India Company. In 1751, aged sixteen, he was a penniless adventurer who signed with the French Foreign Legion as a common foot soldier and was posted to the French colony of Pondicherry on the east coast of India. From there he was seconded to the French East India Company, but when they were defeated by the forces of the British East India Company four years later he was recruited by the latter and never looked back.

One of life's winners, he soon found himself in Lucknow, capital of the state of Oudh or Awadh and indispensable to its Nawab, Asaf-ud-Dowlah. As keen and compulsive a builder as the Nawab, he amassed a fortune as the Mister Fixit between the decadent and extravagant prince and the greedy East India Company—and everyone else in between. In 1785, reputed to be the richest European in India, he started to build a fortress-monument to himself, his own mausoleum, as a European rival to the Taj Mahal. Like a Moghul ruler he kept a harem, which included his original wife Boulone, her three sisters and, it was rumored, eight unrelated spares.

It is a unique building beyond traditional architectural analysis: it has been described as a brick wedding cake but that seems a bit unfair to bricks and wedding cakes. It is certainly a Gothic fortress, a working castle, perhaps the ultimate expression of tropical-Gothic fantasy and enjoyably full of Baroque follies and foibles—and of course is itself a Baroque folly and foible but one that could defend itself. In his will he bequeathed it as a boys' school and it is still one of the top private schools in India; described by the old boy who shows us around as India's Winchester if not its Eton (referring to Mayo College). The old boy couldn't resist mentioning—as indeed does every guide book and here am I doing the same—that its most famous living old boy was a certain Harold Roger Webb, more popularly known as Cliff, Sir Cliff Richard OBE.[68]

By the time of the Sepoy Uprising in 1857 it had fifty pupils and twenty staff (which sounds like a sensible pupil/teacher ratio) who were evacuated to the Residency. During the siege the schoolboys and teachers played important roles as messengers and nurses; the building served as a secret depot and was given Battle Honors by the British for its and its students' and staff's roles in resisting the revolt; and to this day it is still the only building so endowed.

The Twain party's and our last call at Lucknow was to the train station—and very different experiences they were too. In 1897 photographs show a rather undistinguished series of bungalow sheds spread over the width of twelve tracks. It looks at first sight like a staging post for cattle but of course it was for troops; mid-India Lucknow and its cantonment was a major marshaling point for the British Army. The trains were none too glamorous either, and the *Patna Mathura*

---

[68] A British singer of popular songs.

Express 13238 rumbled along at a stately 35 miles per hour, stopping frequently, so the forty miles to Kanpur took over two hours.

The Army is still the major user of the station now, which is certainly why it is in such good condition. Built in 1914 in the style of a Moghul fort—it resembles the shorter north face of the great fort at Agra and is painted the same ochre-red—it spreads beyond the original bungalow sheds and in stature is in keeping with Lucknow's military status. The trains too have been modernized and it is home to the new Lucknow Kanpur Suburban Railway system.[69] It may be more comfortable than the old Patna Mathura Express but don't expect to arrive there much more quickly: the forty miles still take just under two hours—when it's on time.

---

[69] Of course still known by the old name Livy and Clara; "C" for Cawnpore, the old name for Kanpur.

11. KANPUR

"KANPUR", THE POSTER in the Tourist Office boldly declared, "the Manchester of the East". Ye gods, has no-one told them? The irony is wriggling around in the hyperbole: more in keeping might be the "Chernobyl of the South".

For Kanpur is unrelenting grim, shabby, broken down, falling apart, dense, dirt-dusty and dark-brown monotone. This is not the India of the south and west, the India that seduces the visitor by her charm and humor and playful chaos, the India of sensuous explosion and life by the cubic foot, the India of Moghul imagination and Hindu philosophy, the India of momentous weddings and endless festivals—no, this is the India of the flat northern Ganges plains, the badlands, the India of hopeless poverty and dozy illiteracy, the India of gangster politicians and private armies, the India of Maoist insurgents more Maoist than Mao, the India of Naxalites and dacoits, the India of tandoori-oven summers and post-diluvian autumns, the India of tuberculosis and spitting. Even the doorstep size *Lonely Planet* cannot find room for a solitary sentence about Kanpur.

We are only here because on 25 February 1896, in quieter times when Kanpur was called Cawnpore and the only industry was textiles—hence the Manchester of the East—the Twain party passed through here too. It was a strange assignment, born of Twain's growing fascination with the Sepoy Uprising and especially what he saw as the heroic stand of his British hosts. Certainly Smythe would not have been too pleased with the receipts, for Twain's performance was more an after-dinner speech in the officers' mess than the usual Talk in a town hall or theatre.

In fairness to Twain's enthusiasm for visiting the place, one can say that although Cawnpore played only a minor strategic part in the Sepoy Uprising, events here so horrified the British imagination that that the retaliatory massacres were deemed to be justified—and in Twain's account ignored.

*

But we jump behind ourselves. Twain was determined to see all the sites of British heroism and massacre, and as usual Sita, Gillian and I want to follow in his footsteps. The problem is Kanpur. There are none of the usual touts and hustlers one finds in tourist India and who are either annoying or helpful depending on your needs. We decide to start in the Tourist Office and it is there we see the Manchester of the East poster.

The office is up a flight of peeling, grubby Kanpur open-air stairs. Outside holy cows wander past in sack coats, men urinate in the open gutter opposite and electric wires spill in mayhem and profusion from pylons, lampposts and junctions. Inside, decades-worth of dust covers bundled documents lying haphazardly around various equally dusty desks. To one side stands an old rusty chair with dirty grey nylon webbing hanging loosely from the seat frame. Neither of the very elderly assistants speaks English; in fact they look unusually dozy.

Time to wheel out Sita. Gillian and I are by now so used to her breezing around in her tight designer jeans and T-shirts, her long jet black mane trying to keep up, her enormous Gucci sunglasses propped up on her head, her Havaianas sandals flapping around her bejeweled ankles, her Prada bag with its Hermes scarf hanging loosely from the straps, that we forget that she can be a bit of a… sensation. She doesn't exactly pout, not in the Western sense, but she certainly doesn't do demur. In the big cities and tourist towns she merely stops the traffic, but here in Kanpur, in this grubby little geriatric tourist-free Tourist Office she stops the world. The looks of bewilderment and disapproval, of civilizations falling apart, confirm that her snappy high-caste orders in Hindi are making no more progress than our polite requests in English.

Time to wheel out Cultural Attaché Shaura Mark's magic letter from the Indian High Commission. It is tucked into a side pocket of Gillian's camera bag. We haven't used it yet; haven't had to. Written in English and Hindi, it "requires and requests whomsoever read the letter to extend your good offices for India's guests' benefit and convenience"; in effect, a direct order from on-high to make whoever reads it make themselves useful.

Bolt upright does the younger geriatric stand; onto his feet does the elder geriatric struggle. A telephone call does the former make; a cup of tea does latter organize. Sita lays on the pressure in Hindi; I hear the word "babu"—as in "if I were you, babu, I'd get moving sharpish"—as she taps the table. Twenty minutes later the very dark and dapper—and as it transpires utterly charming—Mohit Singh bursts in, all apologies and bonhomie. The younger boss; Mr. Tourism of Kanpur; not a role one imagines is overly taxing.

We take tea as the two elderly incumbents stare at the apparition known as Sita, a real tourist attraction, and Mohit works out how to show us what we need to see. I explain about Mark Twain and the sites he saw: the Hindu temple at the Satti Chaura Ghat from where the signal to attack the British came, the *ghat* itself which in his time was known as the Slaughter Ghat, the well down which parts of the dead and dying British women and children were flung; and the memorial with its lament to the "dying who along with the dead were cast down into the well". I also wanted to see the officers' mess where Twain lectured, now the Cawnpore Club.

*

Cawnpore was an important garrison town with about 10,000 sepoys and a thousand British officers, their wives, children and servants. As word of the Uprising spread from Lucknow a local ne'er-do-well nobleman called Nana Sahib rounded up several thousand malcontent sepoys and for three weeks they besieged the British officers and families in their fortifications.

In the first days of June the aged general, Sir Hugh Wheeler[70] commanding the forces at Cawnpore, was deserted by his native troops. He had with him a few hundred white soldiers and officers, and apparently more women and children

---

[70] Wheeler was a great Indophile, married to a high-caste Indian and even friends with Nana Sahib; thus his guard was down.

than soldiers. He was short of provisions, short of arms, short of ammunition, short of military wisdom, short of everything but courage and devotion to duty. The defense through twenty-one days and nights of hunger, thirst, Indian heat, and a never-ceasing storm of bullets, bombs, and cannon-balls is one of the most heroic episodes in history.

After three weeks the beleaguered British negotiated a truce: there was to be safe passage in barges downstream on the Ganges to Allahabad. They were to board the barges at the Satti Chaura Ghat just south of the cantonment. Most *ghats* have a temple attached, and Satti Chaura Ghat had one—and still does, as we shall see—to Shiva, and it was from this temple that Nana Sahib's lieutenants gave the signal to attack.

When at last the Nana found it impossible to conquer these starving men and women with powder and ball, he resorted to treachery, and that succeeded. He agreed to supply them with food and send them to Allahabad in boats. They came forth helpless but suspecting no treachery, the Nana's host closed around them, and at a signal from a trumpet the massacre began. About two hundred women and children were spared—for the present—but all the men except three or four were killed.

The Satti Chaura Ghat is still there as is the adjoining Shiva temple with the usual eclectic gang of Brahmins and their supporters, human and bovine and canine and goatish, hanging around doing nothing very much in particular. In an early sign of the collective amnesia that events at Cawnpore encourage we find that no one knows from where the fateful signal came, or from where the barges embarked or where in the river the slaughter happened. The scene by the Ganges is peaceful again, even indolent now, and the imagination needs a pause and spurt before summoning up the horrors of the massacre, the screaming of the slain and the lust of the slayers. It all just seems so... un-Indian. Even the famous Ganges vultures have fled the scene.

> The sluggish river drifted by, almost currentless. It was dead low water, narrow channels with vast sandbars between, all the way across the wide bed; and the only living thing in sight was that grotesque and solemn bald-headed bird, the Adjutant,[71] standing on his six-foot stilts, solitary on a distant bar, with his head sunk between his shoulders, thinking; thinking of his prize, I suppose—the dead Hindoo that lay awash at his

---

[71] The adjutant bird is actually a stork and not a vulture. From a distance they look similar.

feet, and whether to eat him alone or invite friends. He and his prey were a proper accent to that mournful place. They were in keeping with it, they emphasized its loneliness and its solemnity.

*

All but one hundred and twenty of the British escapees were shot or slain in the Ganges barges as they were leaving Satti Chaura Ghat. The survivors, all women and children, were brought ashore and sent off to a supposedly safe house, the Bibighar,[72] while Nana Sahib decided what to with them. They were soon joined by a further eighty women and children from nearby Uprising skirmishes; all the men had already been murdered.

As British reinforcements were rumored to be arriving Nana Sahib decided to execute them, but the Bibighar sepoys, who knew all of the survivors at least by sight and in many cases much more closely than that, mutinied against him and refused to murder them. Undaunted, he rounded up half a dozen Muslim butchers from the town and had them dismember the survivors with meat cleavers and throw the limbs, torsos and heads into the Bibighar well to hide the evidence. Not all of the women and children were successfully hacked to death, and with time short the next morning he ordered the remaining living, mostly by now children, to be thrown down the well alive to join the dead.

The infamous well is now in Nano Rao Park, a pleasant enough escape from the squalor of downtown Kanpur. Wrote Twain: "And we saw the scene of the slaughter of the helpless women and children, and also the costly memorial that is built over the well which contains their remains. The Black Hole of Calcutta is gone, but a more reverent age is come, and whatever remembrancer still exists of the moving and heroic sufferings and achievements of the garrison of Cawnpore will be guarded and preserved."

In fact, the well has now been bricked over. As with the Black Hole memorial in Calcutta post-Independence India did not want to be reminded of one of its least glorious moments. Indeed, the terrible events seem to be been wiped out of the collective consciousness, as Mohit has the rather unnerving insistence that this is "where the English jumped into the well" and that next we will go to the memorial to "where the English jumped into the well".

The "costly memorial built over the well" that Twain saw has been

---

72 Literally, ladies; room.

transferred to All Souls Cathedral, a massive, defiant structure built by the British in memoriam fifteen years later. Now renamed (but as usual with Indian government new names ignored) the Kanpur Memorial Church, the cathedral cuts a lonely figure in a wilderness in the cantonment surrounded as it is by Indian Army barracks and installations, with barely a Christian in sight and the barest of congregations come Sunday.

*

With public opinion inflamed at home the British in India retaliated in kind, in what became known as the Cawnpore Massacre. Under the directions of General Neill the rebel sepoys were rounded up and sent to the Bibighar. He then built a series of gallows around the well and had the sepoys lick the British blood off the Bibighar walls; not a pleasant task for a devout Hindu or even a sensitive Muslim. Those who refused were hanged on the spot. Those who licked the blood off the walls were hanged later anyway. When it seemed to Neill that there were not enough sepoys being hanged he rounded up random natives, including women and children, and forced them into the Bibighar. And then he hanged them too.

*

The Indians have moved the British memorial from the well to the British cathedral and ones senses that if they could find somewhere even more mournful to which to remove the memorial *and* the cathedral they would do just that. Only shared shame and regret remain from those terrible, unheroic days in June 1857. The Nana Sahib was lucky; he simply vanished from history.

*

Which brings us finally to the Cawnpore Club, the officers' mess therein and the scene of Mark Twain's low-key after-dinner speech. The Cawnpore Club remains an exact copy of everything it was except for off-duty Indian officers rather than off-duty British ones. The dining room, where he gave his after-dinner speech, has been spruced up recently. For the first time in an Indian club we come across obstreperousness. Gillian wants to take a photograph of me standing where Twain might have stood, behind the top table.

"No madam, you cannot do that," says the aide-de-camp showing us around.

"Cannot do what?" asks Gillian.

"Take photos. You need written permission."
Sita jumps in, eyes ablaze, "You are joking, are you not?"
And that pretty much puts a nail in that coffin.

*

And so ended the tour of the ghastly Kanpur; never before have we been so pleased to see an Indian train and never before so eager to board one, even if it was the same *Patna Mathura Express* 13238 that the Twain party took all those years ago. The change from steam doesn't seem to have helped the journey time: two hours to cover the 35 miles to Agra.

12. AGRA

"Yes, but the Taj Mahal is a curse for us, for Agra," says Dr. Dubeyji, Chief Librarian at Agra University. We had been chatting about the strange phenomenon of being in a relatively uncrowded Indian city, namely Agra. "Relatively" is the word to bear in mind: anywhere else it would be considered uncomfortably full, here it is comfortably empty. It also feels down at heel; all Indian cities could be said to be down at heel but one feels the others are on the up; Agra feels to be on the down.

"Why so? Where has everyone gone?" I ask him.

"You see, the Taj is a world-renowned monument but the government has over-reacted. Here we used to have a famous tannery business and we made carpets for export all over the world. Also an iron-ore foundry. But the government has shut them all to protect the Taj. No industry of any kind is allowed within thirty miles of the Taj. Without growth from business the city is in decline."

"But the tourists, surely they help compensate for the lost industry?"

"Not really," he replies, "nowadays they are mostly groups on long day trips from Delhi."

This answered my next question about the city of Agra: although it is one of the most famous tourist cities in the world there are hardly any foreigners to be seen. I stayed in the Amar Hotel—an overpriced dump as bad luck would have it but we arrived late and tired off the Kanpur train—and apart from a small group of nonplussed Russians we were the only tourists unlucky enough to be there. Likewise, the surrounding streets were foreigner-free.

That changes the minute one enters the Taj Mahal complex on the edge of town. Tourists there are there and a-plenty. In fact, the complex has the same population density as any other Indian city, apart from Agra, except the incumbents are not Indian. After spending two months in unusually close proximity to hundreds of thousands of Indians it is unnerving at first to be surrounded by massed throngs of northern and southern Europeans, Orientals all the way from Thailand to Korea, North and Latin Americans and brilliantly costumed Africans. Only Arabia seems unrepresented at this sight of Islamic munificence; maybe at some other time.

The Taj itself is guarded by four forts, the North, South, East and West Gates. Anywhere else, in any other setting, any of them would be a major attraction in its own right. Most of the tour groups enter through the West or East Gates near where their coaches have to park, but the classic view of the Taj, the one in all the photographs, is best seen through the emptier South Gate. Few of the Delhi daytrip brigade arrive before 11 a.m. and the site opens at 6 a.m. for the sunrise photographs so overnighters—even those stuck at the Amar—can head for the South Gate early and be well rewarded for forgoing breakfast.

The Taj Mahal, 1860s, Samuel Bourne

As well as banishing industry from within thirty miles of the site the government has banned non-LPG auto-rickshaws from coming closer than 500 yards to any of the Gates. They haven't left the tourists free to pollute either. From a long list of banned items are "Eatables such as paan, paan massala, pakoras and samosas, Smokeables such as bidis, cigarettes and match boxes, Music players such CDs, walkmen, etc, Weapons such as firearms, small arms and any knife kind, Accoutrements such as zips, pins and buckle belts, Photography such as videography, including mobile phone videography, flash capability and tripods."

Tourists are given slip-on overshoes for entry beyond the main plinth. The authorities have also made a reasonable attempt to banish the touts and hustlers who were giving a visit to the Taj such a bad name. Once through the Gates one is left alone to wonder in awe—if one wants to, most tourists are so busy snapping away that they never become still enough to experience the beauty shared between their inner selves and the building, settling instead for the rush of objective attractiveness seen through a lens.

*

Well, Gillian and I, and even the more blasé Sita, who has been here twice before, are smitten by the perfection in shades of light and white marble that is the Taj Mahal—and more so than we expected to be. The concept of construction throws up visions of artisans starting in the center and adding layer upon layer of structure until the architect's design is complete. The genius of the Taj is that the vision is of sculpture, reducing and reducing until the architect[73] shouts "Stop!" It seems as if only then, when the mausoleum was complete, did the minaret builders, the garden planters and watercourse engineers set to work.

Mark Twain's reaction was of a different kind. In the strangest chapter in *Following the Equator*, Chapter 59, he settles into a four-page rant against his least favorite people, travel guide writers. I first came across his antipathy towards them when we were together in Jerusalem, when he was working on *The Innocents Abroad* and I on *Innocence and War*, thirty years ago for him, one year ago for me. His beef at the genre can be summarized in one Chapter 59 sentence: "Often the surest way to convey misinformation is to tell the strict truth," of which theory more later.

He started his broadside with:

In Agra and its neighborhood we saw forts, mosques, and tombs, which were built in the great days of the Mohammedan emperors, and which are marvels of cost, magnitude, and richness of materials and ornamentation, creations of surpassing grandeur, wonders which do indeed make the like things in the rest of the world seem tame and inconsequential by comparison. I am not purposing to describe them. By good fortune I had not read too much about them, and therefore was able to get a natural and rational focus upon them, with the result

---

[73] Ustad Ahmad Lahuri.

that they thrilled, blessed, and exalted me. But if I had previously overheated my imagination by drinking too much pestilential literary hot Scotch, I should have suffered disappointment and sorrow.

This seems at best contradictory. If his argument is that he cannot appreciate or describe what has been over-appreciated and over-described before, well perhaps, but it seems a bit of a woolly excuse for such a robust mind. But here he says he won't describe them in spite of the fact that "by good fortune I had not read too much about them… with the result that they thrilled, blessed, and exalted me."

Then there's a further contradiction when he writes about the Taj herself, surely the most important building he could have been referring to in his opening salvo above.

> I mean to speak of only one of these many world-renowned buildings, the Taj Mahal, the most celebrated construction in the earth. I had read a great deal too much about it. I saw it in the daytime, I saw it in the moonlight, I saw it near at hand, I saw it from a distance; and I knew all the time, that of its kind it was the wonder of the world, with no competitor now and no possible future competitor; and yet, it was not my Taj. My Taj had been built by excitable literary people; it was solidly lodged in my head, and I could not blast it out.

He then goes on to quote extensively over several pages from several guide books extant at the time of his visit and by using italics for emphasis, castigates them for building up a false picture of the sites, not by exaggerating them but by telling the truth. His theory is illustrated by using the example of the word "gem". He concedes that all guide writers' individual use of the gem motif is true ("the Taj… where the architect leaves off and the jeweler begins" etc.) but by the cumulative use of the word gem the reader "beguiled by his heated imagination" builds up a picture of the Taj covered not in white marble, as miracle in itself, but in diamonds, "sparkling in the sun, a gem-encrusted Taj as tall as the Matterhorn".

Twain now expands his theory that an individual guide book with a true description of a site leads inevitably to cumulative guide books—even though individually accurate—stirring up hyperbole in the reader's imagination. For this he gives his own experience at the Niagara Falls, "which I had to visit fifteen times before I succeeded in getting my imaginary Falls gauged to the actuality and could begin to sanely and wholesomely wonder at them for what they were, not what I had expected them to be... not an Atlantic Ocean pouring down thence over cloud-vexed Himalayan heights... but a beruffled little wet apron hanging out to dry."

Several pages later, having burdened the reader with a not very well argued non-theory, he delivers his *coup de grace*—for this reader and writer anyway the best paragraphs in *Following the Equator*. It is as if somewhere between the conscious and subconscious he had presented to the guide book writers (of which, of course, he was also one) and the world an example of how it should be done. He chose his subject brilliantly: a comparison of the most familiar man-made miracle, the Taj Mahal, and the most unfamiliar natural miracle, the ice-storm.

> I suppose that many, many years ago I gathered the idea that the Taj' s place in the achievements of man was exactly the place of the ice-storm in the achievements of Nature; that the Taj represented man' s supremest possibility in the creation of grace and beauty and exquisiteness and splendor, just as the ice-storm represents Nature' s supremest possibility in the combination of those same qualities. I do not know how long ago that idea was bred in me, but I know that I cannot remember back to a time when the thought of either of these symbols of gracious and unapproachable perfection did not at once suggest the other. If I thought of the ice-storm, the Taj rose before me divinely beautiful; if I thought of the Taj, with its encrustings and inlayings of jewels, the vision of the ice-storm rose. And so, to me, all these years, the Taj has had no rival among the temples and palaces of men, none that even remotely approached it, it was man's architectural ice-storm.

> Here in London the other night I was talking with some Scotch and English friends, and I mentioned the ice-storm, using it as a figure—a figure which failed, for none of them had heard of the ice-storm. One gentleman, who was very familiar with American literature, said he had never seen it mentioned in any book. That is strange. And I, myself, was not able to say that I had seen it mentioned in a book; and yet the autumn foliage, with all other American scenery, has received full and competent attention.

> The oversight is strange, for in America the ice-storm is an event. And

it is not an event which one is careless about. When it comes, the news flies from room to room in the house, there are bangings on the doors, and shoutings, "The ice-storm! the ice-storm!" and even the laziest sleepers throw off the covers and join the rush for the windows.

The ice-storm occurs in midwinter, and usually its enchantments are wrought in the silence and the darkness of the night. A fine drizzling rain falls hour after hour upon the naked twigs and branches of the trees, and as it falls it freezes. In time the trunk and every branch and twig are encased in hard pure ice; so that the tree looks like a skeleton tree made all of glass—glass that is crystal-clear. All along the underside of every branch and twig is a comb of little icicles—the frozen drip. Sometimes these pendants do not quite amount to icicles, but are round beads—frozen tears.

The weather clears, toward dawn, and leaves a brisk pure atmosphere and a sky without a shred of cloud in it—and everything is still, there is not a breath of wind. The dawn breaks and spreads, the news of the storm goes about the house, and the little and the big, in wraps and blankets, flock to the window and press together there, and gaze intently out upon the great white ghost in the grounds, and nobody says a word, nobody stirs. All are waiting; they know what is coming, and they are waiting, waiting for the miracle. The minutes drift on and on and on, with not a sound but the ticking of the clock; at last the sun fires a sudden sheaf of rays into the ghostly tree and turns it into a white splendor of glittering diamonds. Everybody catches his breath, and feels a swelling in his throat and a moisture in his eyes—but waits again; for he knows what is coming; there is more yet. The sun climbs higher, and still higher, flooding the tree from its loftiest spread of branches to its lowest, turning it to a glory of white fire; then in a moment, without warning, comes the great miracle, the supreme miracle, the miracle without its fellow in the earth; a gust of wind sets every branch and twig to swaying, and in an instant turns the whole white tree into a spouting and spraying explosion of flashing gems of every conceivable color; and there it stands and sways this way and that, flash! flash! flash! a dancing and glancing world of rubies, emeralds, diamonds, sapphires, the most radiant spectacle, the most blinding spectacle, the divinest, the most exquisite, the most intoxicating vision of fire and color and intolerable and unimaginable splendor that ever any eye has rested upon in this world, or will ever rest upon outside of the gates of heaven.

By, all my senses, all my faculties, I know that the ice storm is Nature's supremest achievement in the domain of the superb and the beautiful; and by my reason, at least, I know that the Taj is man's ice-storm.

In the ice-storm every one of the myriad ice-beads pendant from twig and branch is an individual gem, and changes color with every motion caused by the wind; each tree carries a million, and a forest-front exhibits the splendors of the single tree multiplied by a thousand.

It occurs to me now that I have never seen the ice-storm put upon canvas, and have not heard that any painter has tried to do it. I wonder why that is. Is it that paint cannot counterfeit the intense blaze of a sun-flooded jewel? There should be, and must be, a reason, and a good one, why the most enchanting sight that Nature has created has been neglected by the brush.

*

The Twain party stayed in a mansion that is now the headquarters of the Archeological Survey of India. What the ASI has done to the place is typical of what the organization has done to lesser buildings supposed to be under its protection: ruined them. This, apparently is a building it actually owns too. Its regime is the worst of all worlds: a rulebook forbidding any changes to anything, including restorations and improvements, and referees open to… suggestion. One wonders what qualifications are needed, beyond nepotism, greed and bloody mindedness, to work for it.

"Hello, I'm writing a book about Mark Twain's visit to India in 1896."

"I don't know anything about that."

"No, well I do. He was here in Agra on 27 and 28 February."

"He maybe, I don't know."

"And did you know he stayed here, in this very building, when it was used by the Resident, Colonel Loch?"

"No, we wouldn't have any records of that."

"Mark Twain lectured at the Metcalfe Hall."

"I never heard of that."

"Well, it burnt down. Kitchen fire. But you must have records of it. It was the town hall, the main public building until a hundred years ago."

"We wouldn't know about that."

"So what do you know about, historically?"

"No, we are for archaeology."

"And that's not historical?"

"No, I don't know."

Sita gives me a nudge and rubs her finger and thumb: tea money. "When in Rome" and all that, but I'm not in the mood, feeling that the bribee should show a modicum of interest in what one might buy from him—and she has already found out nearly all the information anyway.

Livy wrote:

We are stopping in the most beautiful bungalow—it is a government house occupied by the Political Agent. He is a lovely, interesting man with the most charming house. I wish you could see us here!

We have an immense bedroom more than 30 square feet and it must be about 30 feet high; it has a window onto a large pillared verandah—where, during the night, our servant spreads down his quilt on the stone floor and sleeps. Up high in one of the walls is a sky window which lets in an abundance of light and air. One side of the room has two doors into the dining room, and another side two doors into the entrance hall. By the side of the large window onto a piazza is the door into my dressing room—perhaps 10 x 12—out of that a bathroom a good deal larger. On another side of the room—sleeping-room—opens a door to Sam's bath and dressing-rooms.

It is all most beautiful and delightful—good food, nice, interesting, homelike people, great comfort and great independence.

All the doors in all Indian houses are curtained, so that you can leave the doors open, and so get the more air. In this house I find the best food I have found in India except at Belvedere in Calcutta.

Around this house all the time a patrol marches so that one feels here much protected. You can leave all the doors open if you like without danger.

I do so long for you all to see the pictures constantly before our eyes. These picturesque native servants come and go with their white dresses and white turbans. There are four men to wait at dinner and one little boy of perhaps 10; he is the son of the butler. As you go along a hall or enter a room in these eastern houses there will rise up from the floor, where they are squatting, sometimes from 2 to 6 or 8 servants, sometimes they remind me of monkeys.

Oh, dear. It is as bad as you are imagining. The gardens are destitute, unwatered, uncleaned, uncared for. The main entrance alone has been painted—and that a horrid shade of pink. The window frames are rotten. Tiles have fallen from the roof and not been replaced. The drive is covered in the usual litter. It's some shop window for the headquarters of the people who are meant to be in charge of heritage and preservation.

*

Tourists leaving the Taj Mahal immediately compare the squalor in the tiny medieval lanes around it to the sublimity they have just left behind. This is unfair; it is certain that in the Moghul days Shah Jahan and his court lived in grace and splendor, but the thousands of laborers who built the Taj, the Gates, gardens and watercourses lived in far worse conditions than the modern Indians crowded into the narrow streets, surviving on their cottage industries, just outside the Gates.

More distressing is to see the squalor of the modern architecture that is India's Sub-Continental Hideous. Agra was a Moghul capital and British garrison town and both previous civilizations built many other fabulous buildings here apart from the Taj. Alongside these—and unfortunately quite often on top of these— modern India has built its own new prestige buildings. It is valid to compare these and come to the only possible conclusion: modern Indian architecture is without any merit whatsoever. I'm not talking about the sight of the average new Indian dwelling which is always left unfinished with those twirly steel rods sticking up through the roof, the concrete left unpainted, the blocks unpointed and the builders' rubble left lying in the street outside. No, even prestige buildings like upscale hotels or government offices or the burgeoning shopping malls are uniformly hideous, out of scale, immune to their surroundings and always left unfinished.

At least one's last impressions are more in keeping with happier architectural times. To reach Agra Cantonment Railway Station from the hotel area one has to skirt around the massive walled city that is the famous Red Fort, one time home to the 105-carat Koh-I-Noor diamond.[74] The Red Fort re-surprises on each acquaintance by its imposing scale, exquisite Moghul inlays and poignant irony. Rebuilt, imposingly, by Akbar in the late sixteenth century and rebuilt again, exquisitely, by his grandson Shah Jahan after he had built the Taj Mahal, it was also where Shah Jahan died, imprisoned by his son Aurangzeb, the only view from his cell a perfect one of the perfect Taj Mahal in the middle distance.

A more mundane sight awaits us at 5.40 p.m. at the Agra Cantonment station, the 12965 *Gwalior Udaipur Super Express*; one only wonders how slow the ordinary Express must be as our Super takes nearly five hours to trundle over to Jaipur, 150 miles away into the night.

---

[74] Now part of the British Crown Jewels and on display at the Tower of London.

13. JAIPUR

EVEN TODAY, WITH refrigeration, sterilization and public awareness of sanitation it is hard for foreigners to avoid a touch of tummy trouble in India. In Mark Twain's time here our Western stomachs would have been more robust than the over-sterilized, spoon-fed intestines we sport today, but I am still amazed that the Twain party had been in India for six weeks before being laid low. It has been as if each time a page of *Following the Equator* has been turned and they are all still standing upright a sense of relief and disbelief turns the page too. Who ate what where we will never know, only that Livy missed that meal, for by the time the party arrived at Jaipur Twain, Clara and Smythe were laid low—and would stay laid low for the next two weeks. One can only sympathize with Smythe, feeling deathly and being unable to rearrange all the forthcoming Talks.

They were attended by a remarkable doctor, Colonel Thomas Holbein Hendley, the Residency Surgeon, who was, as we shall see, much more in Jaipur than just a doctor. Hendley not only ordered the lecture tour to halt while the leading light and his supporting cast recovered but also insisted they were all vaccinated against smallpox, an unpleasant procedure in the days when one could almost knit a jumper with the injection needles and vaccine doses were large enough to pass for a snifter in the officers' mess. Back home they were worried. The *St. Louis Dispatch* wrote that "Somehow Jaipur sounds very desolate and far-away-from-home. I'd hate to be sick with rajahs and rickshaws and ajahs and fellahs and punkahs and all that sort about me." The *Dispatch* needn't have worried: Twain loved it all, even from his sick-bed, especially the rajahs and rickshaws and ajahs and fellahs and punkahs. Me too.

They stayed and recovered at the Kaiser-i-Hind Hotel, one of the few genuine hotels in India, which was described by Twain as a "neat little hotel run by nine Indian brothers, and wonderfully noisy". We know from *Following the Equator* that it was in the British cantonment area of Jaipur and so somewhere near the Jaipur Club where the Strathcarron party is ensconced. Livy cheered herself up reading Kipling's "The City of Dreadful Night"[75] and wrote "it gives one a most frightful idea of this country". After a proper American club breakfast, Sita is

---

[75] From *Life's Handicap* and about Lahore·

volunteered to find out what has happened to the Kaiser-i-Hind Hotel and its nine-brother family, Gillian remains immersed in *Autobiography of a Princess,* about the last Maharani of Jaipur, I am off to retrace Twain's footsteps, as he would have trodden on recovery ten days later.

For Twain the *tonga* ride from the Kaiser-i-Hind to the Old City, the center of the famous Pink City of Jaipur, was "a journey which was full of interest for that country road was never quiet, never empty, but was always India in motion, always a streaming flood of brown people clothed in smouchings from the rainbow, a tossing and moiling flood, happy, noisy, a charming and satisfying confusion of strange human and strange animal life and equally strange and outlandish vehicles."

*

Quite so; still is. The journey now is by auto-rickshaw, rather than by *tonga.* The great throng of rainbow-colored, happy, noisy motion is still just as he described; only the volume has changed—and "changed" doesn't begin to describe the change. That "country road" is now a manic highway full of belching buses, lopsided flatbeds and fairy-lit lorries for the offence versus bemused camels

and float carts, sturdy oxen and dogcarts, plodding asses and donkey carts, and heaving humans and flat carts for the defense, all observed and judged by a mass of microbuses with humans hanging onto the roof racks, deranged taxis, agitated auto rickshaws, struggling cycle rickshaws, swarms of amorphous motorcycles, daydreaming bicycles and—heaven help them—terrified pedestrians, all accompanied by the random and blaring blasts of tinny horns and *basso profondo* klaxons. It sounds like an amplified version of the orchestra warm-up for a Stockhausen gig or Miles Davies in one of his more obscure moods.

It is indeed a strange quirk of the human condition than when one puts a representative of *homo indicus* anywhere near a moving vehicle he is transformed from a soul of endless patience and dogged perseverance to a complete maniac with the patience of a weaning grizzly and the perseverance of a tiger shark on its first day off the Dukan diet.

Twain's description of Jaipur holds good today:

> The city itself is a curiosity. Any Indian city is that, but this one is not like any other that we saw. It is shut up in a lofty turreted wall; the main body of it is divided into six parts by perfectly straight streets that are more than a hundred feet wide; the blocks of houses exhibit a long frontage of the most taking architectural quaintnesses, the straight lines being broken everywhere by pretty little balconies, pillared and highly ornamented, and other cunning and cozy and inviting perches and projections, and many of the fronts are curiously pictured by the brush, and the whole of them have the soft rich tint of strawberry ice-cream.

That soft rich tint of strawberry ice-cream, the Pink by which the City is known, has changed in the meantime into a tone of dull orange, not unlike the shade of a dowager's lipstick. Whatever color it is, it needs a make-over and has needed one for quite a few decades. For, as we have seen, it is another quirk of *homo indicus* that he has no interest in maintaining any man-made structure or endeavor. His own religion and culture are as old as any that exists, and are honored in their history and lived to their full glory day-by-day; they are as ancient as the gods and as current as their believers. Could it be that because he doesn't see Hinduism as a man-made religion but as divine and immutable philosophy, that he simply eschews anything that is man-made? After all, by definition it only temporary anyway. Take the Albert Hall for instance.

The same Dr. Hendley who confined the Twain party to Bedfordshire (and having just finished his epic *oeuvre*, *The Medico-Topographical Histories of Jaipur and Rajputna*) also persuaded the then ruler of Jaipur, Maharaja Ram Singh II, to not only paint the whole city pink but also build a splendid monument to honor the 1880 Grand Tour of India by the Prince of Wales, the son of Queen Victoria, Empress of India, later to be King Edward VII. This monument was to be named—like the museum and auditorium in London's South Kensington—after Victoria's late husband, Prince Albert of Saxe-Coburg and Gotha. Like the London building it was to be a museum, but here in Jaipur also a gigantic display cabinet and workshop for local craftsmen and artists.

When Twain visited the building it was only ten years old and he noted

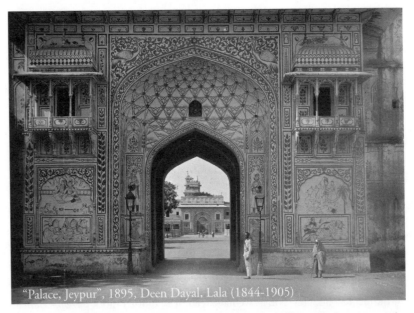

"Palace, Jeypur", 1895, Deen Dayal, Lala (1844-1905)

that: "In the midst of the spacious lawns stands the palace which contains the museum—a beautiful construction of stone which shows arched colonnades, one above another, and receding, terrace-fashion, toward the sky." It is, from a distance, indeed a beautiful building, in a style that its guide book rather airily calls "a serendipitous convergence of Rajput, Moghul and English" but Gillian prefers to think of as tropical-Gothic.

It is up close that, literally, the cracks appear; it is clear that since 1887 the building has been left to decline, unhindered by repair, to from whence it came.

I was there to visit the library in the search for Mark Twain and/or Kaiser-i-Hind references. The library is on the top floor. There is a splendid uniformed guard by the ground floor gate and a typically arcane Indian procedure needed to get past him. I need permission to visit the library; fine, but from where? From the director; fine, where's the director? He escorts me to the office; the director wants a written application; around her enormous desk several other supplicants are filling in forms for permission for this and approval for that in Hindi and English. She gives me a blank sheet of paper; I apply in my best handwriting; she pores over my passport and signs in beautiful black-inked calligraphy, "Lord Strathcarron, foreign historian, allowed acc. and extend hosp, KSS." She then stamps her note twice, the first with precision, the second with a flourish—and a smile. I'm in.

Up the three flights of scuffed stairs, under broken light fittings and peeling walls, is the library. It would seem no new titles have been added or indexing evolved since Dr. Hendley's time. The librarian, a helpful, wiry, very black Tamil named Nattar, immediately directed me to the City Palace library, a proper working library. This one, he said, was a museum library; "the library is part of the museum, not for book browsing". And so why the permission and procedure needed to see the museum-books? He smiled a face full of white teeth and wobbled his head in the Indian way that means everything from yes to maybe to who-knows.

The City Palace is a walled city within a walled city, deep in the heart of old Jaipur. To reach it means traversing Tripolia Bazaar, the main west-east road through the Pink City. It's an overwhelming experience; India condensed; India accelerated; India flagrant and unabashed; India without padding. Just to reach Tripolia Bazaar means walking through a mayhem of side roads, each one a decoction of India in itself. Beggars abound and flaunt their wretchedness competitively, unusual these days in India. Rickshaw drivers pester you and by pestering you while positioned diagonally across the road pester everyone higher up the traffic food chain: motorcycles, auto-rickshaws, small cars, taxis, large cars, town buses, military jeeps, lorries and state buses. While they pester you fester; even in the "cold season" the temperature is uncomfortably close and everyone who can move moves towards the shady side of the street. In the motorized logjam, accompanied by the usual blares going nowhere, the bicycles, oxen, camels, donkeys and humans have to make do as best they can, and as for the foot soldiers... use the pavements you might think? Ha! The pavements are motorcycle parks, the kerbs are car parks and the roads are parks for all of the above plus any form of rickshaw and idle cart. Thus the congestion has come full circle; everyone is everywhere. You, the visitor, along with everyone else must fight for survival in the cacophony of chaos that is the middle of the road. And these are still the side streets.

Then you have to cross the main road. There is no system one can suggest as there is no order to the proceedings, but a wise precaution is to line up downtide of some crossing locals and dance as they dance through the maelstrom keeping them uptide. Eventually one reaches the other side, nerves in tatters and deliria.

From all this madness the City Palace is a wonderful oasis. Calm and traffic free—and thanks to a healthy entrance fee, hustler and beggar free—delightfully low-rise and even until quite recently well maintained, it was the Maharaja of Jaipur's palace until his kingdom was absorbed into India in 1947. Now its collection of halls and receiving rooms has been made into a variety of museums and armories and yes, a working library.

Livy, not being unwell, came here alone. She wrote to her youngest daughter Jean:

> The other day I went to the museum here in the morning. I knew that up to 12:00 no men were allowed to go into the museum, so that the Hindoo women & ladies might be free to go in without being afraid of being seen by the men. I thought it would be a good time to see them with their gorgeous dressings. It was a fine site. Every part of the Museum, even up to the balcony & the second story, & even to the roof was packed full of these brilliantly dressed ladies. Only trouble was that I was as great a curiosity to them as they were to me. They crowded about & shattered & examined me & followed me about. I would go behind cases & get into other rooms to try to get away but ever without success. The crowd was always about me. When they talked I pointed to my mouth & said I could not speak Hindustani. One of them would seem to suddenly understand it & then tell the others.

In the library one can see photographs of Jaipur in Twain's time. The streets are as empty as a Mid-West county town in the 'fifties on an off-market day. It is like that in the City Palace compound now, the equivalent of the Jaipur that Twain saw then; no wonder he loved it so much.

I asked for the curator and was looked after with great enthusiasm by Pankar

Sharma who immediately found several books about late nineteenth-century Jaipur. More to the point he knew all about the Kaiser-i-Hind. Sita had called round earlier that morning; I text her to head back to Pankar's desk.

She arrives moment later looking as fresh as she started the day; I fear I must look like I've been through a desert, which in an urban sense I have. We talk about the Kaiser-i-Hind. "Yes, a wonderful building, in the Baroque style, most unusual here. The porticos have wonderful inlaid Saracenic marbles. It is one of our city's treasures," says Pankar.

"Is it open? Can we go there?" Sita asks.

"Yes, I think so, but it is in very bad condition. It is no longer a hotel, too dilapidated."

"It belonged to nine brothers," I say.

"That right, the Momden family. Muslims, but educated."

"And where is it?" I ask

"Just opposite the Sheraton Rajputna Hotel, a new skyscraper."

We beetle into an auto-rickshaw and beetle off to the Sheraton. Auto-rickshaw travel is fraught at the best of times but mostly because of the noise rather than any danger. The two-stroke engine under the driver is often unsilenced but worse your ears are unprotected and at bus and truck horn height. The danger is diminished because it all happens so slowly, which also of course prolongs the horn exposure.

Eventually, the calm of the City Place long dissolved, we arrive at the Sheraton. But there is nothing there opposite it, save a large empty lot. The building had been demolished two years ago. But not all had gone for one outpost remained.

"It's our family mosque," explains Mujid Momden, a much removed descendant of one of Twain's nine hotelier brothers. Now 35, he has mixed feelings about the old family home and hotel being replaced by the new family fortune.

"It will be a new high-rise hotel, like the Sheraton there. The opposite of the Kaiser-i-Hind."

"You must all be very rich," I suggest.

"Not really, there are so many of us."

"From Mark Twain's nine brothers?"

"When we sold the hotel they were one hundred and eighty-three signatures needed. All could claim part of the old hotel. We inherit like this. We each had to sign saying we knew of no other claimants. But how could we not? The Kaiser-i-Hind had been in our family for two hundred years. The new hotel is American. Ha! They had more lawyers than my family members. We must be sure no tail-end Charlies, popping in the woodwork they said. It took five years to complete the sale. But there must be more family somewhere—we know of some in Canada."

"But the old hotel was a ruin, wasn't it?"

"Yes, nobody wanted to restore it because so many family members owned it. Who spends money on something that is not yours?"

"So everybody owned it yet nobody owned it?"

"That is how it happens here."

"So that could explain why all the beautiful old buildings in India are falling to pieces, uncared for, unloved. No-one is inclined to pay to restore them when so many others own a tiny bit of it."

He wobbled his head in the Indian "yes".

"A-ha!"

*

Meanwhile we are having our own drama. After the latest travel trauma (reaching the Sheraton) we are pausing here in the hotel in the air-conditioned shade for a calming cup of coffee by the fountain. There, as bad luck would have it, Sita picks up a copy of this morning's *Times of India*. She's pale enough already but now turns paler still and gasps "Oh my God."

To backtrack: we had agreed at the outset that she had to take time off the trip to attend one of her interminable cousins' interminable weddings. We agreed it should be while we were all in Jaipur as this is where the Twain party's tour stalled and it would give us a break from the travel too: me a chance to shuffle through all the notes and Gillian a chance to organize the photos and videos, all in the civilized setting of the Jaipur Club. So far so good but we had also agreed that to save time Sita would fly home to Mumbai and back again. First potential problem: Sita hates flying, or more to the point, she hates the idea of flying, as she hasn't actually tried it yet.

"Oh my God," she gasps again, holding up the newspaper. "Listen to this. This morning's *Times of India*, right?"

NEW DELHI: Four persons, including a Civil Aviation official, a pilot and two touts have been arrested by Delhi Police in connection with the latest fake flying license scam. With these fresh arrests, a total number of 10 people have been taken into custody in connection with the racket.

The police have now grounded 14 pilots who have obtained their commercial licenses by submitting fake records. In addition three Civil Aviation officials and two more touts who the police believe were the "other end" of the scam have been questioned and released on bail.

A person is eligible to fly a commercial aircraft only when he or she secures a so-called CPL, which is given out after a person completes 200 hours of flying during the training. This is a costly exercise and the 14 pilots whose licenses have been revoked had allegedly not flown the mandatory hours to skimp costs and are alleged to have bought fake certificates from the government's flying training institute using touts who hang around the training schools.

The Civil Aviation official said they would conduct a third-party audit of all the 40 flying schools in the country in the wake of these scams and even cases of forged licenses coming to light.

Delhi Police say "We believe that we have opened up a Pandora's Box. There seems to be many more people involved in the scam that seems to have grown in the last two years, especially after the proliferation of low-cost airlines."

She reads on in disbelief. Then again, "Oh my God! I'm going on Indigo! Listen":

In the latest incident an Indigo Airline woman pilot, Captain Verah Gulati, was arrested for obtaining a pilot's license on forged documents. It came to light after she was grounded following a series of hard landings.

A Civil Aviation Officer said "We found that she had submitted forged result cards of pilot license examination. She used a tout to bribe a Civil Aviation official to look the other way."

185

She had failed in air navigation paper and was absent in the paper of radio aids and instruments in January 2009. She again appeared in April and July 2009 sessions, but failed both times.

Sources say that more than 1,700 pilots are now under the scanner and insist that several Civil Aviation officials who have been resisting the probe could be directly involved in the scam.

"Oh my God!"

"I'm sure it will be alright," says Gillian soothingly.

"I'm not," says Sita. "I'm going by train," and she whirls off to the Sheraton's Travel Desk to arrange same.

Half an hour later she returns. "I can get the Jaipur Bombay Superfast. It's only eighteen hours each way."

"But you'll miss the wedding," says Gillian.

"A bit, but there will be hundreds of people. Maybe a thousand. It will be alright."

✳

But, as always, we should leave the last word to Mark Twain. On leaving Jaipur he was lucky enough to see one of the Maharaja's processions, a sight he knew then and we know now we will never see again. He wrote:

Then the wide street itself, away down and down and down into the distance, was alive with gorgeously-clothed people not still, but moving, swaying, drifting, eddying, a delirious display of all colors and all shades of color, delicate, lovely, pale, soft, strong, stunning, vivid, brilliant, a sort of storm of sweetpea blossoms passing on the wings of a hurricane; and presently, through this storm of color, came swaying and swinging the majestic elephants, clothed in their Sunday best of gaudinesses, and the long procession of fanciful trucks freighted with their groups of curious and costly images, and then the long rearguard of stately camels, with their picturesque riders.

For color, and picturesqueness, and novelty, and outlandishness, and sustained interest and fascination, it was the most satisfying show I had ever seen, and I suppose I shall not have the privilege of looking upon its like again.

PART FIVE
...WITH A FINAL FLOURISH...

AN HONEST CRITIC.

14. DELHI

EVENTS CONSPIRED TO make Mark Twain's visit to Delhi a short one. Firstly, his schedule was still recovering from the two-week sick leave in Jaipur, delaying pre-booked Talks in Lahore and Rawalpindi[76]; secondly, he himself was still recovering from his illness in Jaipur and wasn't in the physical or mental mood for more than cursory sightseeing, and one can only presume that Clara and Smythe were also still wheezy; thirdly, he had no Talk planned in Delhi and so no reason not to move on swiftly; fourthly, Delhi was suffering from "smallpox & water famine threatened"; fifthly, Delhi was still a quaint, provincial, cultureless city compared to the commercial capital, Bombay, and the administrative capital Calcutta; and lastly, they had every intention to make a more leisurely return to Delhi on their way back to Calcutta when he and the city should be in better health. As bad luck had it, the return trip was never made and so his twenty-four hours in Delhi was only a flying visit, albeit one made in some style residing in some style at the only mansion on top of the only hill.

His party arrived from Jaipur at midnight—nine and a half hours late—at what was the old Delhi railway station, which was then being transformed into the Old Delhi Railway Station we see today. In fact it is now being transformed again with a heavy investment in digital signs, CCTV and even—praise the Lord—a coat of paint. Only the red-coated porters have remained the same down the ages: in Twain's time they were called "coolies" as they still call themselves today. But whether they are coolies or porters their numbers are declining, put out of business by wheely luggage and voracious overpricing, often right under a sign giving the correct rate—half a dollar a bag. Even twenty years ago Indians traveled with their own bedding, it not being expected that hotels or hosts would provide any; another nail in the coolie coffin.

All the modernization does throw up some amusing quirks. At Old Delhi Station they have also invested in a new push button phrase announcer. A delightfully accented English female voice this morning echo-purrs: "The... 12.45... Jandiphur Mail... to Jandiphur Junction... will leave at... 12.45... sharp... we apologize *deeply* for any inconvenience caused."

---

[76] Both now in Pakistan.

Outside the station is the epicenter of Old Delhi, which should more accurately be called Medieval Delhi. This is not meant disparagingly, it's just the prefix "Old" gives the impression of a city far newer than it actually is.

Unfortunately the concept of the medieval only has negative connotations these days, conjuring up images of plague and pestilence in the dark days before sanitation, sleeping quarters, civic pride, footwear, reason and Renaissance. Perhaps Quentin Tarantino sums up the modern image best in *Pulp Fiction* when the gangster-baddie tells the pervert-baddie, "now I'm gonna get medieval on yo' arse," meaning the former is about to torture, in none too pleasant a fashion, if memory serves, the latter. Unfortunately this sort of careless banter gives a bad name not only to medievalism but to sado-masochism as well.

The fascinating point about medieval Delhi, or The MedDel Experience if it were ever Disneyfied, is that it transports one back to the India of Mark Twain's time and to the Europe of Donatello's paintings. The great qualification, of course, is the density of population. Now the Census Board estimate India's population at 1.2 billion; they estimate that in 1900 it was around 150 million[77] or about an eighth of what it is now. In pre-capital Delhi it was less than half a million, a fiftieth of what it is today. An early morning walk, when forty-nine out of fifty people are yet to rise, serves as an indication of the density Twain would have seen here in Delhi.

And it's all still here. The impromptu hairdresser, the trinket salesman, the old notice board, the open sewer, the stagnant mud puddles, the hand-pump well, the ear-cleaner, the cooper, the wheelwright, the beggar child, the sleeping bundle, the urinater, the random roadside pitch, the tailors' stalls, the tea stalls, the liquor stalls, the hawkers and hustlers of the this and the that, the snoozing mange dogs, the shy cats, the boxed fowl, the goats, the cows and the cow pats, the street seamstresses, the street sweet sellers, the street shoe shiners, the street shavers, the street sleepers, the street sweepers, the scavengers and the spitters, the maimed and the infirm, the rats, the open shops with raised floors, the man as a beast of burden worth less than a donkey and more than a child, the cottage industries, houses in the lanes so narrow neighbors can stretch out to touch each other, the lanes strewn with *detritus variosis*, the smell of farmyard and urine and rotting fruit and mulching vegetables, the smell of decay and heat.

And the good news? The people are the good news. Of course, one would

---

[77] Or 250 million if you include India as it was in 1900, so including Pakistan, parts of Nepal and Bangladesh.

prefer not to move back to medieval times, even as a courtier or squire, but we have lost something on the road to long life, freedom and prosperity; the immediacy of our relationships with everyone and everything around us; the immediacy of lives driven by the rather stark imperative: if you don't earn, you don't eat; the immediacy of a life led by the stick and carrot, the snake and the ladder, of religious belief. If one stands accused of patronizing voyeurism it is worth remembering that compassion in its original meaning is to feel *sympathy with* someone and not to feel *sorry for* someone, the latter the meaning the concept of compassion has drifted into.

*

For the late arriving Twain party it was bed-time. They trotted in their *tongas* past the sites they would see the next day: Kashmere Gate, Nicholson's grave, Civil Lines, up Delhi's only hill to The Ridge, past the 1857 War Memorial and so on to the mansion in which they were staying. It was quite a place, in quite a spot, with quite a history.

The Delhi of twenty million now and the Delhi of half a million then is built on the plains, all flatlands but with one exception, a small hill in the center called, reasonably enough, The Ridge. In 1830 the British Indian enthusiast William Fraser[78] built a fabulous white Palladian mansion on top of The Ridge; it was indeed the mansion on the hill and was occupied in 1896 by the Twain party's hosts, Mr. and Mrs. Burne of the Bank of Bengal; bankers clearly did as well than as they do now. Twain remembered it as "a great old mansion which possessed historical interest. It was built by a rich Englishman who had become orientalized—so much so that he had a zenana. But he was a broadminded man, and remained so. To please his harem he built a mosque; to please himself he built an English church. That kind of a man will arrive, somewhere. In the Mutiny days the mansion was the British general's headquarters. It stands in a great garden—oriental fashion—and about it are many noble trees."

It is still here—after a fashion. It has now been absorbed, swamped, by the enormous, sprawling, filthy Hindu Rao Hospital[79] whose turn it now is to occupy the prime location in Delhi. The main part of the old mansion is now the Plastic Surgery Ward; the annex, where the *zenana* would have been, is the Endoscopy Unit. The building itself could certainly use some plastic surgery; the introduction of any kind of endoscope into its foundations would probably cause it to collapse.

The rambling two-story mansion where the Twain party stayed was never the prettiest building in India but next to it now is rotten fruit fallen from the ugly tree. The Sub-Continental Hideous-style Nursing School was erected in 1957 and has not been touched since. What were probably maroon walls have long since faded to a shade of dirty rust; the window frames and lintels are all rotten and crumbling; the ground floor windows are either broken or cracked. The nurses' uniforms are shabby too and the nurses themselves look like they've just crawled out of a glorified squat, which they have. It is adjacent to the old *zenana*. Now say what you like about *zenanas*, but the harems and their inmates were magnificent feats of decoration—at least the ones of my imagination are—and it doesn't seem fair that their memories should have to live next to a squalid block of put-upon nurses.

One constant from Twain's time are the monkeys, who together with the patients and the staff, the pigeons and the bats, the cockroaches and the rats, go to make up Hindu Rao's population. Twain noted that:

...they are monkeys of a watchful and enterprising sort, and not much

---

[78] Also an assistant, almost a disciple, of our friend Ochterlony from Calcutta.
[79] Named after the post-Fraser, pre-Sepoy Uprising owner, Hindu Rao.

troubled with fear. They invade the house whenever they get a chance, and carry off everything they don't want. One morning the master of the house was in his bath, and the window was open. Near it stood a pot of yellow paint and a brush. Some monkeys appeared in the window; to scare them away, the gentleman threw his sponge at them. They did not scare at all; they jumped into the room and threw yellow paint all over him from the brush, and drove him out; then they painted the walls and the floor and the tank and the windows and the furniture yellow, and were in the dressing-room painting that when help arrived and routed them.

Two of these creatures came into my room in the early morning, through a window whose shutters I had left open, and when I woke one of them was before the glass brushing his hair, and the other one had my note-book, and was reading a page of humorous notes and crying. I did not mind the one with the hair-brush, but the conduct of the other one hurt me; it hurts me yet. I threw something at him, and that was wrong, for my host had told me that the monkeys were best left alone. They threw everything at me that they could lift, and then went into the bathroom to get some more things, and I shut the door on them.

*

If the Sepoy Uprising's most heroic resistance was played out at Lucknow and its most shameful episode happened in Cawnpore, it was here in Delhi that some of the most ferocious, close quarter fighting took place. Survival informed every action; Stalingrad springs to mind. There were over thirty actual battles and hundreds of skirmishes during the long summer of 1857 and many of the fiercest took place around the mansion in which the Twain party stayed. No doubt battle scars still remained. The resistance was heroic here too as Delhi, being the seat of the last Moghul Emperor,[80] was the rallying point for sepoys and fellow travelers from Meerut, sixty miles northwest of Delhi and from across the northern plains. The British were outnumbered by perhaps as much as fifty to one and their ranks were depleted by cholera as much as by the attacks.

The next day, 17 March, Mark Twain set off to see the battle sites, still fresh

---

[80] The East India Company had told the 82-year-old Bahadur Shah II that the title would die with him.

as legends in the minds of the British officers showing him around. Next to the old mansion and new—well, quite new—hospital is the 1847 War Memorial set high in the middle of The Ridge. The War Memorial is well cared-for but The Ridge is in a sorry state. What could be a lovely strolling or picnic spot for the beleaguered Delhiites, or a forest or garden park on the only high spot with any hope of fresh air in Delhi, has been taken over by layers of old litter, troupes of reputedly rabid langur monkeys—not all of them of the live-and-let-live variety—and by trollops of *hijras*.

A *hijra* is a eunuch, a breed with a reputable past and a disreputable present. The use of eunuchs[81] may have died along with the harems they served but in India, where change takes its time, they have survived as a kind of sub-caste of transvestites. There are reputed to be a million of them but Indian statistics can be dressed up both ways too. Unlike the TVs of Eastern Asia who can easily pass themselves off as women until the moment of *passione porpora*, the TVs here make no effort to hide their hairy, deep-voiced male origins expect by plastering themselves in cheap rouge and loud lipstick and wrapping themselves in the most gaily colored sarees.

If they make no effort to hide their male origins one has to say they make a massive effort to hide their male organs. Mala, one of the *hijras* on The Ridge, a hideous concoction in bright yellow, his/her black face whitened then rouged like a parody of femininity, explained the process after a hundred rupees helped her remember it. I'm too squeamish to write it down and you'd be too squeamish the read it, but castration is only the half of it... well, use your imagination. Mala claims that the process is entirely safe and the bleeding stops within a day. Older *hijras* perform the cuts and indentation, while the younger ones nurse the new recruit back to health.[82]

Indians see them as a curate's egg; some give them money to bring good luck to a bride or new child, some give them money not to be touched by them, especially at traffic lights where they camp up and down the lines. Others give them money for sexual favors, the trade they ply up here on The Ridge: they are after all the girly-boys of Arnold Schwarzenegger's disdain and indeed Mala's first

---

[81] Etymologically from the Greek "bed guard".

[82] Meanwhile, trained doctors perform the lucrative operation known as genitoplasty, turning an estimated 300 girls a year into boys by grafting a penis and injecting hormones. At US$5,000 parents reckon it is cheaper than a wedding and dowry—and morally better than sex selection abortions which have left India with seven million more boys than girls under six.

thought was that I was a great white punter.

Eventually one finds one's way past the unpredictable monkeys and hideous *hijras* to the octagonal Gothic steeple that is the War Memorial. The Inscription reads: "This monument was erected in 1863 in memory of those who died in the fighting of 1857 during the Mutiny. It is built on the site where Tailor's Battery defended this position. The names of the Officers and Jawans are inscribed herein, in memory of their bravery and sacrifice in defeating the enemy."

Below it is another plaque erected twenty-five years after Independence: "The 'Enemy' of the inscriptions on this monument were those who rose against colonial rule and fought bravely for national liberation in 1857. In memory of the heroism of the immortal martyrs for Indian freedom." So there.

After the War Memorial they rode down the hill to the area still known as Civil Lines, the scene of some of the bitterest fighting. Many of the buildings still showed their scars. Today one better take an auto-rickshaw down as the monkeys lie in wait on either side of the road. I say to myself: whatever you do, don't take a banana out of your pocket. Then, silly, you don't have a banana. True, but they don't know that.

Civil Lines was from where the British governed Delhi in the nineteenth century, a sort of Old Delhi version of New Delhi, which of course is exactly what it was: where all the great and the good lived before being decanted into Lutyens' new city. Civil Lines is still a broad, tree-lined avenue with comfortable bungalows behind high walls. When King George V visited India in 1911 he announced, on what with hindsight seems like almost a whim, that the capital would move from Calcutta to Delhi and the empire would build a new Delhi, New Delhi, to accommodate it in the most sumptuous, jewel-in-the-empire style. Civil Lines, the old New Delhi of old Delhi, then went into a decline and one feels particularly sorry for the owners of the opulent Maidan's Hotel, who opened in grand style in 1903 in the prime spot in Civil Lines only to find their hotel more often empty than full ever since.

(I still find it amazing that the British should have built New Delhi at all, let alone built it so generously: they must have known by 1911 that the end was nigh, yet they chose to build this one last magnificent statement, nothing less than a capital city, in honor of empire and their idea of good government. Any other imperial power would have taken the money and run—although there are many Indians who would suggest the British already had.)

In Twain's time the bungalows were occupied by the great and the good of Delhi. Now they are occupied by the officers of the dozens of lesser spotted government departments that Indian bureaucracy spawns; it has become a sort of civic cantonment. Next to Maidan's is the Indian Police Officers' Mess—the same officers whose average wage is $2,500 a year but who drive up to the mess in cars worth an average $25,000. Maybe they all play the lottery and win every week.

Their next stop on the Delhi tour was the famous Kashmere Gate, famous for its elegant symmetry and famous for being a bloody witness to some of the toughest battles in the Sepoy Uprising. For three hundred years before the British arrived Delhi had been the capital of Moghul India and its most famous builder, the Taj Mahal's Shah Jahan, had built a wall around what was then called Shahjananabad. The Red Fort red-stone wall is beautifully sculptured, both decorative and defendable. In retrospect, the one-and-a-half-mile wall was more decorative than defendable. Fifty years after it was finished, with the Moghul Empire in decadent decline, the Persian Emperor Nadir Shah (whose first name lives on to describe a low point) sacked Delhi and massacred over one hundred thousand of its inhabitants in one night in a Christian crusader-style killing spree. It was with this memory still fresh that the East India Company was welcomed, initially at any rate, by the remnants of Moghul Delhi.

The Kashmere Gate now has the misfortune to be under the care of the

nincompoops of the Archaeological Survey of India and as such combines the worst of all worlds: reliance on officialdom and hostility to visitors. There is no sign of the fighting that took place there and it is now just another bashed-up ruin heading towards a rubbly future. The British started the vandalism in the Red Fort itself immediately after the Sepoy Uprising was put down, demolishing the old harem and out-palaces and building a row of completely inappropriate barracks. But worse is seen all around its walls: the immediately adjacent section of the old Moghul wall at Kashmere Gate has been bulldozed to make way for a massive and meritless concrete monstrosity, a shopping mall-cum-metro station. The Barbarians have been at the Gates since 1856 but are now fuelled by revenge and bulldozers rather than revenge and philistinism.

Next to the still-proud Kashmere Gate was the grave and pedestal to Brigadier General John Nicholson. Never was there a better example of history being open to interpretation. To the British of the time, especially back home, he was the Hero of Delhi; to the Indians of the time he was the Butcher of Delhi[83]; it is safe to say now that all agree he was a thoroughly unpleasant man who happened to be a brilliant soldier—not the first one of that particular breed. After Independence the new government decided to move his grave out of India and sent it back to Ulster, to his old school, the Royal Dungannon.

*

Whilst in Delhi Gillian and I have to apply for a Pakistani visa at the local High Commission. Sita has no wish to go behind enemy lines and the enemy probably wouldn't let her in anyway.

One needs at least a tourist visa to enter Pakistan but it soon becomes clear they don't really want any tourists—at least not in a joined-up thinking kind of way—and they don't really like issuing visas much either.

I started—and gave up—the process in London. There in Knightsbridge stands the beautiful Regency building that is the Pakistani High Commission. The High Commission had a visa department; so far so good. I went through a gate into the gardens and found a scene resembling a refugee camp. There were five tents marked A, B, C, D and E. There was no explanation for the system and no lines within any of the tents, just a mad scramble. On the other side of

---

[83] He believed in the idea of exemplary punishment pour encourager les autres: having decapitated a local hoodlum he kept the head on his desk.

the garden was an open-air desk with piles of forms in English and Urdu. It had been sprinkling rain London-style on and off all morning and the top ones were soaked; they were held in a pile by a broken brick which had left its crumbs all over the place.

I asked a fellow lost-looking-soul, a Pakistani, if he knew what was happening. He said, you fill in the form three times, add the photos, and take them to the correct line. Ah, but how do you know which is that line? He shrugged and said he had heard that in theory A was for enquiries, B and C were for handing in the forms in Urdu and English, and D and E were for collections, but in practice everyone just piled into what seemed like the shortest line.

I had already printed off our forms from the High Commission website and attached our photos so I joined the end of the jumble of the C line. There were no ropes separating the lines and people were jostling and pushing and raising their voices not only within each so-called line but across lines too. There was no point in being English about this; the tactics were arms and elbows and the strategy pushing and shoving. After twenty minutes I was standing sideways one line back from the front. At the desk a harried looking official—poor man!— looked up, saw a foreigner and reached out for my forms.

"Wrong forms," he shouted.

"But I printed them this morning from your website".

"New forms now. New security. Forms are on the table." He turned back and grabbed another sheaf from another supplicant. Case dismissed.

This was a double disaster as on the internet forms it had asked that the passport photos be glued to each of the three copies—and they were. Starting again was the only way forward. Outside the sprinkle had turned to London light and the forms were soaked at the top, sodden in the middle and damp at the bottom. I took three damp ones and retired home via a revisit to the photo booth to try again the next day. I had been at the High Commission for an hour and a half, plus a further hour to-ing and fro-ing. I am writing this in Delhi and have been in the Sub-Continent for two months—and two and half hours wasted hereabouts seems like nothing at all, almost time well spent. Western readers living in a busy capital will agree that two and half hours wasted in a working day is a lifetime.

I tried again the next day, making sure I was there well before the 10 a.m. kick-off time. (They close at noon—no, I don't know either.) The new form was a lot more detailed and complicated than the previous one, requiring notification in advance of exactly where and when one was going to be at any given time, as if every tourist was on a pre-arranged package tour. I did my best but there was one part with which I couldn't legally comply: they asked for our last three months' bank statements. Now, it's illegal in most Western countries to reveal anybody's bank statements, including your own. I wrote a little note to that effect and gave our banks' names and addresses.

It was forty-five disorderly, frustrating, barging minutes before I reached the front—or near the front—of the C scrum. The same poor man was there, dealing simultaneously with eight outstretched arms and four raised voices. He grabbed our forms, gave them a quick glance and put them on a pile. I asked him to check the bank boxes were alright as completed. "No problem. It's just a form. Come back in four weeks. Phone first."

"Four weeks? You mean four days, it said five days on your website."

"That was the old form. Now four weeks. New procedure. All forms must go the Foreign Ministry in Pakistan."

I didn't even need to think about it for a nanosecond; apart from anything else our flight to Mumbai was leaving in ten days. I took back my passport and forms and retired for a rethink.

I have a good friend who herself has a good friend at the American Embassy in New Delhi. I had the latter's contacts and she in turn was expecting my call—and dinner—once we had arrived here. Did she know if it was possible to obtain a tourist visa from the Pakistan High Commission in Delhi? Ten minutes later the phone rang. Yes, no problem but it will take three days. Three days! Job done, see you in Delhi.

Fast forward to Delhi. Scene: four days ago outside the Pakistan High Commission. We are in the diplomatic quarter. Delhi, like other artificial capitals such as Canberra and Brasilia, has such a quarter. Built around wide, gridded, litter-cleared boulevards and open, grassy, tree-lined spaces, the embassies crouch behind high security walls. Only the flags on top of the poles give each country's game away. Outside each embassy is a sentry box, maybe two in the case of the American, and that's it. It's clinical, empty and quiet, except outside the Pakistan High Commission when suddenly, as one turns the corner into the entry road, one is back in India—except, of course, it's Pakistan-in-India. There are squat tents, lean-tos, people sleeping on the pavements, dogs sleeping in the road, chai-stalls, litter everywhere, auto-rickshaws arguing, a kind of functioning anarchy—the general Sub-Continental melee.

Actually it's even worse than London as there is not even a hat tilted toward the lining-up tradition. But I've been in India a couple of months and become quite accomplished at what would have seemed like ungentlemanly conduct two months ago. Push, shove, manhandle, elbow, trip, shoulder, fart, shout, then start all these again, repeat three times and I'm within shouting distance of the front of the ruckus.

"I'd like two tourist visas please."

"What is your mother country?"

"UK."

"Then you must go to London. Here is just for Indians."

"I can't go to London. I'm here. Look, is there someone on the cultural or diplomatic side I can see?"

"Are you a VIP?"

"Yes." Forgive me Lord, for I have sinned.

He dials a number and above all the shouting supplicants and jostling hubbub speaks to someone and gives me the phone.

The phone says: "Where are you staying?"

"At the India International Centre."

"Give the man at the desk your card. I'll be there at seven this evening. Let me speak to him again." I hand the phone back to the desk jockey and give him my card.

*

Like the diplomatic quarter, the India International Centre is in New Delhi but not in India, not in India-India; in fact it's a UN and NGO outpost that doubles up as a Foreign Correspondents' Club for visiting journalists. Into this oasis of tranquility, only half an hour late, wanders our potential benefactor. For the next twenty minutes, over a beer in the bar, he and I discuss my visa requirements and all the very many problems associated therewith.

"But maybe there's a solution," he eventually says.

I want to say straightaway: "Go on then, how much?" but years in Arabia tell me to play the face game.

"Oh well, it would be wonderful if you could, somehow, you know, think of a solution. Of course anything I can do to help..."

"Well, I have a friend in the High Commission. You see, he has family worries. His wife is ill and not able to look after his son who needs special treatment."

199

"And doctors are expensive, even here."

"Yes, that's the trouble. Doctors. He cannot afford to pay the doctor," he says.

"I can imagine. Dentists are just as bad. Meanwhile his wife and son are becoming worse."

"Yes, nothing is easy. We feel sorry for him but what can we do?"

A long pause into my beer glass. "If it isn't too expensive perhaps I can help with the doctor. For your friend."

Another long pause, this time into his beer glass. "I see what you mean. That would be much appreciated."

"And could he help me? I mean, with my tourist visa?"

"Oh, I'm sure that could be arranged. It's only a formality after all, nothing compared to a doctor's help."

Another pause, this time into my beer glass. "And did your friend mention a doctor's fee?"

"No, but I believe such an Indian doctor would be two hundred and fifty US cash."

"Would an Indian doctor take pounds and euros instead? I believe I have that much upstairs."

"Oh yes, I'm sure that would be quite acceptable."

"And if I give our passports when could I have them back?"

"This time tomorrow."

And so it was done. I'm sure his friend's wife and son made a quick recovery; for our part we have two six-month tourist visas issued three weeks ago in Brussels, Belgium.

Whatever minor thrill there was at beating the system was tempered by the sadness of saying goodbye to Sita. Pakistan was not for her; nor she for it. She has been a constant source of amazement and amusement—and knowledge. Her last words are, "I really hope the book gets published" so if she is reading these words she will know her wish has come true.

15. LAHORE

I AM ANXIOUS—as ever—to not just follow the same route as Mark Twain but also to use the same form of transport. From Delhi to Lahore then was a simple and quick train journey on the *Flying Mail*, one of the fastest and most prestigious Raj train routes connecting Karachi, Delhi and Lahore. Not so today. Since Twain's time we have had the disaster of Partition in 1947 and Lahore now finds itself in Pakistan. Between Delhi and Lahore the India-Pakistan border is one of the tensest in the world, especially now since roguish tendencies in the ISI, the Pakistani intelligence agency, have been shown to have sponsored the 2008 terrorist attacks in Mumbai. It is also one of the most poignant train journeys in the world, the scene of inter-tribal religious massacres just prior to Independence and Partition when half a million people died—and as many as sixty thousand of them making this very train journey, massacred along these very tracks.

*

It is beyond the scope of this book to rehearse the events and massacres leading up to Partition except to make a few quick points as events today are still affected by the horrors perpetrated then. Between the end of World War 1 and the outbreak of World War 2 it became obvious to the more thoughtful imperialists on the ground that India would one day be independent; the "if" was becoming the "when". As ideas and plans for the "when" were floated during the late 1930s the British and Indians envisaged one large country to replace the Raj; this would include the three countries that are now Pakistan, India and Bangladesh.[84]

By the early 1940s a counter-move grew to have a Muslim homeland in the west and east of India and out of this grew the idea of a West Pakistan and East Pakistan. The one country divided into two only lasted until 1971 when a particularly nasty civil war resulted in the western half becoming Pakistan and the eastern half Bangladesh. The man behind the idea of dividing India, a brilliant advocate and natural leader named Mohammed Ali Jinnah, is now a national hero in Pakistan as its founding father; everywhere else he is blamed for, inadvertently, causing the horrors of Partition—and by extension the horror that

---

[84] Burma, now Myanmar, although part of the Raj, always had a different fate.

is Pakistan today. (Interestingly enough, in view of these horrors, Jinnah was not a particularly religious man. Neither, for that matter, was his Indian counterpart Nehru, although both men used religion as a rallying point and power base.)[85]

I think this common view of Jinnah's culpability is a little unfair. True, he rabble-roused the groundswell that grew into the Muslim side of the massacres but by then events had spiraled out of his and everyone else's control; once again religious fervor was humanity's enemy. It suits all sides now—and Hindus, Muslims and Sikhs massacred with equal ferocity—to blame a British policy of divide and rule for Partition. That is a little unfair too as both Britain and India were equally aghast at the idea of a divided country, especially one divided along religious lines—the mixing of politics and religion as surely incendiary as a spark to gunpowder.

The British viceroy, Lord Mountbatten, is now especially blamed for the massacres by his decision to bring Independence and Partition forward from 1949 to 1947, a date at which Pakistan in particular was not ready for self-governance and way before the great twelve-million soul shift of populations along the religious divide could have been completed—or even the final frontiers of the divide drawn. If there is any irony in his defense, it is that he did so in an effort not so much to stop the massacres, which were already long beyond stopping, but at least to minimize the time in which more of them could take place.

No one will ever be able to second-guess that decision but he took what at the time the British—and a great many Indians and future Pakistanis—thought were the two least worst options: for the sake of the Sub-Continent an early Independence and Partition and for the sake of the war-depleted British Empire an early cut and run.

To travel along this train track now is to be reminded of the impossibility of a smooth Partition. There is no natural border. Hindu and Sikh families who had been living as far north as the Afghan border fled to Hindu-controlled Indian Punjab, while Muslims families who had settled right across the plains of northern India under centuries of Moghul rule fled to Muslim-controlled Pakistani Punjab. Punjab, now a state in both countries, could equally well be its own country, a Sikh country, as India is a Hindu one and Pakistan is a Muslim

---

[85] Mahatma Gandhi, like Jinnah and Nehru a London-trained lawyer, seems to have created a new religion of his own—using elements of Hindu and Buddhist ascetic practices.

one.

Since Partition the normalization of relations between India and Pakistan is what one might call a moveable feast. Pakistan has started, and lost, four wars against India. Both countries have armies they cannot (Pakistan) afford and should not have to (India) afford. Both have nuclear weapons aimed straight at each other. Suspicion and paranoia about each other come before reason and reconciliation. They are after all the same race of people; only their man-made religions—and whatever politically or culturally spins off from these—are dividing them.

Nevertheless, from time to time, efforts are made to be reasonable with each other. From the ebb and flow of negotiations someone had the good idea to resurrect the old railway line between Delhi and Lahore that the Twain party took on 17 March 1896. They gave the new train a name, the *Samjhota* (in Hindi) or *Samjhauta* (in Urdu) *Express*, depending on where it was originating; either word means concord or agreement in English. The train would make the round trip twice a week. The original plan was to have the whole rake complete each round trip and although Pakistani locomotives and carriages didn't mind trundling two hundred miles across the Indian Punjabi plains—any more than the Indian version minded delving the twenty miles into the Pakistani Punjabi plains—the trade unions and security wallahs on both sides soon agreed it would be less stressful to have the passengers disembark and re-embark across the respective frontiers.

In Mark Twain's notes he reported that he left Delhi at midnight and arrived in Lahore at 05.30 a.m. next day, 18 March. I can only presume something is wrong with the note as no train then, not even the *Flying Mail* on which he would have been traveling, turned in that sort of speed. Nevertheless one thing is certain, it would have been a lot quicker then than the slow chug of a folly that makes the journey today.

As I am sitting, swaying and jolting on the *Samjhota Express* it is good to read his notes again, if only to remind myself why we are making this trip this way at all: only to follow in his train tracks, as every guide book and tourist forum insists this is the worst possible way to journey from Delhi to Lahore. And the border crossing complications haven't even started yet. And two sets of unpleasant, deadly memories are right here with us on these tracks.

Apart from the Partition massacres, on 18 February 2007 a bomb exploded on this train, killing 68 passengers and injuring a hundred more. It was just days before the two governments were due to meet for peace talks. The case remains unsolved. WikiLeaks reveals that the CIA's top suspect is David Headley, a name-changed, Pakistani-American, Pakistani-intelligence-sponsored terrorist behind a number of other massacres, including the 2008 Mumbai terrorist atrocity. Other investigations point the finger at Abhinav Bharat, a right-wing Indian group with links to retired Indian Army officers. The memories of that blast and the religious hatred of humanity behind it haunt the slow train journey now; the very slowness of passing through the scene of the horror stops the memory moving on.

Is there an easy way, a pleasant way to go from Delhi to Lahore? Yes, and an amusing way too. One takes the Delhi to Amritsar train, the *Sachkhand Express*. This ends twenty miles from the border, and taxis and buses abound to help with the final leap. Once at the border the respective armies put on a display of bravado and machismo as they strut and goosestep round their countries' flagpoles and barriers. It has become quite the tourist attraction with numbered seats and postcard sellers—photography in theory being forbidden. The show—and there is no other word for it—lasts for half an hour. Rumor has it that once the tourists have gone they all muck in together, not surprisingly as they are all Punjabis after all.

Border show over, one then walks through the two frontier posts without excessive botheration. Once into Pakistan an equal number of taxis and buses abound to take one the final twenty miles into Lahore. That's the easy way, the amusing way.

And there is the other way, this way that the Mark Twain sleuth hounds are taking. Eventually the *Samjhota Express* reaches Attari on the Indian side of the border. All change! I had noticed that we were the only people in our carriage and when I went to find a serviceable loo saw that there were only three other passengers in the next carriage—backpacking tourists from the Far East. Now as we jumped down onto the shale (there is no platform as such) it is clear we are the only five passengers from all of the six carriages.

If you don't mind I'm going to compress the next four hours into four sentences. Exciting it was not (1). Ironical it was; the fact that there were just the five of us clearly aroused both sets of guards' suspicions and so prolonged the process: why would anyone sensible chose such a stupid way of travelling from Delhi to Lahore? (2). A further complication was completing "Occupation" on the forms: I didn't want to put "Tourist" as just a quick look through my cases, crammed with books and notes and the "magic letter" from the Indian High Commission would reveal I am slightly more than that, leading to unknown further delays (3). "Writer" could mean—dread word—journalist; "Historian" won the day. And there was plenty of idle time for mathematics: five people, four hours, twenty-two guards equals five and a half guard/hours per entry (4).

*

An hour later the Pakistani version of the *Samjhota Express* grinds its way into Lahore station, Platform 1 no less. Lahore Station, like the one at Lucknow we visited three weeks ago, was designed post-Sepoy Uprising to be both train station and fort. At first sight it looks like the son of St. Pancras in London but in fact the turrets are reinforced and the clock towers bomb-proof; it's a classic piece of Oriental-Gothic Raj style and a classic piece of once-bitten-twice-shy Raj intent.

Lahore Station is as busy as any in India and one is met by the usual hordes of porters and taxi touts. Luckily I had said "yes" when the nice PRO at the Avari Hotel in the Mall not only asked, but insisted that we should be met. And so it is done; a tall, young, spring-footed, tousle-haired British Pakistani meets me—and greets me with a British Midlands accent. He is Muji from Birmingham, here on a three-month hotel management placement and the sort of chirpy person to whom one warms immediately. He is good news but he has bad news: we cannot reach the hotel; there's a full-scale demonstration on outside, probably for the next hour. What's it about? Blasphemy.

"For or against?" I ask.

"Not for," Muji replies.

We cross the square outside and find a *chai* shop to watch the show. The marchers holler past the station, a mass of green and white flags and placards, black or white clothing, anger on the faces and hatred in the voices. They all look like they have been cloned from the same anger/hate hybrid gene.

"They all look alike," I say and sip. To a man they all seem to be twenty-two years old with unshaped beards, no moustaches, and shaking right raised fists.

"They *are* all alike. Fuckin' nutters," says Muji.

"I'm pleased you said so first. What are they shouting about?" There seems to be only one slogan shouted.

"My Urdu's a bit shaky and I don't read it, but something like 'Hang Munrid a thousand times!'"

205

"Gosh, who's Munrid?" I ask.

"Fucked if I know. Blasphemy is a big deal here now. Every day, that and the CIA yank they've locked up. Or something else. Have you heard much about the blasphemy business?"

"Only the headlines," I reply. I retrieve yesterday's *Times of India* out of my carry-on. Under the headline "Pakistan Assassinations Highlight Sway of Radical Clerics", I read out "Yousaf Qureshi made headlines when he offered $6,000 to anyone who kills a Pakistani Christian woman convicted of blasphemy. She was seen in public making a sign of the cross, a definition of blasphemy in today's Pakistan. Now, the cleric told worshippers packed into his 17th-century mosque his followers had done a 'marvelous job' days before, by assassinating a cabinet minister who had defended the woman."

"Yeah," says Muji, "there've been two assassinations of cabinet ministers here lately. The last one, guy called Bhatti, was shot by his own bodyguard. They're all fuckin' batty if you ask me. There's no police at all; they're all bent as fuck anyway. Mind you, the whole country's bent. It's run by the army and they're rippin' everyone off too. I just keep me head down, that's what the hotel says we all have to do. Not that I'm that interested. I hate politicians in England too." He looks up and out at the emptier street. "I reckon we can go if some bastard hasn't nicked the car. We're meant to have a driver waiting. Last one we employed drove off with one of our cars. That happens all the time too."

"How come you're staying at the Avari?" Muji asks as we drive through the rickshaws and rubbish. I notice the English road names: Aikman, Tollington, Club, Davis, Durand, Shalimar, GT.[86] "Not that there's anything wrong with it. Best in town I think."

I explain: the Twain party all stayed at the Nedous Hotel in Mall Road. It was sold in 1946, revamped and renamed the Park Luxury Hotel. That was knocked down and made into the Lahore Hilton. Then they gave up and now it's the Avari Hotel. I had emailed them after the visas were sorted and asked if by any miracle they had any of the Nedous archives. They said no, but come and stay anyway. Too expensive, I said. Not with a media discount—you are a travel writer, aren't you? I am now, I said, and so here we are. And, it has to be said, they didn't exactly have to squeeze us in.

---

[86] For Grand Trunk. There are GT Roads in towns all along the old Grand Trunk Road that connected Peshawar near the Afghan border to Calcutta, via Rawalpindi, Lahore, Amritsar, Meerut, Cawnpore, Allahabad and Benares.

*

That first night Mark Twain lectured at the Railway Theatre, but it has sunk without trace. I am disappointed because this is the first time I've drawn a compete blank: elsewhere even if no Twain venue still stands there have been records and a location, somewhere to go and mope about. Actually I couldn't have gone to the Railway Theatre for a show even if it had existed: the 10 p.m. Karachi curfew had been extended to Lahore.

"Not that it's an official curfew," says Ahmed from a bar stool in The Tollington Pub in the depths of the Avari Hotel. "You are somehow just meant to know."

We introduce ourselves. Ahmed is a 45-year-old Pakistani Canadian, a researcher from Toronto working on a new HBO series about the Mujahideen. This is his first trip to Pakistan; he's been here a month, up north, and is only in Lahore overnight to fly home out from here tomorrow. His family was Kashmiri; his father a railway engineer working where Ahmed has just been, in the North West Frontier, at Partition. His parents were not worried, Muslim Kashmir was bound to be part of Muslim Pakistan; it wasn't, another Partition disaster. His family was homeless but at least his father was well trained and qualified and Commonwealth Canada welcomed them, with generosity too. He cannot say enough good about Canada, the home he has come to have, and enough bad about Pakistan, the home he never had.

He is interested in India and the contrasts, there and here.

"I haven't been here long enough for the contrasts," I reply, "but you can't help being impressed with India. I love the way they live in the past and embrace the future. If knowledge will be this century's most valuable raw material they are a generation or two from being on top of the world. Everywhere you look in India are colleges or advertisements for colleges. You could write a pamphlet with all their exam initials."

Ahmed says, "There's no education happening here. It's another scam. They call it the ghost-school racket. The politicians take money from foreign aid and NGOs for new schools and put up a shell. There's a big opening, VIPs cutting tapes, usual bullshit. Then they go and that's it. All the money for books and teachers—even students—gets no further than the politicians' pockets. Even if you can find a teacher, they're paid squat. If they are paid at all. They were out on strike in Peshawar last week. Hadn't been paid for months. If you want to take a

207

higher exam you slip some money into your answer sheets. If you want to pass you slip some more in. No wonder they got madrasahs everywhere."

"How does that work?" I ask.

"Only a quarter of girls—a quarter right?—and half of boys complete primary school. The literacy rate in the country as a whole is only fifty percent, much less among the under thirties. They are way behind Nepal and Bangladesh—and as for India..."

"But the madrasahs?"

"They spend half the day teaching the children to learn the Koran by rote in Arabic. Imagine your schooldays learning the New Testament in Aramaic by rote. But the other half they do spend teaching them how to read and write. And they are free, Saudi money mainly, and the kids get fed, fed well too. If you're a poor Muslim anyway and you want your children to read and write you send them to a madrasah."

"That's all they learn, the Koran in Arabic, and reading and writing Urdu?"

"That's it. No sports, no culture, no technology. No computer skills, not in the Koran. No English, not in the Koran. No science, especially no science, not in the Koran. You think the literacy rate at fifty percent is bad enough, but that fifty percent know nothing about the world at all. Half the population is under 25 and half of them illiterate."

"And the rich?"

"Pakistan is run by 27 families, extended families. Some are in politics, some the military, some in business but one way or another they have the place all sewn up. None of them pay any taxes. They couldn't give a shit. They're all educated abroad, a lot of them only speak English. Switzerland is where they all bank. But even the Swiss got fed up with President Zardari, told him not to be so blatant, even took him to court. The Swiss!"

"The famous Mr. Ten Percent."

"That name started when he was married to Benazir Bhutto at the time she was Prime Minster. Man, she was a crook, big time, a real scammer. He is even worse. Now he's President. When he was sworn in he had to declare his worth. The world was watching so he couldn't put nothing. He put down 1.9 *billion* US dollars. Transparency [International] reckons he has stolen ten times that amount and five times more than that if you include his cronies. It's like Nigeria without the oil. They don't need oil, they've got US aid. And that's not all."

After a month of buttoning his lip Ahmed was in full flow. "Zardari has been in prison for murder, twice, and indicted for four more, then mysteriously they were both pardoned—Benazir for corruption and him for ordering the murders—including, by the way, her brother."

A few beers later and we have put the world to rights. The Americans created a lot of the problems by throwing money at the Pakistanis to spend on the Mujahideen when they were fighting the Russians in Afghanistan. Once the Russians had been defeated the Mujahideen were left to stew. Some became the Taliban and now the Americans are throwing more money at the Pakistanis to fight them. Meanwhile the Pakistani Taliban are gaining ground rapidly as the drones policy, bombing Pakistan territory in search of the Taliban, is backfiring on patriotic hearts and minds. The politicians let it continue as the army feeds some of the American money back to them. The 100,000-strong ISI, the army's intelligence unit, is riddled with Taliban sympathizers and assassins, such as the dead cabinet minister Bhatti's bodyguard. The ISI created various terrorist groups to fight the army's wars by proxy in Afghanistan and Kashmir and these have now become self-funding through guns and drugs and are no longer under anyone's control. The best any outside government can do is stop giving the Pakistanis foreign aid or military funding which simply disappears and encourages corruption—and irony-free American politicians please note, the Taliban, which brings us back to where we started. In fact, if you sat down with a blank piece of paper and US$20 billion you would not be able to invent a more counter-productive, ill fitting and yes, morally bankrupt set of policies however hard you tried. SNAFU, I believe is the appropriate acronym, or as Mark Twain said "Politician and idiot are synonymous terms", or even Sita's favorite: "Suppose you were an idiot. And suppose you were a member of Congress. But I repeat myself."

*

The next day I knew I was going to be disappointed even before I was disappointed. This was one of Mark Twain's favorite days, lunch with the Lieutenant Governor in Government House and then a ride through Lahore on one of the governor's elephants. Government House is reputed to be surrounded by troops. A bit late, one would have thought: only a few months ago the resident Governor of Punjab, Salmaan Taseer, was assassinated too over his support for repealing the blasphemy law. Taseer was a highly successful international investment banker turned politician, a sort of Pakistani version of

Michael Bloomberg but without the annoying prissiness. And as for finding an elephant...

> In Lahore the Lieutenant-Governor lent me an elephant. This hospitality stands out in my experiences in a stately isolation. It was a fine elephant, affable, gentlemanly, educated, and I was not afraid of it. I even rode it with confidence through the crowded lanes of the native city, where it scared all the horses out of their senses, and where children were always just escaping its feet. It took the middle of the road in a fine independent way, and left it to the world to get out of the way or take the consequences.

> I am used to being afraid of collisions when I ride or drive, but when one is on top of an elephant that feeling is absent. I could have ridden in comfort through a regiment of runaway teams. I could easily learn to prefer an elephant to any other vehicle, partly because of that immunity from collisions, and partly because of the fine view one has from up there, and partly because of the dignity one feels in that high place, and partly because one can look in at the windows and see what is going on privately among the family.

> The Lahore horses were used to elephants, but they were rapturously afraid of them just the same. It seemed curious. Perhaps the better they know the elephant the more they respect him in that peculiar way. In our own case—we are not afraid of dynamite till we get acquainted with it.

It's only a short walk along the extension of Mall Road and into the Mayo Gardens from the Avari Hotel to Governor's House. For once I don't take a guide as I know about the Nedous Hotel and the Railway Theatre. Governor's House is close at hand and although unvisitable is, I presume, photographable and gawpable. Instead we amble through the city streets and market, keeping Governor's House on our left, somewhere. There's no hurry and the amble turns into a half-marathon, ambling-wise.

Lahore is noticeably poorer than Delhi, Old or New, and I suspect that outer or tribal Pakistan is noticeably poorer than outer or tribal India. Certainly its religion-bound, education-free prospects are much poorer. Delhi's streets are covered in trash but occasionally, just occasionally, it is swept up and sifted for

Street scene, Lahore, 1890s

trinkets and, even more occasionally, bits of it for recycling. Here in Lahore the trash is denser and older and without the benefit of cows and goats chomping on it as a first line of attack. Twice I saw makeshift bonfires near the market; when the garbage gets too bad someone takes the initiative and burns it, creating more pollution. In Delhi they are making some effort to tackle the foul air, introducing four-stroke and LPG rickshaws, gas-powered town buses and the like, while here the smelly old two-stroke rickshaws and old, old cars and buses belch out smoke unabashed. In Delhi if one is lost it is certain that at least a shop owner will speak enough English to set you back on track; here even the pharmacy owner I ask doesn't speak English. In Delhi beggars have their pitch and are, by and large, passive; here they wander around and are active and persistent. In Delhi one sometimes feels like one is in the twenty-first century, with hope and pride in the air; here in Lahore one more often feels like one is in the nineteenth, with fear and despair in the eyes. And I miss seeing women out and about, especially brightly dressed and bangled women.

Eventually, with many vague attempts at left turning, we come out on Staff College Road, the wrong side of, but still adjacent to Governor's House. There's another demonstration but this one is very different from yesterday's. The demonstrators are older, quieter and are waving sheets of paper and not placards. There is no sign of Islam or hatred. Simply anger.

I find a man in a suit and ask him, "What's all this about?"

"Oh, the electricity. Wish I was with them but I need to be in my office."

"What about the electricity?"

"Haven't you noticed the generators?" Actually I have, especially around the market. "The Lahore ESC just sends out these enormous bills whether you are there or not. There are no meters. And no electricity for a lot of the time. These are mostly shop keepers and stall holders. They've had enough."

"But if there's no electricity there should be no bills."

"Ha, then they cut you off. Then only reconnect with baksheesh. The supply company was denationalized, then given to one of Zardari's cronies. Ever since it's become another scam. They sell to the highest bidder. It's called hot-wiring, a guaranteed supply. But you pay. Where are you staying?"

"The Avari."

"Ask them. I better go."

I cannot get anywhere near Governor's House, another fine architectural example of Raj confidence, not just in an endless future but in experimenting with different classical motifs from the Palladian portico to the Moghul sepulcher rear and Oriental-Gothic wings. It is indeed surrounded by troops. Gillian's one noble attempt at photography is instantly banned by frantically waving lines of incoming camouflage.

Decision snaps sometimes replace camera snaps and I decide to bale out of Lahore there and then rather than wait for tomorrow. I've seen all there is to see here, story-wise, my bar buddy Ahmed has left and Lahore is sinking in anger. I walk back to the train station and for a while enter a parallel Pakistan, one with purpose and old world charm and one without testiness and disruption. The unkind thought arises that the railway track is an umbilical chord back to an easier, more pleasant life in India.

16. RAWALPINDI

TRAINS TO RAWALPINDI, combining with its neighbor and Pakistan's capital Islamabad, run every other hour and three hours later I am on the 4.30 p.m. *Subak Kharmam Express* up towards the North West Frontier. Gillian has joined Livy and Clara on strike; all three need a rest and stay behind in Lahore while Mark Twain and Carlyle Smythe and I make the trip up to Rawalpindi.

Once out of Lahore one sees yet another Pakistan, Pakistan the picturesque. Twain made this same journey but made no comments about it but here I'm reminded of his impressions of Bengal more than I had been in Bengal; or maybe—apart from the nakedness—it was the insidious Pakistan-now-equals-India-then mindset:

> And everywhere through the soft vistas we glimpse the villages, the countless villages, the myriad villages, thatched, built of clean new matting, snuggling among grouped palms and sheaves of bamboo; villages, villages, no end of villages, not three hundred yards apart, and dozens and dozens of them in sight all the time; a mighty City, hundreds of miles long, hundreds of miles broad, made all of villages, the biggest city in the earth, and as populous as a European kingdom. I have seen no such city as this before.

> And there is a continuously repeated and replenished multitude of naked men in view on both sides and ahead. We fly through it mile after mile, but still it is always there, on both sides and ahead—brown-bodied, naked men and boys, ploughing in the fields. But not a woman. In these two hours I have not seen a woman or a girl working in the fields.

He wouldn't see one outside a house now either, but that's a different matter.[87]

*

Three hours and a glorious sunset over the plains later, I reflect on how good

---

[87] It's sobering to reflect that a woman who leaves the house and is even suspected of tarnishing her owner's "honor" can be sentenced to gang rape by a village kangaroo court, some members of which carry out the "punishment"—*with the woman's owner's consent.*

the trains are—and such excellent value; presumably a service not yet farmed out to one of Zardari's crook-cronies. In fact this Rawalpindi railway line was a source of great pride to the British and Indian—and of course future Pakistani—engineers and managers who built and ran it. The terrain up to Rawalpindi and beyond was difficult and the rush for a quick completion, caused by the need to have a reinforceable garrison in place near the Afghan border, made the building of it even more challenging. It was only finished eight years before Mark Twain and Carlyle Smythe arrived, by which time the garrison had become the largest in the British Empire with 40,000 soldiers encamped, including "one regiment of British and one of Native cavalry; two regiments of British and two of Native infantry".

It is still a large garrison town now and the headquarters of the Pakistani Army and Air Force. Twain stayed and lectured in The Club, Rawal Pindi, in the cantonment area, so attached to but not exclusive to its military clientele. From old photographs it looks remarkably like the Poona Club and it met the same fate: burned down by a blaze started in the open-fire kitchen. It was rebuilt as the Artillery Officers' Mess, a status it maintained through Partition and its take-over by the new Pakistani Army.

Like much else it has now been semi-privatized by an unholy alliance of politicians and generals and when not in use by the officers can be hired for special occasions. I wander in late morning the next day and share a soft drink with three young officers at the bar. They all speak perfect English. Like the Indian Army, the Pakistani Army is cloned from the British Army—the commercialization here, with advertisements for wedding hosting, BBQ & Tombola Parties and Karaoke Evenings are a later development. I'm still trying to imagine a sober karaoke evening, or wedding reception for that matter. Outside are the famous old tennis courts where the first ever Davis Cup was held but now half full of paying parked cars. A ticket booth stands where the main court umpire must have sat.

The eldest officer, Humza Yousaf, striped up as a captain, asks me where I am staying. I say Flashman's Hotel opposite. (I couldn't resist it, being a lover of George Macdonald Fraser's yarns; it is also the nearest hotel to what was The Club.) It turns out he has family in England only thirty miles away from mine and our prep schools used to play against each other at soccer and cricket. We agree to dine together tomorrow evening; and a very informative dinner it will be too.

The area around Flashman's Hotel is Saddar Bazaar, a wonderful collection of alleys and shops and a thriving business center, a self-contained town within a city. Wandering further afield reveals Rawalpindi, or just Pindi as the locals say, to have a distinct and robust flavor. One warms to its cool atmosphere, welcome even now in late spring. The people reflect the geography: although we are still in Punjab it is nearing its end and more exotic-looking mountain tribesmen mingle with local traders and a disproportionally high number of men in military and mullah uniforms.

Unfortunately it also attracts its share of fanatics. This is where, in the old

East India Company grounds, Benazir Bhutto was assassinated in late 2007. It was also where her father was hanged by General Zia, a particularly unpleasant religious maniac-cum-military dictator-cum-serial-embezzler, and from whose rule the psychotic warrior-gangster-priest nature of Pakistan has never recovered. It was also where in 1951 the first elected Prime Minister of Pakistan, Liaquat Ali Khan, was assassinated. One would be a brave Bhutto, or any politician, to go anywhere near the place. Sometimes it feels like a politician in Pakistan has the life expectancy of a rear gunner in World War 2.

It's not just politicians. More than three hundred people have been killed and many more hundreds injured in the eighteen bomb blasts here since 1987. All have been religiously inspired and politically driven. The nature of the outrages has changed too: up to ten years ago anonymous car bombs were in vogue but now the suicide bomber holds sway. And it's getting worse. The recent attacks on mosques were inter-Muslim internecine affairs, an ominous shift pointing to a religious civil war.

The rampant terrorism affects everything. The Cricket World Cup is being held right now. Pakistan is cricket mad and was due to co-host the tournament. Then some Islamists sprayed the Buddhist Sri Lankan cricketers' bus with AK-47 bullets and the World Cup games were taken away from Pakistan. One of the venues was to have been the local Army Cricket Ground, already host to a test match, in the grounds of The Club and now adjacent to the Artillery Officers' Mess. Many Pakistanis cannot even bear to watch it on television being played in India, Sri Lanka and Bangladesh, and unlike in India, where the World Cup is talked about constantly, the country's shame has made it taboo in Pakistan.

*

Flashman's Hotel, with its low-rise and evocative colonial fort front and prominent position on Mall Road, is a joy. It has recently been refurbished and they have resisted the temptation to carve up the old Raj suites into smaller bedrooms as has been done in hotels elsewhere. I am the only foreigner staying so maybe it's not driven by good taste but good business. It was owned by the Pakistan Tourism Development Corporation but that has since been privatized, possibly why they insist on guests paying cash. Sleep is sound but broken at dawn by an hour long amplified prayer melee. One gets used to the pre-dawn muezzin all over the Muslim world; the call to prayer echoes out over the loudspeakers and normally only lasts for a minute, leaving enough time for the visitor—and most of the faithful—to turn over and snatch another hour or two sleep. Here in Rawalpindi they broadcast the whole service and the combined and echoed noise from the half a dozen minarets in earshot not only makes re-sleep impossible but sends the day off with a most discordant racket, an electronic Babel.

I meet my new officer friend Humza for dinner. Inevitably the subject turns to Pakistan, the failed state. A few glasses of Pakistani beer, aka mineral water, later we conclude that it is a failing but not yet a failed state; it is certainly a rogue state. There is one more leader in it to turn it around. Another Zia or Zardari and it's finished. The problem is no leader is on the horizon, hardly surprising given the constant assassinations of leaders and hopefuls.

Gillian and I had been in pre-1979 revolutionary Iran a couple of times and Pakistan now reminds me of being there then. There the state, in the shape of the Shah and his coterie of crook-cronies, had abandoned responsibility for governance and had descended into outright gangsterism; the same could be said here. This quickly spirals into a self-fulfilling prophecy: the regime knows the good times cannot last forever, so uses what time may be left to focus solely on getting even richer even quicker.

True, there is as yet no outstanding mullah, no Ayatollah Khomeini around whom the illiterate and dispossessed could rally, but one feels that if a new leader is to arise he will be religious rather than political or military. Right now the danger is not much the strength of the mullahs but the chronic weakness of the state, which is allowing the fundamentalists to push towards their Sharia goals without any resistance. As in old Iran, the reality for the mass of the population is uneducated joblessness with no hope of reprieve while they stare aghast at the blatant misuse of power by their elite. Also as in old Iran, growing anti-Americanism, due to their pursuit of the Afghan War on Pakistani soil with increasing Pakistani causalities, is leading to a corresponding mistrust of all Western values. Most of those with these Western values may scoff—albeit politely—at the primitive theology behind the mistrust, but if all you know comes from a man-made interpretation of a man-made religion the resulting world views are going to be, well, primitive. There are now no fewer than thirty Islamic parties who all unite around toppling the civilian government and creating an Islamic state.

The politicians take the blame for the American presence in Pakistan, but by a sort of internal *Pax Pakistanica* control of foreign policy and national security lies with the military and both parties are making respective fortunes from skimming off American spending, now at US$22 billion and increasing by a further US$3 billion a year. In fact, Pakistan has been under total military rule for half of its existence and it is no surprise to find that—like the Prussia of old—it is not a country that has an army but an army that has a country. Under its wing it then has two statelets answerable only to itself: the ISI, now out of control, and the nuclear weapons program shrouded in effective secrecy.[88] It consumes an extraordinary twenty percent of the national budget, employs a million people

---

[88] Only by chance did the CIA find out that three top-ranking officers on the nuclear team were Taliban double agents. All attempts to find out about others have been repeatedly rebuffed.

and runs extensive business interests all over the country, including raw material and import monopolies and extensive property portfolios unhampered by any planning restrictions.

It doesn't take a genius to see that American foreign policy in South Asia is as foolhardy now as it was in Southeast Asia forty years ago. Reasonable people in Pakistan are helpless, as with one hand the Americans throw money at the deeply unpopular activities of the military-intelligence establishment while on the other demand that the hapless civilian-gangster government wrest back control of the country.

The terrorist groups that the ISI has sponsored with US money are now so drug- and gun- rich and out of control that they have taken to attacking the ISI's paymasters, the Army itself to protect their fiefdoms or, more accurately, thiefdoms: 2,300 military personnel have been killed by the ISI's proxies in the last five years. Of more concern to my dinner companion is the other 100,000-strong force, nominally under military control, which controls the 110-strong nuclear weapons program. Already Pakistan has sold nuclear technology to North Korea, Libya and Iran against all international rules and even harbors the scientist, A. Q. Khan, responsible (harbors is a polite way of saying openly fetes). Quite why America has funded it all in the first pace is unclear, especially as the sole purpose of the weapons is to blow up the West's neighboring ally, the multiracial, multicultural, secular democracy of India.

The real danger is one that everyone acknowledges but seems powerless to prevent. The Taliban has turned its attention from Afghanistan, where it is suffering such heavy losses that even it cannot sustain them, to the much easier pickings of Pakistan. The worst-case scenario, that the Taliban acquire Pakistan's entire arsenal of nuclear weapons, is not at all beyond the realms of possibility.

On that happy note we say goodnight. Like Mark Twain, I "had intended to penetrate the north west Frontier as far as Peshawar, only a few miles from the Khyber Pass, portal of Afghanistan", but sickness had dislocated his schedule and two more days were lopped off by a message that his ship was sailing from Calcutta ahead of time. I needed—well, wanted—to get back to the life afloat too.

*

The next morning I wish Rawalpindi good-bye, and back in Lahore Gillian good morrow. Then we both wish Mark Twain, Livy, Clara and Smythe goodbye; they are re-shugging along old train tracks to reach Calcutta quickly, as it were, to catch the steamer to South Africa, following more of that equator. Pakistan we wish good-bye too as we fly out from Lahore to Dubai and then on to Istanbul to rejoin *Vasco da Gama* in southern Turkey.

Good bye to everyone, it's been fun... if a little exhausting; ten weeks on the road in India is boxing enough for that writer then—and this writer now.

FOLLOWING
THE EQUATOR
A JOURNEY AROUND THE WORLD
BY
MARK TWAIN
SAMUEL L. CLEMENS

HARTFORD   NEW YORK

AMERICAN PUBLISHING CO.   DOUBLEDAY & McCLURE CO.

MDCCCXCVII

Ian and Gillian returned to their yacht Vasco da Gama in southern Turkey to write this book and edit the photographs and videos.

Sita found work as a producer's assistant in Bollywood.

Satan found new work as a bearer.

Smythe returned to Sydney and took over fully the family business managing tours.

Livy and Clara returned to London and New York respectively.

Mark Twain wrote *Following the Equator*, also in London. There's a happy ending.

The New York Times

January 1, 1898

Mark Twain Paying His Firm's Debts

Samuel L. Clemens ("Mark Twain"), says The Publishers' Weekly, has just made a payment of 25 percent to the creditors of C. L. Webster & Co., which failed in 1894, and in which Mr. Clemens was heavily interested. The assignee, Bainbridge Colby, of 120 Broadway, managed to realize 28 percent of the liabilities out of the assets of the firm and of the personal estate of Mr. Clemens, which was turned over to him at once. With one or two exceptions, the creditors offered to settle with 50 cents on the dollar, and this sum Mr. Clemens paid last year. He, however, stated that he should take no advantage of any bankruptcy law, but would, if given time, pay dollar for dollar of the indebtedness. He has kept his word, and has now made a payment that wipes out 75 percent of his liabilities. Mr. Clemens hopes inside of four years to make his final payment. It is to be hoped Mr. Clemens may be granted the satisfaction of seeing his great undertaking accomplished. He is sixty-four years old.

The New York Times

March 12, 1898

Mark Twain's debts as paid. Lecture Tour and "Following the Equator" raise the funds

Mark Twain has paid all the debts that led to the bankruptcy of the publishing firm with which he was connected. It is a fine example of the very chivalry of probity, and, in the circumstances, as an admirer has pointed out, it deserves to rank with the historic case of Sir Walter Scott. The firm came to grief; Mark Twain might, if he had pleased, have confined his share of the loss to the amount of his liability under the partnership. He preferred to make good the entire loss, and to this end he had to make a fresh start in life at the age of sixty. He accomplished it, and with this and the profits of his latest book, Following the Equator, he has carried out his high-minded and generous purpose.

He has gained the esteem of all men of honor throughout the world. This act is the best of all critical commentaries on the high moral teaching of his books. He needs all the encouragement of sympathy. He has paid his debts, but he has still to make another fortune, and he is sixty-three!

INDEX